# MODERNISING BRITAIN

## Central, devolved, federal?

*edited by*
**Stanley Henig**

**THE FEDERAL TRUST**
*for education & research*

This book is published by the Federal Trust, whose aim is to enlighten public debate on federal issues of national, continental and global governance. It does this in the light of its statutes which state that it shall promote 'studies in the principles of international relations, international justice and supranational government.'

The Trust conducts enquiries, promotes seminars and conferences and publishes reports and teaching materials. The Federal Trust is the UK member of the Trans-European Policy Studies Association (TEPSA), a grouping of fifteen think-tanks from Member States of the European Union.

Up-to-date information about the Federal Trust can be found on the internet at www.fedtrust.co.uk


This book is part of the Federal Trust's 'Governance in Europe' series. Further volumes will include *European Governance: British Perspectives*, *Governance – European, National, Regional* and *Regional Governance in Europe*.

Federal Trust for Education and Research 2002

ISBN 1 903403 13 8

NOTE: All contributors to this volume are writing in a personal capacity. Views expressed are those of the authors and do not represent the position of their institution.

The Federal Trust is a Registered Charity No. 272241

Dean Bradley House, 52 Horseferry Road,

London SW1P 2AF

Company Limited by Guarantee No.1269848


Marketing and Distribution by Kogan Page Ltd

Printed by MFP Design & Print

*My late father, Sir Mark Henig, was a member of the Royal Commission appointed in 1969 under the Chairmanship of Lord Crowther to examine the constitution of the United Kingdom. Its massive report published four years later gives extensive consideration to many of the ideas and concepts which underpin 'New' Labour's plans for modernisation. Sir Mark Henig devoted much of his life to public service. This book is dedicated to his memory.*

*Stanley Henig*

# Contents

## Part 4: A Federal State in a Federal Europe?

## Part 5: Conclusion and Beyond

## Appendices

# Contributors

**Alex Bax** is a Senior Policy Officer at the Greater London Authority. He works on a wide range of topics including e-government, e-commerce and technology change, strategy consistency and integration, and London's night time economy. From 1993 to 2000 he was assistant to the Chief Executive at the London Research Centre.

**Sir Jeremy Beecham** has been a member of Newcastle City Council since 1967, and was Leader from 1977-1994. He was Chairman of the Association of Metropolitan Authorities from 1991-1997 since when he has served as the first Chairman of the Local Government Association. He is a member of the Labour Party National Executive Committee and the NHS Modernisation Board, and is President of the British Urban Regeneration Association.

**Dr Alan Butt Philip** is Jean Monnet Reader in European Integration in the School of Management, University of Bath. He was specialist adviser for regional policy and the structural funds attached to the House of Lords Select Committee on European Community Affairs from 1980 to 1989. He contested the European elections in 1979 as a Liberal, and in 1999 as a Liberal Democrat.

**Louise Ellman MP** has been MP for Riverside since 1997. From 1981 to 1997 she was Leader of Lancashire County Council. She is a member of the House of Commons Select Committee on Transport, Local Government and the Regions.

**Professor Stanley Henig**, Senior Research Fellow at the Federal Trust, is a former MP and Leader of Lancaster City Council. Until 1999 he was Secretary of the Labour Group on the Local Government Association. He is the author and/or editor of many books on British and European politics of which the most recent are *The Uniting of Europe: from discord to concord* (Routledge, 1997) and *The Kosovo Crisis: America's last war in Europe?* (Reuters, 2001).

**Baron Isherwood** is currently Director of Regeneration at the North West Development Agency. He manages a staff of 100 with an annual budget of £200m spent on a variety of land and property, regeneration and rural development schemes across the region. He was previously Regional Controller in the Government Office for the North West, dealing with housing, urban affairs, environment and planning issues.

**Barry Jones** is Reader in Politics and Director of the Welsh Governance Centre at the University of Cardiff. His research interests include the Labour Party, European regionalism, and the politics of Welsh devolution. His most recent publications include *The Road to the National Assembly for Wales* with D. Balsom (UWP, 2000) and *The Committee System in the National Assembly* with J. Osmond (IWA, 2001).

**Elizabeth Meehan** has been on the staff of Queen's University Belfast since 1991, first as Professor in the School of Politics and now as Director of the Institute of Governance, Public Policy and Social Research. Her research and publications cover: women and politics; European citizenship; citizenship and participation in the UK; constitutional change in the UK; and British-Irish relations in the context of the EU with particular reference to the peace process in Northern Ireland and freedom of movement of persons between the two islands under European arrangements.

**Ines Newman** is Head of Policy at the LGIU. She was appointed to head the policy and research team in the economic development unit at the London Borough of Hackney in 1984. In 1988 she set up the economic development unit in Harlow District Council and was the co-ordinator of the South East Economic Development Strategy Group (SEEDS). She has published widely on issues around economic development, regions, democracy and social exclusion. She is reviews editor for *Local Economy.*

**Ulrike Rüb** is Research Officer at the Federal Trust, where she specialises in devolution, regions in Europe and European citizenship. During her studies in both Germany and the UK, she has undertaken research on the EU and the regions, with a particular focus on the German Länder.

**Jane Saren** is currently Managing Director of the Edinburgh office of GPC International, Scotland's leading public affairs consultancy. In this role she has closely monitored and analysed the unfolding of the new constitutional settlement in Scotland, with a particular focus on the evolution of co-ordinating mechanisms (both formal and informal) between the tiers of government. Prior to joining GPC in 1996, she was a senior manager in local government, with experience north and south of the border.

**Dr Wilfried Swenden** completed his DPhil in politics at Oxford University in 2000 on 'Federalism and Second Chambers: Regional Representation in Parliamentary Federations', an analysis of the role which the German Bundesrat and Australian Senate have (or have not) been playing in articulating regional interests. He is currently a Post-Doctoral Fellow of the Flemish Fund for Scientific Research at the University of Louvain (KU Leuven), Belgium.

**Dr John Tomaney** works in the Centre for Urban and Regional Development Studies at Newcastle University, where his current research focuses on questions of devolution and regional governance. His most recent publications include 'End of the Empire State? New Labour and devolution in the United Kingdom' (*International Journal of Urban and Regional Research*, 2000) and 'Reshaping the English Regions', in *The State of the Nations 2001* (Imprint Academic, 2001).

**Dr Alan Whitehead MP** was appointed Parliamentary Under-Secretary of State at the Department for Transport, Local Government and the Regions (DTLR), responsible for local government, in June 2001. He has been Member of Parliament for Southampton Test since 1997. He was Leader of Southampton County Council from 1984 to 1992.

**Dr Alex Wright** is Lecturer at the Department of Politics, University of Dundee. He also holds a visiting research fellowship at the Institute for Advanced Studies in the Humanities, University Edinburgh, during 2002 where his research will focus on Scotland's agenda in the EU. His publications include *Scotland: The Challenge of Devolution* (ed.) (Ashgate, 2000). He was appointed to the Scottish Consumer Council in 1998.

# 1

# The Agenda for Modernisation

# Foreword

## Dr Alan Whitehead MP
### Parliamentary Under-Secretary of State
### Department for Transport, Local Government and the
### Regions

I am delighted to have the opportunity to write an introductory piece to welcome this new book by the Federal Trust. It provides a thought-provoking perspective on the development of devolution within the United Kingdom.

Devolution and decentralisation are crucial features of the Government's programme for modernising our constitution, and for revitalising democracy. The creation of the new devolved legislatures and administrations in Scotland, Wales and Northern Ireland, followed by the establishment of the Greater London Mayor and Assembly, were among the highlights of our first term. In the English regions, meanwhile, we saw the setting up of the Regional Development Agencies and regional chambers, and the strengthening of other regional structures.

This book is particularly timely as a contribution to the growing debate on the way forward for the English regions, in the run up to publication of our White Paper on Regional Governance. This will explain our plans to provide for directly elected regional assemblies, in those regions where people decide in a referendum to support this, and where predominantly unitary local government is established, while also setting out the way ahead for regions which do not opt for elected assemblies.

# Preface

## Sir Jeremy Beecham
### Chairman
### Local Government Association

Ever since the 1960s when the late Lord Hailsham responded to the economic difficulties of the North East of England by injecting considerable public investment into the area, and sporting a cloth cap, regionalism has been on the political agenda.

From the Redcliffe -Maud report on, there was a general recognition that whatever changes were made to local government, many strategic functions needed to be exercised in a regional context. The 1973 local government reorganisation achieved something of a halfway house in those areas where metropolitan county councils were established, though these of course were subsequently abolished in the 1980s. The North East created the North of England Development Council which later was replaced by the Northern Development Company, an alliance of local government and the private sector, supported by central government. Other institutional developments, however, ranging from the Regional Economic Planning Councils of the 1960s to the Government Offices for the Regions of the 1990s, were essentially manifestations of central government's presence in the regions, accountable to Westminster and Whitehall, rather than the regions themselves.

As the pressure for devolution in Scotland and Wales grew, and as the strength and success of regional governments in Europe became apparent, not least in the competition for European funding and influence over EEC policy directives, a demand for more accountable regional structures developed.

Strong as a sense of regional identity was evident in the North East, North West and Yorkshire and Humberside, the tide has been flowing increasingly strongly in other less well defined regions such as the South West and the West and East Midlands. After all, regional government exists everywhere, albeit in an unco-ordinated, unaccountable fashion. Scepticism in the leadership of New Labour may now give way to a growing recognition that, if only in the interests of effectiveness, all cannot be ordained by central government.

Local government is anxious that new regional institutions should not take to themselves functions, which, in the spirit of subsidiarity, are best discharged locally. It recognises the need for accountable, strategic decision-making in areas such as transport and land use planning, sustainable environmental policy, economic development and regeneration, and the provision of major arts and sports amenities. The forthcoming White Paper on regional government presents a real opportunity to develop the case and refine the proposals. It could permit the UK to emulate the successful pluralist systems that have helped many of our EU partners to modernise their economies, increase competitiveness and tackle the problems of social disadvantage.

# Introduction

## Stanley Henig

This book has been written and published in what might be termed the interim year between the first and second periods of office of Tony Blair's Labour Government. Modernising Britain's constitution is a central feature of 'New' Labour's programme: it certainly includes devolution. The first term of office witnessed the re-establishment of devolved government in Northern Ireland, its inception in Scotland, creation of a Welsh Assembly and some tentative steps towards the creation of regional authorities in England – including a directly elected assembly and mayor for London and the creation of regional development agencies. On the agenda for the second term are directly elected assemblies for English regions – triggered by referenda.

A key feature of any analysis of the British constitution must be the excessive centralisation of formal political power. The most formal legal/technical phrase is that sovereignty belongs to, and flows from, the 'Queen in Parliament': Parliament is sovereign and no Parliament may bind its successors. From time to time specific formal powers may be granted to lesser, or lower, authorities. But what is given may be taken away. This analysis is in no way altered by the fact that in any modern society there are countervailing forces – economic, financial, industrial, media etc.

The establishment of devolved government in Northern Ireland after the First World War was part of a hoped for solution to the so-called Irish problem. It embodied a first challenge to this overwhelming centralisation. However, the very phrase 'United Kingdom of Great Britain and Northern

Ireland' is a reminder that these arrangements were seen as, somehow, exceptional. Devolution had been introduced to solve a particular problem and not as a result of any belief or commitment to decentralisation as such. A half-century later, the re-imposition of direct rule offered a fresh reminder of the essential characteristics of our constitution.

For the purposes of this introductory chapter, Northern Ireland can to some extent be placed on one side. A necessary, if not a sufficient, condition for ending thirty years of conflict was the setting aside again of direct rule, which had been re-imposed with the near collapse of civil order and the creation of a new, devolved regime. Whilst the Conservative Government, led by John Major, which initiated the process, was a strong supporter of the concept of 'subsidiarity' as it might apply to the European Union, it had no belief in devolution as a principle of government for the United Kingdom. By way of contrast, the New Labour Government which successfully negotiated the 'Good Friday' settlement, also had a major commitment to modernising the British constitution and, *inter alia*, extending the concept of devolution to Scotland, Wales and, ultimately, the English regions.

The chapter by Elizabeth Meehan demonstrates the extent to which the 'Good Friday' agreement and the institutions it spawned stand apart from other devolution arrangements. In attempting to build bridges between two communities and also to lock the Irish Republic into a settlement for Northern Ireland, the Westminster government has used many devices more frequently found in federal systems – Belgium is a particularly interesting parallel. Given that the problems of Northern Ireland are widely perceived as unique, it is possible to argue that these arrangements cannot be considered a precedent. Nonetheless they will stand as a reference point. The federal aspects of the settlement, including the involvement of the Irish Republic in what successive British Governments had always considered to be the domestic affairs of the United Kingdom, cannot but have an impact on the theoretically inviolable concept of the sovereignty of 'Queen in Parliament'. In a strict sense Parliament may not have bound its successors, but the British Government has nonetheless effectively renounced any right or capacity for Westminster to make unilateral decisions about future constitutional arrangements for Northern Ireland.

The roots of devolution for Scotland and Wales are quite different. In political terms the settlement in Northern Ireland remains a compromise between nationalists whose goal is to merge into the Republic and advocates of the United Kingdom some of whom might have preferred the province to be part of Great Britain, along traditional Scottish or Welsh lines. By way of contrast, it has been the concept and challenge of independence – the equivalent would be unimaginable in the context of Northern Ireland – which has driven forward the devolution process in Scotland. In her chapter, Jane Saren looks at the new constitutional arrangements in their own right, whilst Alex Wright – by way of contrast – considers that they may be ephemeral and assesses the prospects for independence and/or a federal solution for Scotland in the UK and/or in Europe.

As the devolved regimes for Northern Ireland, Scotland and Wales 'bed in', the question of what to do about England has inevitably moved up the political agenda. There are two aspects of what might be termed the 'English question'. For orthodox constitutionalists it seems anomalous that MPs from the other three countries can discuss and potentially determine legislation affecting England whose MPs do not have the same rights for certain issues which affect Scotland and Wales. Whilst theoretically the same holds true also for Northern Ireland, this is widely regarded as being a small price to pay for a settlement of civil strife. Equally, so long as Labour enjoys a huge parliamentary majority in England as well as Scotland and Wales the issue is unlikely to surface in the real world. However, it is worth bearing in mind the differing political histories of the three countries. During the years of Conservative supremacy at Westminster from 1979 until 1997, the party never won a majority of seats in either Scotland or Wales. It was consequently easy enough to mount a case for devolution on the grounds that the Westminster Government did not represent either country. However, from 1970 until 1997 the Conservatives always won a majority of seats in England – a situation which may well recur if and when the gloss on 'New' Labour diminishes.

For the present the other aspect of the English question has greater political salience. This concerns the perceived impact of devolution on relatively deprived regions in Northern England. These regions with a record of strong Labour support are looking increasingly enviously at the financial arrangements accompanying devolution for Northern Ireland, Scotland and Wales. Closer to London, regional boundaries are much more fuzzy and there is markedly less enthusiasm for a new tier of government. Labour's response is to propose an *à la carte* approach. Directly elected assemblies will be available to regions 'on request' as and when they are sanctioned by referenda. Taken together with the devolved regimes in the other three countries and the differing types of local authorities, this suggests that for the immediate future sub-Westminster government will resemble a patchwork quilt.

At this stage the principles behind Labour's modernisation programme remain constitutionally subordinate to the formally unchanging sovereignty of the 'Queen in Parliament'. It follows that stitches to hold the quilt in place are essentially pragmatic and political. Nonetheless the emergence of a new tier of sub-Westminster governance at national and/or regional level must generate interest in structures of governance and their inter-relations. In bringing Britain much closer to the European Union norm, it also focuses attention on federal theory with its interest in the impact on governance of the separation of political and constitutional power between different tiers.

Few concepts have been so (wilfully) misunderstood in British political life as federalism. In large part this reflects the success of anti-Europeans opposed to the development of what they call federalism which they equate – erroneously and disingenuously - with the fantasy of a European super-state. It is sometimes suggested, with total disregard for history, that federalism is somehow intrinsically anti-British. The reality is quite different. We bequeathed federal structures as a constitutional norm for the British dominions and sought to do the same in Central Africa and the West Indies. Britain also played an important role in planning and facilitating the constitution for the post-war Federal Republic of Germany. None of those involved seemed to have any serious doubt that federalism was a respectable, indeed desirable, form of governance which could safeguard liberty by checking too great a concentration of power at the centre, whilst at the same time offering effective government. Perhaps there is an unspoken assumption that such matters simply have no resonance for a unitary Great Britain and a *United* Kingdom. It is part of our popular political culture that our government is more efficient than any other (even though the media which help promote such a view devote even more time to undermining public satisfaction) whilst our liberties are protected by parliamentary democracy.

Labour's modernisation programme can be posited as a challenge to this traditional rather smug view which in the twenty-first century has seemingly little relevance to the real world. Britain has 'imported' human rights to reinforce, or substitute for the failures of, our parliamentary democracy, whilst there has been a depressing litany of instances where the administrative machinery of government has simply failed to deliver what either its theoretical political masters or the wider public have demanded. What is particularly fascinating about devolution is that it throws into sharp relief those issues of governance with which federalism is centrally concerned. The new sub-Westminster tier is, or may become, a repository for national or regional loyalties and it will be taking on a variety of governmental functions – even if these are devolved on a highly pragmatic basis. Such a context makes it impossible to disregard the whole complex of intergovernmental relations and how they are to be organised and regulated. We may finally opt for muddling through, preserving what one contributor (Ines Newman) describes as an institutional mess, but there is a need to be aware of the problems and their consequences. Another contributor (Baron Isherwood) gives a graphic description of the interface between deconcentrated government regional offices (pre-1997) and the new Regional Development Agencies. All told it is perhaps not surprising that few of our contributors believe that federal theory has contributed much to date towards the programme of devolution. New Labour modernisation of the British constitution rests on an essentially pragmatic framework, which may not provide solutions to the problems and conflicts inherent in inter-institutional relations.

By way of contrast federalism offers not only a coherent philosophy with a set of principles, but also a great deal of practical experience of the working of government at different levels and its inter-relationships. A major concern of this book is to look at the extent to which arrangements currently being made do, by design of accident, in fact contain within them federal aspects. In looking at the ways in which devolved powers operate, authors will seek to identify problems and assess the extent to which federal thinking could contribute towards solutions.

The chapter by Wilfried Swenden will examine practical issues involved in the management of federal structures and will also look at a number of federations. There is an incredible diversity of federal structures. However, all are underpinned by certain principles and fundamental concepts: for this reason it may be useful to devote some space in this introductory chapter to federalism and federal theory. Central to federalist philosophy is the institutional dispersal of political power. The key feature is that power is shared between different levels or tiers of government. The sharing is enshrined in a constitutional settlement, which regulates relations between these levels of government. Revocation of, or amendment to, that settlement requires agreement from both levels. It follows that the central authority cannot simply wipe out the sub-national authorities as the then British Government did with the Greater London Council. It seems to me equally to be the case that secession by a part of the federation could only take place by some kind of mutual agreement enshrined in a legal process.

The key concept is that of 'entrenchment' – equivalent to legal protection. This will operate in slightly different ways depending on the nature of the federation. It may be worth exploring two contrasting models. The first envisages a federal system created within a single state or country. The 'lower' levels of government need legal protection so that they cannot be removed or their powers significantly changed by simple fiat of central government. In the second, the federation is a grouping of separate states or countries: the European Union is the obvious example. In this case the newly created central authority must be entrenched. The most likely safeguard would be a requirement that removal of, or significant changes in, its powers would require the agreement of all or most of the states or countries. Of course, at their extremes these two models are essentially theoretical. There are federations, Switzerland is a good example, which have characteristics from both and where both tiers of government are entrenched.

It is worth pointing out that British entry into the developing federation of the European Union represented a significant undermining of the sovereignty of the 'Queen in Parliament', breaching the operating principle that no Parliament can bind its successors. That principle has not been formally breached by any of the devolution settlements to date, although that with

Northern Ireland may come close in certain respects. Entrenchment clauses require a basic law – in effect part of the constitution. Whilst the procedure for amending the constitution may be largely political, the preservation of the federation has to be underpinned by legal guarantee – in effect enforced by the courts. Thus, the European Court of Justice supersedes 'Queen in Parliament' on issues concerned with the European Union.

There is one other crucial feature of any federal system. Each tier of government must have its independent source of revenue which cannot be turned off by the other tier. Again there are different ways of achieving this. Taxation powers may be distributed by kind between the different tiers or there may be a formula which automatically divides the proceeds of some or all taxes. There has not been the remotest suggestion that Labour's modernisation programme encompasses the relaxation of Treasury control that this would imply. Indeed, many would see this is a key difference between devolution and federalism.

Advocacy of a federal structure for the United Kingdom is not the purpose of this book. All the authors recognise the inherent difficulty of 'producing a federal scheme satisfactorily tailored to fit the circumstances of England' because 'a federation consisting of four units – England, Scotland, Wales and Northern Ireland – would be so unbalanced as to be unworkable.'[1] Any idea that this problem could somehow be circumvented by equating individual English regions with the other three countries would seem to be a fantasy. However, much of the philosophy and many of the concepts and structures which underpin, and are spawned by, federalism have considerable relevance and resonance for a centralised 'super-state' which embarks on the path of decentralisation and devolution. One aim of this book is to look at just what contribution federal ideas and federal practices can make to the modernisation of our constitution.

The bulk of this book falls into three substantive sections. The first includes chapters on Northern Ireland, Scotland and Wales by Elizabeth Meehan, Jane Saren and Barry Jones. All pay some attention to the performance to date of the devolved institutions. The second substantive section of the book focuses on English issues with chapters devoted to the establishment of the GLA and the election of a Mayor for London (Alex Bax); the ongoing plans for regional devolution outside London (John Tomaney); the administrative interface between Government Offices for the Regions and Regional Development Agencies (Baron Isherwood); and the relationship between local government and regional authorities (Stanley Henig). By way of contrast Ines Newman re-assesses the devolutionary process in England in a wider European context.

The third part of the book shifts the focus right into that wider context – the European federation or, as some would have it, quasi-federation of which we are already a part. Wilfried Swenden relates devolution to federal thinking and practice in Europe. Alan Butt Philip in a sense reverses Newman's approach by focusing on devolution from a European viewpoint. Alex Wright grasps the federal dimension and examines its possibilities from a Scottish viewpoint.

Going back, the book actually begins with a foreword by Alan Whitehead MP, Parliamentary Under-Secretary of State at the Department of Transport, Local Government and the Regions and an introduction by Sir Jeremy Beecham, Chairman of the Local Government Association. These are balanced at the end by what might be termed an epilogue from Louise Ellman MP. She assesses the progress of devolution, gives the background to the forthcoming White Paper and offers a vision for the future.

The authors all share the prime interest of the Federal Trust in governance. We do not intend this book to be prescriptive or to be structured around a dominant over-arching theme. Rather it is a series of essays inspired by the concept and process of changing our traditional constitution and intended to offer a contribution to the debate.

### Notes

[1] Royal Commission on the Constitution, London: HMSO, 1973.

# 2

# The Celtic Challenge to our Unitary State

# The Implications of Devolution for Scotland:
## 'Shaken, not stirred'

## Jane Saren

### Introduction

The establishment of the Scottish Parliament in May 1999 was potentially an enormous challenge to the traditional, centralised British state. This chapter examines the political thinking within Scotland leading to the demand for devolution and suggests some frameworks which can help explore where the process of devolution may be heading. In particular it looks at how the principles of national identity politics could evolve to assist the UK as a whole in the transition to a modern European Member State.

Undoubtedly devolution was a shock to the concentrated authority which has characterised the British political system. The Scottish Parliament in particular was deliberately designed as a break from the traditional Westminster model of centralised power and executive control. Features such as the electoral system, the power of the Committees and the power of the Scottish Parliament vis-à-vis the Executive are a testament to this intent.

Nonetheless it is questionable how far this impact has affected the overall functioning of the British state – thus far.

### Why a Scottish Parliament?

What was the impetus for creating the Scottish Parliament? It is impossible to make predictions about where Scotland may be headed without some consideration of how we have arrived at the current position.

When asked the reason for the establishment of the Scottish Parliament, many would now answer 'Margaret Thatcher' – and it is undoubtedly true that it was the repeated experience of Scotland voting for a different party to govern the UK at successive General Elections in the 1980s and early 1990s which stoked the demand. From this perspective, Holyrood is an insurance policy that this situation will not arise again.

However there is a much older pedigree to demands for 'Home Rule'. Ever since the Union of 1707 there had been those who sought to undo it. Home Rule was a principle of the Scottish Liberals, significantly boosted in the 1880s when Gladstone took up the cause of Home Rule for Ireland. The Scottish Home Rule movement spans a number of political traditions including the early years of Labourism in Scotland. Then, as now, the motivation was complex. Arguments in favour included the need to defend the Liberal Party's Scottish base against nationalist advance. A case was made on grounds of good governance typified by Asquith's depiction of Westminster as 'a congested centre' overloaded with business pertaining to only one of the 4 nations of the Union. There was also an element of assertion of nationalist or Scottish identity politics evident, for example, in Ramsay MacDonald's diagnosis in 1915 of the weakness of the pre-First World War Labour movement in Scotland being, in part, it 'had not been Scotch enough'.

It was as a response to the threat of Nationalism that devolution for Scotland was adopted as Labour and Conservative policy in the 1970s. In the February 1974 election the Labour Party, by then a straightforwardly Unionist party, polled 37 per cent and won 40 seats in Scotland. The party's own internal polling (contrary to received wisdom, an activity undertaken long before Peter Mandelson's reign as Director of Communications) indicated that 13 of these seats were vulnerable to the SNP at a future election. With the help of some old-style fixing of trade union votes, Harold Wilson foisted a commitment to 'a directly elected assembly with legislative powers within the context of the political and economic unity of the UK'. Edward Heath had similarly manoeuvred a top-down adoption of a policy of mild devolution within the Conservative Party, which featured in its 1970 General Election manifesto, but was edged aside by local government reform when the Tories took power.

J.P. Mackintosh provided the seminal intellectual case for devolution as part of a UK-wide process of decentralisation, which was argued on the grounds of efficacy and good governance, in 'The Devolution of Power: Local Democracy, Regionalism and Nationalism'. Mackintosh (1929 –1978) was Professor of Politics at Strathclyde University before being elected Labour MP for Berwickshire and East Lothian in 1966. He brought an analytical and academic rigour to the debates on the structure of 'Government *outside* Whitehall' and supported devolution for Scotland within a comprehensive framework of 'workable regionalism' covering Wales, Northern Ireland, Greater London and the English regions.

At the same time, he was aware of the emotional impetus behind nationalism, 'the answer to so many of the present discontents'. His prognosis in 1974 was that the other parties could never win so long as they fought 'on the ground chosen by the SNP, namely what can these parties do for Scotland?' He argued that devolution or favourable spending allocations for Scotland could never counter the appeal of the SNP without a challenge to the fundamental nationalist perspective:

> 'And anything that they suggest will always be inadequate [...] so long as there is no proper pride in being British. Only one thing will halt or reverse the onward march of the SNP and that is a period of government in London which is really successful so that it ends with a satisfied electorate eager to vote positively for a party that has once again restored the feeling that Britain is a successful, worthwhile country to belong to for those who do have other places where they can go and other traditions and titles to which they can turn.'

Following the October 1974 General Election the Wilson Government undertook the long process of steering devolution legislation through Westminster. The subsequent referendum in 1979 produced a modest majority on a 64 per cent turnout, famously falling below the threshold of 40 per cent of the electorate which had been set in the Act (by a successful amendment from George Cunningham, a Scot and Labour MP representing a London constituency).

Those involved on both sides remember this as a period of intense, passionate and bitterly divided Scottish politics. However traumatic it may have been at the time, the extended rehearsal of the arguments almost certainly strengthened the devolution plans of the 1990s, which took on board many of the earlier criticisms and offered responses.

After the 1979 referendum, a new generation of political activists arose for whom constitutional reform for Scotland became the central question. Wendy Alexander, now Minister for Enterprise and Lifelong Learning in Scotland and an erstwhile member of Scottish Labour Action, the Home Rule faction of the Labour Party, stated in an Edinburgh International Book Festival lecture: 'All my contemporaries were preoccupied with what it meant to be a Scot.' A further indication of the extent to which the Conservative governments of the 1980s and 1990s fostered support for some form of Home Rule is her statement:

'[...] for many in Scotland national identity has become a way of expressing a commitment to social justice – in a way that has not been available to English socialists and social democrats.'

One wonders whether William Morris and George Orwell would agree.

Lindsay Paterson, Professor of Educational Policy at the University of Edinburgh, has gone further in suggesting that the dominant ideology in Scotland in the post-war Union was social democracy. He describes a distinct and complex process of consultation on policy, which he calls 'the Scottish instance of political pluralism – the governing of complex welfare states by means of negotiation between the state and organised interest groups.' It was when the Conservative governments began to move away from this consensus approach of 'Scottish democratic unionism' that 'a memory of its successes became a leitmotiv of the campaign for home rule.'

The notion of a democratic deficit in Scotland also relied on a sense of national identity. Writing in an Institute for Public Policy Research publication on the politics of devolution in 1996, James McCormick and Wendy Alexander commented that 'for most Scots, Scotland's democratic claim rests on a cultural and political identity which is distinct from a British identity.'

The traditional left wing inside, and indeed outside, the Labour Party had up until the 1980s seen 'the national question' in Scotland through a socialist prism. According to this analysis, nationalists sought to impose a spurious concept of a unified Scottish interest on the whole country, ignoring genuine conflicts of interest between different classes. In 1970, for example, Tom Nairn was a Marxist, employing his gift for crafting a baroque phrase to denounce the quest for Scottish Home Rule:

> 'It is not at all evident that the forms of autonomy one can reasonably foresee – whether partial or total – could cure the disease. They might perpetuate it, crystallising the long central hopelessness of Scottish history within a framework of archaic bourgeois nationality.'

The view of national identity as a historical construct with a specific role and place in human history now appears to be utterly out of fashion within Scotland. It may be that the predominant ideology has changed. On the other hand, perhaps the years of Thatcherite rule dimmed the solidarity of the Scottish Labour representatives with their English brothers and sisters and made the politics of national identity more compelling. Eric Hobsbawm observes dryly that a local, regional or sectional interest is strengthened if it can don a national costume:

> 'The Cornish are fortunate to be able to paint their regional discontents in the attractive colours of Celtic tradition, which makes them so much more viable. [...] They are luckier than, say, Merseyside, which can mobilise in defence of the equally or more hard-hit local interests only the memory of the Beatles, of generations of Scouse comedians, and the proud traditions of its rival football teams.' (*Nations and Nationalism since 1780*, p. 178)

The view that Liverpool and Glasgow had more in common than Glasgow and Edinburgh, once held widely on the left in Scotland, was eroded by successive General Election defeats suffered by the Labour Party. One consequence of the centralisation of power under the Conservatives was a tendency in Scotland to equate England with the South East and London. Devolution began to look like an attractive alternative to waiting for the politics of individualism south of the border to recede.

A further strand in the complex interweaving of support for a Scottish Parliament was expressed in 'The Claim of Right' produced by the Scottish Constitutional Convention in 1995. At a time when political activists in the Labour party south of the border were grappling with the need to revisit shibboleths such as Clause Four, interventionist economic policy and the internal democracy of trade unions, Scotland was more exercised with devolution as the route to modernisation, a new politics and maintaining a connection with the party's traditional base.

The Scottish Constitutional Convention was established after the 1987 election as a vehicle for communication between the Campaign for a Scottish Assembly, and the political parties. It gained the support of Labour and the Liberal Democrats in Scotland. The Scottish Constitutional Convention saw itself, and was talked about by devolutionists, as representing the whole of Scottish society; in reality it was closer to 'Scotland's anti-establishment establishment', as Andrew Marr puts it. It may be that this partial engagement with the population of Scotland now represents a challenge which the Scottish Parliament has to overcome.

Does all of this history matter? Certainly, it does. As Kierkegaard said, life has to be lived forwards but can only be understood in retrospect. After only two years of the new Scottish Parliament, it is far too soon to reach conclusions about where Scotland's relationship with the rest of the UK is headed. At the same time, an understanding of what is expected from the new institution is essential in order to make sense of how it is being judged.

### The mid-term assessments

Much has been written about the first two years of the Scottish Parliament. The assessments of the first year of the Scottish Parliament in the summer of 2000 were mixed, but – with the exception of Canon Kenyon Wright, the chair of the Constitutional Convention – scarcely laudatory. The sudden death of the First Minister, Donald Dewar, in November of that year was a harsh reminder that politicians are mortals too. Criticism became somewhat more muted for a brief time, but Dewar's successor Henry McLeish was soon the subject of excoriating media comment. It is tempting to agree with

Presiding Officer David Steel's sentiments about 'bitch journalism' in Scotland – much of the Scottish print media has been scathing. James Naughtie, however, cautioned that press comment on the House of Commons in the era of Gladstone, Disraeli, Palmerston and other Parliamentary giants, illustrates that politicians are always subject to harsh scrutiny. Indeed Naughtie suggests that historians may well look back to the early days of the Scottish Parliament as a great advance in how politics is practised.

The more supportive, and reflective, commentators have made allowances for the challenge of starting such an institution from scratch and have concentrated on the achievements: getting the committee system functioning in its combined role of scrutiny and policy formation; the passage of overdue legislation of modest scope; and the increase in political participation which has ensued. There is also a sense of satisfaction that there are now discernible areas of policy divergence in Scotland, such as student tuition fees and the funding of long term care of elderly people (whatever the criticisms of the substance).

Graham Leicester, Director of the Scottish Council Foundation has produced a report card on devolution at the end of each year of the Scottish Parliament. In the first of these, he concluded that devolution had not lived up to its potential and pointed to the 'frustration of the actors **within** the system' (my emphasis):

> 'That frustration is felt by ministers who cannot force through innovations and blame their civil servants; by civil servants who cannot find any coherence in fragmented ministerial policy driven by press releases, glossy initiatives and set piece speeches; by the Parliament's committees either tied down with government legislation or else daunted by the scope of their remit and an inability to prioritise; by individual MSPs living an itinerant lifestyle based more around the demands of local newspapers and the constituency mailbag than the vision they all hold of a better Scotland.'

By July 2001, Leicester was reflecting on 'one of the most prolonged 'silly seasons' in modern politics' in the months following the death of Dewar. He argues that this period demonstrated devolution's 'feet of clay' and yet simultaneously endeared it to the Scottish public by making its institutions and personalities 'part of the furniture':

'Devolution really does now seem a perennial feature of the landscape – for which we hold an affection but no great expectations.'

The long history of the campaign for the Parliament and the patchwork of expectations that have been pinned onto it go a long way to explaining these harsh judgements, made of its performance to date.

What is incontrovertible is that the Scottish Parliament is here to stay for the foreseeable future. Iain McWhirter, political commentator and columnist, suggests that 'anyone who looks objectively at the achievements of the Scottish Parliament in its first year would have to conclude that it has had a major impact on Scottish civil society.' Joyce MacMillan, journalist and theatre critic, is a long-standing champion of devolution and was a member of the Constitutional Steering Group, established by Donald Dewar as Secretary of State after the 1997 General Election to produce detailed plans for the operation of the Scottish Parliament. She has spoken of her frustration with those who indulge in fundamental criticisms of the new institution, and suggested that such critics should be obliged to state what they would prefer to see in its place. They should make explicit their support for the *status quo ante*, for separation from the UK, or else state precisely how they would improve the existing constitutional settlement.

MacWhirter makes the acute observation that the level of complaint is, paradoxically, another sign of the acceptance of devolution as a given fact of life:

'[...] Scotland seems to have stopped blaming London for everything that is wrong in Scottish society. They now have someone else to blame in Edinburgh. If you like, the grievance culture has been repatriated: instead of girning about Westminster, Scots are now girning about the Scottish Parliament.'

## Policy making in a devolved Scotland

Magnus Linklater, a former editor of the Scotsman, has noted that much of the criticism directed at the Scottish Executive has been for a perceived lack of radicalism in its programme. The Executive is a Labour – Liberal Democrat coalition. Linklater mused that it may be in the nature of coalition politics to lead to over-caution. At the same time, he acknowledged that in the aftermath of major constitutional change, a sound case could be argued for pursuing a strategy of building confidence in 'safe' government.

An alternative view is that the national identity politics, which fuelled Scottish devolution, rendered 'national self-determination' the ultimate aim. In this atmosphere of Hegelian nationalism, the policies that could be enacted by the new institution were a secondary concern. Had J.P. Mackintosh still been alive, one can imagine far more energy being devoted to the policy detail.

One of the first bills passed by the Scottish Parliament, the Incapacitated Adults Act, is a perfect example of the kind of specifically Scottish legislation which Mackintosh argued was crowded out in the Westminster timetable and justified the creation of a special institution (in *A Diverse Assembly*, p.84). Whilst not a headline-grabber, this was an important technical piece of legislation required to remove an area of ambiguity in Scots law regarding the management of the personal affairs of adults affected by mental illness and dementia.

Such modest and worthwhile legislation was never going to meet the level of expectation fostered about what devolution would deliver. There was a particular irony in the juxtaposition of the presentation-conscious Blair Government at Westminster with the restrained and understated style of the Dewar administration in Edinburgh.

This was highlighted when the major announcements of the NHS Plan, 10-Year Transport Investment Plan etc. were made for England and Wales towards the end of the 1999 – 2000 Westminster session. Scotland was in a slightly odd and somewhat unsatisfactory position. Under the Barnett Formula, additions are made to Scotland's block grant pro rata when Whitehall Departmental budgets are increased. The money is not ring-fenced and it is up to the Scottish Executive to determine its own allocation across spending departments.

On health, it was clear that the commitments did not apply north of the border and that decisions about the allocation of increased funding would be made by the Scottish Executive in the autumn.

This suggested a plethora of issues. First, there remains a public expectation of a *National* Health Service with equitable levels of provision throughout the UK: indeed, Tony Blair said in his speech to the 2000 Labour Party conference, 'the best NHS for each of us is an NHS for all of us, throughout Britain.' Second, in a limited and mobile labour market, the NHS in England was able to recruit additional staff in advance of the Scottish Executive determining its additional staffing requirements.

The delay before the announcement of the Scottish Health Plan created an opportunity for a campaign to build in Scotland, to match or better the English Plan. In this case the particular focus was the full implementation of the Sutherland Commission report on long term care for elderly people. Perhaps this is a fortuitous means for popular pressure to be exerted on the priority setting of politicians. However it is important that the public debate acknowledges that this involves a choice about spending priorities and goes beyond a determination to match England for every penny when government spending increases are announced. Susan Deacon, the Health Minister in the Scottish Executive, is unusual (and brave) as an MSP who is prepared to acknowledge that the NHS in Scotland is already well-provided in comparison with the health service south of the border. She has suggested that the Scottish Parliament should concentrate its efforts on ensuring the effective use of those resources, rather than pledging itself to maintain the exact level of current differential advantage.

Finally, in this era of performance management and accountability of public services to their consumers, it seems reasonable to ask how Scotland's NHS provision compares to England, Wales, and Northern Ireland. The majority of British people still regard the NHS as a British institution and expect some equity of provision across the land. However devolution makes such comparisons increasingly difficult without a shared commitment to maintaining data using common definitions and bases.

The UK Government's review of energy policy has highlighted the limitations of a stark dualist approach, which draws a line in the sand between reserved and devolved powers. Energy policy is a reserved matter. However, both planning and environmental protection are devolved. Concern has already been expressed by the SNP and Green Party in the Scottish Parliament that one outcome of the review may be the commissioning of new nuclear power stations. Robin Harper, the Green MSP, has already pointed out in an article entitled 'Facing up to the intricacies of devolution', that since Scots have

> 'under the Scotland Act, control over our environment, [...] we should, if we choose to, be able to set higher standards than the rest of the UK. [...] I would suggest that it is extremely urgent that we investigate all the legislative and democratic means by which we can resist any attempt by Westminster to impose a new nuclear power development on Scotland.' (*Holyrood Magazine*, issue 52, Sept 2001, p. 9)

Harper's view will attract much sympathy in Scotland. Yet Scotland currently sources over 40 per cent of its energy needs from nuclear power and all three of its nuclear power stations are scheduled to cease production over the next ten to fifteen years. Investment in renewable energy cannot come anywhere near to bridging the gap. At the same time, Scotland trades energy over the North-South interconnector and is part of a British energy market. Any decision by Westminster regarding nuclear new build in Scotland is no more or less an imposition than a decision to build a new plant in Cumbria or Wales. What value can be put on citizenship if standards of environmental protection in respect of nuclear safety vary from one part of the United Kingdom to another? Can it be satisfactory for one tier of government, which lacks responsibility and the detailed policy expertise on energy generation to seek to stymie the policy initiative of another?

I raise these questions not as a proponent of nuclear new build but in order to illustrate the potential for the current devolution settlement to throw up enormous tensions in policy making and implementation. Combined with the emotion attached to the nuclear power debate and harnessed to the Scottish desire for a deal of self-determination, one can envisage the circumstances in which a defining constitutional conflict is created.

### Joined-up government for the post-nationalist age?

The challenge for the bedding in of Scottish devolution is to establish a paradigm for the policy process to match the shared governance approach epitomised by J. P. Mackintosh. It is now commonplace amongst political theorists to assume that globalisation has heralded the post-nationalist age. It is no longer the case that national identity has to be an exclusive category, fitting the 'either – or' mindset beloved of the Scottish press and our less imaginative parliamentarians (and betrayed by the mishmash of ethnic and national identity questions served up in the Scottish version of the census). One can hold parallel allegiances to a range of identities including Scottish, British, European, Asian, African etc and these may be greater or stronger in degree depending upon the context and over time.

Similarly, there is no reason why an element of non-exclusive cultural nationalism should not exist, without challenging a broader political authority. Nonetheless, this demands the development of a political language and new policy co-ordinating mechanisms, which acknowledge the new pluralism and do not keep bringing us to T-junctions at which we must choose one direction or another. Writing about Ireland, Richard Kearney notes that 'inherited notions of absolutist sovereignty are being challenged both within nation states and by developments in international legislation.' He cites the British-Irish Council of the Isles as 'a **practical** form of joint sovereignty.'

Turning back to Westminster-Holyrood relations, the Joint Ministerial Committee 'has grown to become the central piece of political machinery in underpinning the devolution settlement.' (Hazell, 2000) There is a certain irony in the lack of transparency of the main co-ordinating mechanism in the light of the civic principles of openness, accountability and transparency on which the Scottish Parliament was founded.

Much has been said and written about the need to reconnect politicians and the electorate, following the lowest turnout under universal franchise in the UK, in the General Election of June 2001. The creation of the Scottish Parliament was in itself meant to lessen the distance between the political elite and the governed. Perhaps some means can be devised of enabling wider popular participation in policy making on knotty issues such as health service prioritisation or meeting future energy needs whilst protecting the environment, which supersede the prickly sensitivities of institutional sovereignty and help to address the real concerns of the population, north and south of the border?

The unionist political parties also need to develop more sophisticated means of dealing with policy making for the new, devolved Britain. To date, the British parties have tended to adopt a de facto franchising approach to policy making for the party bodies within Scotland. Whilst it is entirely sensible to insist that devolution means different policy positions may be taken in England and Scotland, there remains a need for an overall, encompassing ideological mission statement which renders the whole coherent. Since party activists tend by nature to be locally focused, consideration also needs to be given of ways of fostering dialogue across the geographical parties. The alternative would seem to be a growing resentment of central control whenever the British party is forced to intervene to establish consistency. Doubtless we can learn from overseas experience in building the machinery by which political parties can retain an overarching identity and at the same time operate in a multi-tiered pluralist democratic state. Such an approach is also relevant to the relationship between Parliaments and local government, and to the European Union.

The EU is a good example of the need to engage party activists and politicians in the development of a popular political language which can accommodate the realities of differential sovereignty. Because of the impulse behind devolution, it is Westminster rather than Brussels, which is the *bête noire* for MSPs and the Scottish media. Nonetheless the challenge of meaningful political accountability and inclusive democracy is a common denominator in our era of complex multiple governance. A simple illustration of the maze of accountability is that each voter in Scotland now has 19 elected representatives across their local council, the Scottish Parliament, Westminster and the European Parliament.

**Local government**

Local councils remain heavily dependent on grants from the Scottish Executive to finance their expenditure – 80 per cent of their funding comes from this source. Local government was somewhat wary of a loss of power with the creation of the Scottish Parliament and has sought to enshrine its role and rights, initially in a concordat and now in a Partnership Framework document between the Scottish Executive and local government. This defines the working arrangements and requirements for consultation between the layers of government.

The establishment of the Scottish Parliament has created a stronger executive at the centre, and a greater interest in and scrutiny of local government in the Parliament. Alongside this, the Scottish Executive has discovered that local government holds most of the levers for action and remains crucial even when new partnerships such as community schools and Social Inclusion Partnerships are established. Local government feels under a degree of threat; many Scottish Executive ministers admit privately to frustration. Councillors resent the constant calls to improve from a set of central institutions, which have yet to demonstrate their own effectiveness in performance management and modernisation. However unless the Scottish Executive develops an appetite for the political challenge that real reform of local government would entail, the stand off will continue.

**Refereeing the settlement**

Writing in 2000, Robert Hazell considered that 'intergovernmental relations in the UK have got off to a gentle and remarkably smooth start.' Hazell contrasts this with the 'fierce tensions and major disputes with political wrangling and court battles which can characterise [...] federal systems' and ascribes it to the 'pragmatic and gradualist approach' adopted by the UK Government.

Thus far the cases of dispute have been internal to Scotland rather than requiring the involvement of the Privy Council. The Scottish courts have been used to challenge the processes of the Scottish Parliament, by the *Scotsman* newspaper regarding the holding of Committee sessions in private; and by the Countryside Alliance in relation to the involvement of a charity in the drafting of Mike Watson's Private Member's Bill which seeks to outlaw fox hunting.

Now that Scottish devolution has comprehensive cross-party support, the political imperative for the existence of the Scottish Parliament appears to be sufficient guarantee of its continued existence. There has been no real demand for its entrenchment beyond the Scotland Act. The area of dispute lies rather in the strategy of the separatist parties to push at the boundaries of the devolved powers and paint a picture of how much more, in their eyes, could be achieved with independence.

In a very real sense, H.M. Treasury is an important referee between the UK Government and the Scottish Executive. The latter has appealed to the Treasury for additional financial assistance to enable it to implement its policies in respect of writing off Glasgow City Council housing debt and provision of free personal care for the elderly. Given the political sensitivities of using the Scottish Parliament's discretionary personal income tax powers, there has been considerable discussion of the virtues of 'fiscal autonomy'. This would replace the block grant to the Scottish Executive from the Treasury with a system whereby the Scottish Parliament would collect Scottish taxes (whatever the definition) and make payment to the Exchequer for Scotland's share of UK reserved services, such as defence and social security. Unless there is a suggestion that Scotland is a net contributor rather than beneficiary from the Treasury's present division of the spoils, this is a zero sum game. In practice this system would not obviate the need for the Scottish Executive and Parliament to grapple with priorities in its spending commitments and confront the fiscal implications of its political preferences. It also sits oddly with the alleged social democratic preference of the Scots that we should wish to set up a balance sheet relationship with the rest of the British Isles rather than accept the liberal principle of citizenship whereby the legitimacy of the state's redistributive role is accepted.

## Conclusion

Where is Scotland headed? And what are the implications for the future of the UK?

After only two and a half years of devolution, it is extremely early to offer a definitive judgement of the predominant direction. Even within the Labour Party, views of the ultimate destination range from the 'motorway with only one exit' (Dalyell) to 'modern governance in the information age' (Wendy Alexander).

The centralised, traditional British state has thus far proved more resilient than either champions or opponents of devolution had expected. The predominance of the small 'n' nationalist paradigm in Scotland has slowed, or perhaps helped to prevent, a domino effect of constitutional reform encompassing the monarchy, House of Lords, electoral reform and English regional government.

It may be that the most important contribution which Scotland can make to modernisation of the British state is to provide an example of a country which can embrace the principle of subsidiarity whilst maintaining a robust and confident national identity. If we accept that the pursuit of unfettered national sovereignty in the 21$^{st}$ century is, in the phrase quoted by Francis Fukuyama, ' a game played at the end of history', then our challenge is to create the more sophisticated political discourse and mechanisms which protect the values of democracy, pluralism and accountability in a complex and multi-tiered series of political units (Francis Fukuyama, 'Don't do it Britannia', in *Prospect*, May 2000).

A focus on the requirement to create a political culture which embraces complexity yet strives for meaningful accountability could also usefully inform the debate on the number of MSPs following the reduction of Scottish representation at Westminster. The Scotland Act requires a concomitant drop in the number of first-past-the-post MSPs in order to maintain co-terminosity of Westminster and Holyrood constituencies. The discussion in Scotland to date has been determined by one of two perspectives: the busy-ness of the current 129 MSPs and the 'Westminster is trying to take something away from us' outlook. Given the level of popular disappointment in the Scottish Parliament – a poll in 2001 found that a substantial majority said it had made no impact on their lives – it might be that the legislative requirement to reconsider numbers is a great opportunity for reform in the public interest. The MSPs could review the operation of the Parliament, determine realistic priorities in areas in which it can exert influence and/or legislate and consider how it can operate more effectively. They could seek to co-operate with Westminster in increasing the transparency and public understanding of the liaison machinery. In many ways the issue will be a test of the maturity of the institution and of the political debate in Scotland.

Central government has to maintain a consistent, but not controlling, interest in the operation of the devolved institutions. It should play a facilitating role in promoting new fora for dialogue, exchange and debate. The political parties could also seek means of enabling activists to engage across geographical boundaries. Certainly, the unionist parties must develop positive and explicit defences of the Union, the best defence being the practical demonstration of the benefits of intergovernmental partnership.

Some of Donald Dewar's papers have recently been donated to the nation by his children, including a copy of the Scotland Act inscribed by Tony Blair. The inscription reads: 'To Donald – It was a struggle; it may always be hard; but it was worth it. Scotland and England together on equal terms!'

Indeed it probably will always be hard – but meeting these challenges is the only certain route by which we can hope to channel the abundant energy, vast talent and enormous promise of modern Scotland.

**Key dates**

May 1997          Election of a Labour government with the manifesto commitment to legislate within its first year for a Scottish Parliament, dependent on the endorsment of the Scottish electorate in a pre-legislative referendum.
Publication of the White Paper 'Scotland's Parliament'.

July 1997          Referendums (Scotland and Wales) Act receives Royal Assent.

September 1997     Referendum held in Scotland.

December 1997     Scotland Bill introduced at Westminster.

November 1998     Scotland Act receives Royal Assent.

May 1999          Scottish Parliament elections held.

**Outcome of the first Scottish Parliament Elections**

Votes and seats: May 1999

| Party | FPTP % | FPTP seats | $2^{nd}$ vote % | $2^{nd}$ vote seats | Total seats |
|---|---|---|---|---|---|
| Lab | 39 | 53 | 34 | 3 | 56 |
| SNP | 29 | 7 | 28 | 28 | 35 |
| Cons | 15 | 0 | 15 | 18 | 18 |
| LibDem | 14 | 12 | 13 | 5 | 17 |
| Other | N/A | 1 | N/A | 2 | 3 |
| | | | | | 129 |

**Notable features of the Scottish Parliament**

The Scottish Executive is a coalition, formed by Labour (the largest party, but without an overall majority in the Parliament) and the Liberal Democrats.

The structure of the executive departments is similar to that in the previous Scotland Office, although some titles have been changed.

The committees have substantial powers. In addition to scutinising and amending legislation, they can initiate legislation. They conduct inquiries and have the power to call witnesses. The activity of the Scottish Executive is subject to committee scrutiny, including its financial proposals and administration.

The role of chairing committees is allocated to Members across all 4 main parties, not solely to those parties which make up the Scottish Executive.

# Welsh Devolution
## *Balancing opportunities and frustrations*[1]

## Barry Jones

### Introduction

Devolution was described by Ron Davies, a Welsh Secretary of State, as a process not an event. His intention was to persuade the Welsh electorate that the limited powers devolved to Wales could, with experience and the passage of time, be increased. Many people including the majority of members in the National Assembly for Wales could agree with that assessment. This chapter, however, takes a longer-term view of the 'devolution process' looking back to the 1880's and even beyond.

The historical review shows how nationalism in Wales far from burning brightly, as it did in Ireland and Scotland, fluttered only intermittently. Wales' relationship with England has been close (it could not have been otherwise given the geography) but uncertain and sometimes strained. Demands first for Home Rule in the early twentieth century and later for devolution in the last quarter of the century, always fell short of independence and were couched in constitutional terms; a more accountable bureaucracy, a more sensitive application of government policies, and a greater understanding of and sympathy for the Welsh interest and the Welsh language. Welsh aspirations fell well short of independence but for a more semi-detached relationship with England.

During Mrs Thatcher's premiership there were widely held Welsh concerns that the Welsh case was being discounted or even ignored. Even then, however, the logic of Welsh demands led not to political independence but to democratic accountability. Consequently, legislative devolution, on offer to Scotland and Northern Ireland, was not granted to Wales. Instead executive devolution meant that Wales would continue to depend upon Westminster legislation.

The argument of this chapter is that this unique arrangement poses difficulties between the two levels of government and that the tensions generated could lead to a more extensive devolution of legislative powers akin to those exercised by the Scottish Parliament. Given this scenario, devolution in Wales would appear to be a continuing process the end point of which cannot be determined with any certainty.

**Historical context**

There is no clear historical pattern of Welsh demands for devolution, still less for independence. Indeed there is evidence to the contrary. The sense of a separate Welsh identity has always been problematic given the widely held view that the Welsh are descended from the Ancient Britons. Consequently early Welsh aspirations were not so much a desire for separation from England as the restoration of the historic unity of southern Britain. It was a sentiment so well exploited by Henry Tudor prior to the battle of Bosworth, that his army was substantially Welsh. This Welsh connection was recognised by contemporary observers; the Venetian Ambassador expressed the opinion that 'the Welsh may now be said to have recovered their former independence for the most wise and fortunate Henry VII is a Welshman.[2]

Despite these expectations the 1536 Act of Union incorporated Wales with England. It was not until the nineteenth century and the industrialisation and radicalisation of Welsh society that a sense of national identity emerged, not steeped in the misty traditions of ancient Britain but stimulated by the modern nationalisms of mainland Europe and Ireland. Initially, its expression was not political but administrative. The Welsh Education Act of 1889 created a modern system of secondary education administered by the Central Welsh Board and supplemented in 1907 by the Welsh Department of the Board of Education. National institutions also emerged – the University of Wales in 1893, the National Library and National Museum in 1907 and the Welsh

Health Insurance Commission in 1913. In 1919 the Welsh Board of Health and the Welsh Department of Agriculture were created. Thus the Welsh identity was recognised by progressive administrative decentralisation.

In the 1930's the Welsh Parliamentary Party campaigned for political reform: to establish a Welsh Office and Welsh Secretary of State with a seat in the cabinet. The proposal was rejected by two prime ministers, Chamberlain and Churchill. It was not until 1964 and a new Labour Government headed by Harold Wilson that Wales finally achieved a Welsh Secretary of State and a Welsh Office. Even then, however, powers were extracted from a reluctant Whitehall bureaucracy.

While it could be argued that the campaign for political devolution was sparked into life by Plaid Cymru's Carmarthen by-election victory in 1966, other factors and forces sustained it. Plaid Cymru failed to make a significant electoral breakthrough, while its association with the Welsh language issue antagonised many anglophone Welsh voters. The aim of independence, central to SNP strategy in Scotland, was quite unrealistic in Wales, which lacked a valuable natural resource equivalent to North Sea oil. However there was a small, but growing element of devolutionists in all the Welsh parties. Throughout the period from 1966 to 1997 a substantial minority in the Welsh Labour Party supported devolution and were frequently described as nationalists with a small 'n'. Furthermore, the tradition of Welsh radicalism with a nationalist tinge had never been extinguished in the Liberal Democratic Party. But it is doubtful if these forces would have brought about devolution were it not for Mrs Thatcher's Government during the 1980s.

In the 1979 referendum the Welsh electorate had rejected devolution by an overwhelming 4 to 1 majority and the project appeared to be dead. The Labour Government was defeated subsequently on a vote of no confidence and in the following general election Mrs Thatcher and the Tories came to power committed to a programme of privatisation and rolling back the frontiers of the state. The programme had a draconian impact on Wales. The two basic industries, coal and steel, were decimated. Between 1979 and 1995 the number of coal miners were reduced from 43,000 to less than 2,000 and the Welsh steel industry contracted from 70,000 to 15,000 workers. Whatever the economic case for the policy, the speed and intensity of its application in Wales produced resentment. Fundamental constitutional questions were raised about the legitimacy of a government pursuing policies so detrimental to the Welsh interest while lacking a Welsh mandate.

A similar disenchantment with central government emerged as a result of changes to the administrative structure. Under Mrs Thatcher the Welsh Office acquired new powers and responsibilities including negotiating with the Treasury the level of the local government support grant, and increased responsibilities for agriculture, education, the health service and secondary, further and higher education. Confronted with Labour dominated local authorities the Conservative Government created a raft of quangos to administer many of its reform policies. By the early 1990s the quangos were responsible for £1.5 billion expenditure a year, a situation which led to charges by the Welsh Labour Party of a 'democratic deficit'. A similar accusation was made about the reform of Welsh local government. Despite the unanimous opposition of all the Welsh MPs the Conservatives pressed ahead with the proposals. S.O.86 which stated that any bill relating exclusively to Wales should be considered by all the Welsh MPs in its committee stage was suspended, and Conservative MPs from English constituencies were drafted in to ensure the Government's majority.

**Ambivalent steps to devolution**

Unlike the 1979 referendum the Welsh electorate in 1999 was not asked to endorse government legislation. The 1999 referendum was designed to produce a popular mandate prior to the passage of a government bill. This 'pre-legislative referendum' was concerned with the general principles of devolution rather than detailed proposals which the Government feared might open up divisions in the Welsh Labour Party.

The referendum results were counted in the 22 Welsh unitary local authorities under the supervision of the national returning officer, Professor Eric Sunderland, in the Welsh College of Music in Cardiff. Here the cumulative national total of votes was declared. The final result was very close; the 22 districts were split 11 for and 11 against devolution. In the national vote 50.3 per cent voted 'Yes' to the Government's devolution proposals and 49.7 per cent voted 'No'. The overall majority was wafer-thin, just 6,721. Significant differences in the Welsh electorate were revealed. The traditional north/south split was replaced by an east/west split. The more affluent and anglicised east produced a clear majority of 'no' votes, while the poorer and largely Welsh speaking west gave a similar majority of 'yes' votes. There were also significant variations in turnout; in the most Welsh areas up to 60 per cent of the electorate cast their votes compared with less than 50 per cent in the anglicised eastern districts. Some commentators, noting the nature of the east/west divide, concluded that the first task of devolution was to bind the nation together. In the wake of the referendum a general consensus emerged; no matter how narrow the majority, devolution was now a reality and efforts should be directed to making it work.

The first election to the National Assembly was held on 6 May 1999. The Labour Party was understandably optimistic; in the 1997 general election it had won 55 per cent of the vote in Wales. However, the party faced unexpected problems. Ron Davies, the Welsh Secretary of State who had led the 'Yes' campaign in the referendum, was obliged to resign over a personal scandal. Alun Michael, a Cardiff MP and a minister at the Home Office, was appointed Welsh Secretary and subsequently endured a bitter and bruising leadership contest with Rhodri Morgan, during which claims were made that he was Blair's man: not really an enthusiastic devolutionist but part of the Millbank control system. Large sections of the party were disillusioned not only by the leadership issue but also by the 'twinning system', a mechanism brought in to ensure that a high proportion of women were selected as Labour candidates.

The main conflict in a bitter campaign was between Labour and Plaid Cymru. In a significant departure Plaid declared in its manifesto that it had never wanted 'independence' but self-government, an ambiguous phrase and one which incensed the Labour Party which condemned 'nationalist madness' and the 'independence agenda'. Plaid accused 'New Labour' of being an English party more concerned to win the votes of 'middle England' than to meet the needs of the Welsh working class. Surprisingly Plaid appeared to get the better of the exchange and its denial of 'independence' ambitions made it more attractive to working class voters in the Valleys.

An HTV / NOP poll on the eve of the election suggested that there might be an upset. It revealed that Labour voters were less likely to remain loyal to Labour in a National Assembly election (because it was a Welsh election) and Plaid supporters were more likely to vote than Labour supporters in the Assembly elections. Despite these indications the actual result confounded everyone. Labour lost three rock solid seats, including Rhondda, and the party failed to gain an overall majority winning only 28 of the 60 seats in the Assembly.

National Assembly Election 6 May 1999

| Constituencies and Regional Lists | % Votes | No. of Seats |
|---|---|---|
| Cons | 16.2 | 9 |
| Lab | 36.5 | 28 |
| Lib Dem | 13.0 | 6 |
| Plaid Cymru | 29.5 | 17 |

The Labour Party, either unable or unwilling to form a coalition with the Liberal Democrats, determined to soldier on with a minority administration giving all parties on the subject committees the opportunity to influence policy. This was never entirely satisfactory. Labour found it difficult to come to terms with its failure to win an overall majority and on 9 February 2000 Alun Michael, the First Minister, lost a vote of no confidence and resigned. Subsequently, his adversary in the leadership election, Rhodri Morgan, was elected as Labour leader and First Minister and proceeded to construct a coalition with the Liberal Democrats. Depending on one's viewpoint, devolution had either experienced its first success or first disaster. However, that a new Welsh political system was emerging seemed undeniable.

**Making the system work**

The difficulties of defining the character of devolution in the United Kingdom are exacerbated by the manner in which powers were devolved to Wales. Whereas Scotland was empowered to pass legislation and raise revenue by varying the rate of income tax, the Welsh National Assembly cannot enact primary legislation or raise taxes. The Westminster Parliament continues to legislate for England *and* Wales as it has since the 1536 Act of Union. The Assembly can pass secondary or subordinate legislation in those areas in which the Welsh Secretary of State had previously been constitutionally competent. This is a much more limited form of devolution than that enjoyed by either Scotland or Northern Ireland.

There is another complication. The National Assembly for Wales does not have cabinet-government in the classic Westminster mode. The Welsh cabinet provides political leadership but is not responsible exclusively for policy-making. This deviation from the cabinet norm came about largely because the debate on Welsh devolution embraced a commitment to a more inclusive political process in which all political parties would play a role in 'policy formulation'. Consequently, the six National Assembly subject committees (partly concerned with policy-making) contain representatives of all political parties in the National Assembly.

Finally, confusion was compounded by the Labour Government's decision to retain the two Secretaries of State for Scotland and for Wales so as to represent Scottish and Welsh interests in the United Kingdom cabinet. This arrangement had rather less to do with the devolution settlement than with central government's intention to maintain a role in the post-devolutionary context. While there is little logic for such an arrangement in Scotland, where extensive legislative and revenue raising powers have been devolved, there is a good argument for retaining the Welsh Secretary of State. Given the nature of executive devolution, the Welsh Secretary continues to exercise significant powers in the operation of the Welsh devolution settlement.

While the National Assembly has been denied primary legislative powers, it does possess a legislative capacity. Secondary or subordinate legislation, frequently expressed as statutory instruments, is an important element in the new Welsh policy process. It has the same legal force as primary legislation and is more extensive; on average for every page of primary legislation there are three pages of secondary legislation. In some cases secondary legislation can amend previously enacted primary legislation. Secondary legislation is not simply second class legislation. Significant powers covering 18 policy areas are now the responsibility of the National Assembly (see Appendix, p. 244-245). They include, for example, the ability to restructure the National Health Service in Wales, to organise school examinations and curricula and, not least, to authorise expenditure of approximately £8 billion per annum.

It would be a mistake, therefore, to presume that the National Assembly does not exercise a significant degree of political power. But the exercise of that power is dependent upon the development of a complex set of inter-governmental relationships. It is ironic that as a consequence of executive devolution Wales is obliged to be more pro-active in the procedures of the Westminster Parliament whose legislative programme continues to apply to both England and Wales. The Assembly, together with the Welsh Secretary, must seek to ensure that legislative proposals take full account of the 'Welsh interest'. It will not be alone in this activity. Many public and private organisations from across England will be in competition for the government's support. Much of this activity takes place during the 'pre-legislative consultation' period, characterised by regularised procedures and access to government departments, guaranteed for 'insider' groups but less certain for 'outsiders'. It is not yet clear what kind of preferential status will be accorded to the National Assembly in this consultation exercise. Given the civil service links between the pre-devolution Welsh Office (now part of the National Assembly) and central government departments in Whitehall, one would assume that the Welsh case would be given a sympathetic hearing. Whether this would apply to the same degree if there were different parties in control in Westminster and Cardiff is a moot point and one yet to be tested.

The Government of Wales Act specifically allows the National Assembly 'to make representations about any matter affecting Wales' (Section 33). This could mean promoting legislation specific to the needs of Wales. There is very little historic experience of such legislation. Those Acts of Parliament specific to Wales have usually been concerned with the Welsh language, although the Disestablishment of the Church in Wales Act (1922) is a conspicuous exception. An alternative procedure would involve the attachment of specific clauses to general legislation relating to England and Wales in order to meet specific Welsh needs as identified by the National Assembly. In either case the Assembly can look to the two Westminster parliamentary committees, the Welsh Grand and the Welsh Affairs Select Committee. The Welsh Grand composed of all the Welsh MPs possesses legislative functions and could take responsibility for the committee stage of Welsh Bills. However, the government of the day can always suspend standing orders and appoint MPs from English constituencies to ensure its majority. By contrast the Welsh Affairs Committee is an investigative body, the product of the Welsh electorate's rejection of devolution in the 1979 referendum and based on the departmental committee system created by the newly elected Conservative Government. It shadowed the Welsh Office and scrutinised public policy in Wales. It is a small committee with regular meetings and specialist advisors, but has no legislative role.

As a result of devolution, responsibility for reviewing the activities of the Welsh Office (which in practice is a putative Welsh civil service) has been assumed by the National Assembly. Some academics have suggested that the two Westminster committees should be merged into a single committee, with both scrutinising and pre-legislative functions rather like US Congressional Committees. However, the Commons is a conservative body and although the Procedure Committee was sympathetic, the consensus of Welsh MPs was that both committees should remain. At some stage, a more coherent role, in support of the National Assembly, must be found for the two parliamentary committees.

Another apparent anomaly in the wake of devolution is the Welsh Secretary of State. Most of his functions are now performed by the National Assembly but in a more transparent democratic manner. However, there are still policy issues effecting Wales that are determined in London, most notably macro-economic policy. The Secretary of State is a member of the cabinet and, as such, participates (through Cabinet committees) in determining government strategy and legislative programme. One could describe this as a quasi-ambassadorial role; in certain circumstances it could be crucial to the Welsh interest. But the main justification for the retention of the Welsh Secretary of State is the Block Grant. This is determined each year by the Treasury and is related to the UK level of public expenditure as applied by the 'Barnett Formula'. The process involves the National Assembly, through its First Minister, making representations to the Secretary of State as to the level of the Grant required together with justifications. The Secretary of State presents the case to the Treasury as part of the annual round of interdepartmental financial allocations. In the final analysis, however, there is no certainty that the National Assembly will get all it wants.

The case of Objective One Funding from the European Union and the requirement that there should be 'matched funding' has illustrated vividly the difficulties implicit in the funding arrangements. The issue sparked off a crisis in the National Assembly, exacerbated relations between the opposition parties and the minority Labour administration, provoked conflict with Westminster and, eventually, the resignation of Alun Michael the Assembly First Minister. He resigned first as leader of the Welsh Labour Party, subsequently as a member of the Assembly and eventually returned to the backbenches in the House of Commons. The episode confirmed what many political commentators had suspected, that the financial basis for devolution was suspect. There is no guarantee that the Secretary of State will accept the National Assembly representations uncritically nor that the Cabinet will side with the Welsh Secretary of State against the Chancellor. Quite the reverse, the Treasury always rules! Difficulties have already emerged despite the Labour Party being the party of government in both London and Cardiff. If there were to be a Conservative government in London and a Labour administration in Cardiff, the evidence suggests that the potential for financial and constitutional disputes would increase significantly.

The devolution of executive functions to Wales will probably stand or fall on the levels of effective co-operation between civil servants in Whitehall and Cardiff. The importance of this matter can be gauged by the *Memorandum of Understanding* (1999) which laid down the principles for co-operation followed by more specific agreements. These included the *Agreement on the Joint Ministerial Committee*; the *Concordat on the Co-ordination of Financial Assistance to Industry*; the *Concordat on Financial Assistance to Industry*; the *Concordat on International Relations*; and the *Concordat on Statistics*. The Memorandum seeks to make more explicit the procedures and practices of the civil service. In effect, the UK Government, after due consultation, has drafted a code of behaviour and co-operation for civil servants at both UK and regional levels of government to bring transparency to procedures previously hidden away in the corridors of power. In typical British fashion the introduction to the memorandum declares:

'The memorandum is a statement of political intent, and should not be interpreted to be binding agreement, [...] it is intended to be binding in honour only. [...] Concordats are not intended to be legally binding, but to serve as working documents.'

The infinite flexibility of the British constitution would not appear to be seriously threatened by this document. Conventions and procedures, based on the memorandum, will doubtless evolve in the light of experience and circumstance. Nevertheless, the guidance is a detailed and sensible basis for developing good relations between the administrations in London, Edinburgh, Cardiff and Belfast. It argues the case for: good communication, early on in the policy process, to alert other administrations to proposed developments and to enable arrangements for joint policy development where appropriate; co-operation on matters of mutual intent and shared responsibilities; full exchange of information, statistics and research between the administrations subject to restrictions of confidentiality or freedom of information; mutual respect for information received in confidence – the administration providing information should be able to state restrictions upon its usage.

The guidance also clarifies functional responsibilities, viz. that: UK Parliament will not normally legislate on matters devolved without the agreement of the devolved administrations but retains the 'absolute right' to enquire into or make representations about devolved matters; devolved legislatures (assemblies) will be entitled to debate non-devolved matters. International and EU relations are the responsibility of the UK Government which however recognises that devolved assemblies will have an interest particularly in the application of EU policies; while relations between the administration should be carried out on a departmental multi-lateral or bilateral basis there will be a need for a Joint Ministerial Committee (JMC) consisting of ministers of the four administrations.

It has been argued that these concordats, or non-statutory agreements, are a species of 'pseudo-contract' (Rawlings, 1998) in the sense that they are not enforceable in the courts. Nevertheless, they are extremely important. Given executive devolution and the horizontal division of law making powers, Wales will depend upon a harmonious operation of these concordats, to a far greater extent than is the case in Scotland and Northern Ireland which both possess primary legislative powers. However, for the concordats to be effective in delivering significant political devolution to Wales, certain conditions will have to apply. Concordats will have to be amended and updated on a regular basis and much will depend on the personal relations between key civil servants who provide support and advice for the Assembly with a different political complexion from that in Westminster. In the early days of devolution, before generally agreed conventions have been established, the degree of good will at the civil service level and a consensus at the political level will be critical. Neither requirement can be absolutely guaranteed.

As noted above Ron Davies, when Secretary of State, referred to devolution as 'a process not an event'. The experience to date of the concordats supports that view. On 29 November 1999, the Welsh Secretary, Paul Murphy, in an address to the National Assembly announced a new Legislative Protocol whereby legislation requested by the Welsh Cabinet would be treated as government legislation so as to ease its passage through the Commons. On 10 December 1999 a new concordat, on Assembly/Treasury relations was published explaining how disputes on financial matters could be raised in the Joint Ministerial Committee (JMC) and confirming that the Assembly's Principal Finance Officer would be able to attend the regular meetings of Principal Finance Officers of central government departments. In the same month the Chancellor of the Exchequer, Gordon Brown, announced that the JMC would have a sub-committee system to facilitate the development of pro-active policies across the four administrations.

Although these are promising developments the National Assembly is concerned that its secondary legislative powers might be reduced progressively by the injudicious drafting of parliamentary bills which fail to specify devolved functions to Wales. As a consequence the Assembly resolved on 2 February 2000:

> '[...] to support the principle that primary legislation affecting Wales should confer all appropriate functions to the Assembly in a flexible way and commits itself and the Cabinet, through the Subject Committees, to continue to press for this approach in all government Bills.'

Dissatisfaction with the legislative situation continues to feature in discussions amongst Assembly Members. In the opinion of John Osmond,

Director of the Institute of Welsh Affairs, the legislative issue will 'run and run'. This view was confirmed in the year 2000 St David's Day speech given by the Assembly Presiding Officer Dafydd Elis Thomas to the Welsh Governance Centre in Cardiff University. He indicated that the National Assembly might well set up a constitutional convention (which he would be prepared to chair) to consider clearer and more extensive devolution of legislative powers.

An additional factor further complicates the operation of multi-level governance in the new 'devolved' United Kingdom. The most distinctive feature of the National Assembly is the organisation of its committees. The initial intention was to run them along local government lines, with 'Subject Committees' assuming responsibility for the determination of policy. During the passage of the Government of Wales Bill, the opposition parties argued that such a diffuse power structure would reduce the status and authority of the National Assembly. It was argued that a Cabinet system of executive authority was necessary to provide effective political leadership and clear lines of accountability. However, the local government style committee system was not discarded but preserved to act as a counter-weight to the cabinet. Labour argued that this would ensure that the policy making process was inclusive of all members of the Assembly, and not confined within the ranks of a small political elite. Consequently the Government of Wales Act was a constitutional hybrid involving a balance of power between the Executive Committee (Cabinet) and the Subject Committees of the Assembly (Jones, in Osmond, 1999). If the Assembly is to have an input into the Westminster legislative process, to ensure that Welsh interests and needs are taken into account in the drafting of legislation, then the Subject Committees will need to develop appropriate procedures. It may be argued that such an input into the Westminster legislative process should be the responsibility of the Executive Committee (cabinet) and in strictly constitutional terms this is probably so. But the National Assembly Advisory Group recommended that the Subject Committees should develop House of Commons Select Committee characteristics, that is to say sounding out interested parties, taking evidence, identifying problems and making recommendations. Such committees would be participating in the pre-legislative consultation process exercising both a policy formulation function as well as a scrutinising function.

So far the signs are promising. Organised interests have submitted evidence which, according to one committee chair with Westminster experience, is at least on a par with that presented to Westminster Select Committees. Furthermore, all committee members participate fully in the process, in contrast to the Westminster experience. A more inclusive policy formulating process is developing in the National Assembly in which a co-ordination of public and private sectors, social groups and institutions is coming into being with clear aims and objectives. An original form of regional governance is evolving (Le Galès and Lequesne, p. 243). However, if this process is to survive, let alone develop, it will have to be 'legislatively fruitful'. The enthusiastic involvement of interest groups and other organised interests is conditional upon them playing a meaningful role, and a perception that they can make a difference. If the legislative concordat delivers more opportunities for National Assembly involvement through the government promotion of Assembly legislative proposals, or more opportunities for 'Welsh' amendments to general legislation, then the newly emerging Welsh policy communities will become more influential. The 'inclusive' policy process advocated by the pro-devolutionists in the referendum campaign and seen as a utopian aspiration by critics would become firmly established with executive devolution regarded as a more viable basis for Welsh governance.

**Conclusion**

By any measure the National Assembly's formative years have been stormy. The wafer-thin majority in the referendum raised doubts about the commitment of the Welsh voters and the legitimacy of the whole project. The departure of one Welsh Secretary (Ron Davies) and the appointment of another (Alun Michael) did little to enhance the devolutionary process. Furthermore, the failure of the Welsh Labour Party to win an overall majority in the first Assembly elections frustrated the expectation of strong and consistent policies, arguably one of the main justifications for devolution. The resultant scenario of 'all-party inclusive policy making' was less than convincing and eventually led to Alun Michael losing a vote of 'no confidence'. While the creation of the Labour/Liberal Democrat coalition and a three-year policy programme marked a significant improvement the situation was confused by the decision of the Liberal Democrat, Mike Germain, to withdraw from the posts of Deputy First Minister and Economic Development Minister following a police investigation of a fraud case.

It is against this background of institutional initiatives, political experimentation and plain damage limitation that a poll of Welsh public opinion was taken in the summer of 2001 to measure general attitudes towards devolution and the National Assembly during the first two years of its operation. A majority (51 per cent) were in favour or strongly in favour of devolution with only 32 per cent against.

| Attitudes to devolution | % |
|---|---|
| Strongly in favour | 11 |
| In favour | 40 |
| Against | 19 |
| Strongly against | 13 |
| Don't know | 17 |

ESRC & Market Research Wales (June 2001)
*Western Mail* 6 August 2001

Against this general feeling in support of devolution, there were criticisms of the National Assembly's performance in specific areas. Over 60 per cent were critical of the inability of the National Assembly to deliver on improving public services, such as health and education. This is to be expected and it is a criticism also levelled at the Westminster Parliament. But the Assembly is barely two years old and still has to prove its worth to the Welsh electorate.

There is a widespread feeling that it is a 'talking shop', a view held by those devolutionists who believe that executive devolution is inadequate and that full legislative powers should be devolved to Wales as they have been to Scotland and Northern Ireland. Anti-devolutionists reject the National Assembly outright, but while a return to the pre-devolution system is unrealistic, it does mean that the National Assembly is vulnerable to criticisms from both sides. The Welsh devolution settlement is not yet finalised.

*Notes*

[1] The research for this paper is funded by the ESRC Award for Devolution and Constitutional Change Research Programme.

[2] in Williams, D., *A History of Modern Wales*, London: John Murray, 1950, p.20.

# Making a Difference[1] or More of the Same?

## Devolution in Northern Ireland

### Elizabeth Meehan[2]

## Introduction

'The Belfast Agreement of 1998, while conferring a similar, though not identical[3], raft of powers upon the new institutions there to those transferred to Edinburgh, did not arrive from the same democratic will. While the 'democratic deficit' [...] was keenly felt, there was no collective commitment to democratic-pluralist institutions [...] and the agreement was seen primarily by all concerned as an attempt to end the violence [of] the prior three decades.' (Wilford and Wilson, 2001)

As this quote shows, the political reasons for [re-]devolution to Northern Ireland are different from Scotland and Wales: crisis resolution rather than a new consensus about the meaning of democracy being the mother of invention. The first part of this chapter provides something of that historical context in Northern Ireland.

The contrasting motivations for change influenced the institutional and procedural arrangements for renewed self-government in Northern Ireland. Either despite violence and crisis or because of them, Northern Ireland was on the road to devolution before reformers in Scotland and Wales achieved what they wanted by constitutional means. However, the distinctive backdrop in Northern Ireland has subverted the new institutions. Periods in 'shadow' mode and suspension mean that Northern Ireland has fallen behind Scotland and Wales. Nevertheless the persistence of the legacy of the past somehow coexists with the beginnings of what has begun in Northern Ireland - long after the term became familiar elsewhere – to be called the 'new politics'. The drive to give this a chance can be seen in the frantic attempts at the time of writing (early November 2001) to find a way of ensuring the re-election of David Trimble as First Minister. This was against the opposition of anti-agreement forces led by the Democratic Unionist Party (DUP), but with the support of two renegade members of the Ulster Unionist Party (UUP). A reflection perhaps of constitutional changes potentially implicit in devolution, the DUP opened legal proceedings against the essentially political manoeuvre of redesignating members of the Northern Ireland Women's Coalition (NIWC) and the Alliance Party of Northern Ireland (APNI) as 'Unionist' (see below). In accordance with longer established political norms in the United Kingdom the courts declined to be involved and kicked the matter back into the political arena, thus ensuring the continuation of devolved government.

# Historical context

At its foundation under the Government of Ireland Act 1920, Northern Ireland was governed through legislative and administrative devolution. At the time, there was a discreet hope in Great Britain that a federal solution to the Irish Question might come to prevail through the creation of a Council of Ireland linking the parliaments in Dublin and Belfast. Obviously, this did not happen. Direct Rule was established in 1972 in the wake of the failure of the civil rights agenda and in response to escalating violence. Thereafter, there were two attempts at re-devolution – in the 1970s and 1980s – both of which failed. The first arose from the Sunningdale Agreement, recalled by Seamus Mallon, now Deputy First Minister, when he famously dubbed the 1998 Agreement as 'Sunningdale for slow learners' (Wilford, 2001).

The key features of the 1998 Agreement can be traced to the germination of ideas in those two decades; that the constitution of Northern Ireland (Irish or British) should be determined by consent[4] and, in the absence of Irish re-unification, a settlement should be based on three strands - power-sharing in a devolved assembly, north-south co-operation, and an east-west relationship that introduced something of a partnership between the Governments of the

Republic of Ireland and the United Kingdom with respect to Northern Irish affairs. The period of Direct Rule coincided with accession to the European Union by both states. EU membership played some part in the capacity of the two Governments and parties in Northern Ireland eventually to finesse the ideas noted above into a package that could become the basis of a contrived consensus.

Developments on two fronts were crucial. On the one hand, talks between Sinn Féin's (SF) Gerry Adams and John Hume, leader of the Social and Democratic Labour Party (SDLP), which had failed in the late 1980s, resumed and led to an agreement which the Irish Taoiseach, Albert Reynolds, was able to transform into a peace proposal, albeit in its original form unacceptable to the British Government and northern Unionists when presented in 1993. Meanwhile, the British Government had also indicated the possibility of a new initiative (Morrow in Wilson, 2001; Patterson in Wilford, 2001). In 1990, Peter Brooke, the new Secretary of State for Northern Ireland, while making it clear that an end to violence was necessary, announced that there was no 'selfish strategic or economic' British interest in Northern Ireland. He authorised secret contacts between the intelligence services and the IRA, which continued for several years. Peter Brooke also initiated 'talks about talks' – which included placing on the agenda a potential change to the Irish constitution to remove its territorial claim on Northern Ireland. These talks failed and the security situation worsened. But the momentum continued, if painfully (talks were again unsuccessful in 1992), under a new Secretary of State, Sir Patrick Mayhew.

On 15 December 1993, the Taoiseach, Albert Reynolds, and Prime Minister, John Major, made a joint statement on Northern Ireland's future - The Downing Street Declaration - formalising the new outlook adumbrated by Brooke and Mayhew. To republicans, this was a retreat from the Hume-Adams approach but they could not ignore the role of a Fianna Fáil Taoiseach and approval in Washington. Thus nine months ensued in which 'clarifications' were sought before the announcement of an IRA cease-fire on 31 August 1994. As Morrow (in Wilson, 2001) points out, the cease-fire raised expectations whilst, at the same time, the political pieces were not yet in place for these to be met. The so-called Frameworks Documents, proposed by the two Governments in February 1995 as the basis for negotiations, were rejected by unionists while republicans were disconcerted by the increasing emphasis on decommissioning as a pre-condition. The two Governments agreed to ask Senator George Mitchell to head an International Body on Decommissioning in the hope that the issue could be resolved before a forthcoming visit to Northern Ireland by President Clinton. The International Body's Report, published on 23 January 1996, stated that all parties to negotiations should make a 'total and absolute' commitment to:

• democratic and exclusively peaceful means of resolving political issues;

• the total disarmament of all paramilitary organisations;

• agree that such disarmament must be verifiable to the satisfaction of an independent commission;

• renounce for themselves, and oppose any effort by others, to use force, or threaten to use force, to influence the course or the outcomes of all-party negotiations;

• agree to abide by the terms of any agreement reached in all-party negotiations and to resort to democratic and exclusively peaceful methods in trying to alter any aspect of that outcome with which they may disagree;

• urge that 'punishment' killings and beatings stop and to take effective steps to prevent such actions. (Mitchell, 1999)

The Report suggested that the parties might consider some decommissioning during the negotiating process. David Trimble, leader of the Ulster Unionist Party (UUP), and the British Government had proposed that negotiations be preceded by elections, whereas John Hume felt that the delay this would incur might stretch the cease-fires to breaking point (as it did in the case of the IRA which bombed Canary Wharf on 9 February 1996). Both points of view about an election were recorded whilst the Report merely suggested that a democratic election process could contribute to the building of confidence.

Elections to the Forum, from which successful parties derived eligibility to send delegates to the talks, took place in May 1996 and SF did well. A potential impasse over the possibility of a walk-out by the Democratic Unionist Party (DUP) and other hard-line unionists at the prospect of SF participation was removed when the new Labour Secretary of State, Dr Marjory (Mo) Mowlam, assured SF that the resumption of the IRA cease-fire (after Canary Wharf) meant they would be included. David Trimble, elected leader of the UUP in 1995 with a hard-line reputation, now came under pressure from business and church leaders 'to take up the challenge'. (Morrow in Wilson, 2001)

Multi-party talks opened on 15 September 1997 with Senator George Mitchell in the chair. On 22 May 1998 the people were asked: 'Do you support the agreement reached at the multi-party talks on Northern Ireland as set out in Command Paper 3883?'. A simultaneous referendum, which was held in the south and which entailed the abolition of the territorial claim over Northern Ireland, secured a 95 per cent 'yes' vote. The result in the north was 71.12 per cent in favour of the Agreement. Nationalists were strongly in favour and it seems that 'no' votes were cast mostly by unionists (especially in Dr Paisley's - DUP leader - constituency). However, exit polls indicated that between 51 per cent and 55 per cent of Protestants had voted 'yes' (Elliott in Wilson, 2001). The first elections to the new Assembly were held on 25 June 1998. The results favoured pro-agreement parties but made David Trimble's position difficult since, for the first time, the UUP came second in the proportion of first preference votes and SF crept up on the SDLP. However, in terms of seats, the UUP were the largest with 28, followed by the SDLP with 24. The DUP and other anti-agreement parties gathered 28 seats between them. Other unionists, the Progressive Unionist Party (PUP) brought the pro-agreement unionists to 30. Adding the SDLP seats plus 18 SF, 6 Alliance Party of Northern Ireland (APNI), and 2 Northern Ireland Women's Coalition (NIWC), pro-agreement parties made up 80 out of the 108 members.

# Arrangements

### Powers and constraints

The Belfast or Good Friday Agreement consists, as Hadfield (in Wilford, 2001) explains, of the double annexation of two Agreements. First, there is the multi-party Agreement, preceded by a Declaration of Support and secondly, there is an Agreement between the British and Irish Governments dealing with aspects of the multi-party Agreement which have inter-state dimensions. The Northern Ireland Act 1998 gives effect to the multi-party Agreement and deals with aspects upon which it is silent. This and other legislation is the framework for devolution (Hadden in Wilson, 2001; Hadfield in Wilford, 2001). The other legislation relates to UK responsibilities such as provision for elections, release on license of paramilitary prisoners, human rights, equality, and policing. The intergovernmental Agreement led to four Treaties, entered into on 8 March 1999, dealing with north-south and east-west aspects, the related statutory powers having been provided in the Northern Ireland Act 1998 and, further, in the North/South Co-operation (Implementing Bodies) (Northern Ireland) Order 1999.

As in the Government of Ireland Act 1920 and the Northern Ireland Constitution Act 1973 and unlike legislation for Scotland and Wales, the 1998 Act outlines three forms of powers - transferred, reserved, and excepted. Transferred powers are those devolved to Northern Ireland institutions. Reserved powers are those which were devolved between 1921 and 1972 when they became the responsibility of the Northern Ireland Office but which in due course may become devolved again – criminal law, police, public order, emergency powers and the courts. Reserved powers also include some which were not previously devolved – banking and financial services, telecommunications, certain import and export controls. These are particularly relevant for relations with the Republic, but it is not clear whether they will ever become devolved. Excepted powers are those 'regarded as the prerogative of the sovereign state' – international relations, defence, security, nationality, Parliament, elections, and taxation.

Some constraints on powers are similar to those in Scotland and Wales; legislation and administrative action that would contravene the European Convention on Human Rights (ECHR) and EU law, that discriminate on unlawful grounds, or be inconsistent with UK international obligations. In the event of a dispute over competence, provisions in Northern Ireland are parallel to those for Scotland and Wales: referral to the Northern Ireland Court of Appeal and ultimately to the Judicial Committee of the Privy Council.

**Powers and constraints – quasi-federalism and sovereignty?**

Assessment of the extent to which these provisions provide evidence of embryonic quasi-federal elements varies according to whether the question is approached from a legal or political point of view and to the relationship between the internal and external dimensions of the Northern Irish settlement. As noted, both the multi-party Agreement and intergovernmental Agreement (and its consequent Treaties) are effective only on the basis of statutes enacted in Westminster. However, with respect to the internal provisions, it may be that the Scotland Act gives a little more scope for the competence of the Scottish Parliament vis-à-vis Westminster than is the case for the Northern Ireland Assembly.

As Hadfield (in Wilford, 2001) points out, excepted powers in Northern Ireland equate with reserved powers in Scotland. She also points to differences in the wording of the relationship between devolved competences and excepted and reserved powers. These differences may enable the boundary in the Scottish case to be more open to adjustment than is possible under the Northern Ireland Act. She suggests that prior jurisprudence on *vires* questions implies that different wordings in the two Acts may mean that any future questions about putative quasi-federalism would find more scope in Scotland than Northern Ireland.[5]

Subsequent to the Scotland and Wales Acts, conventions for relations with the centre were developed in a Memorandum of Understanding, drawn up in 1999, and in the terms of reference of a new Joint Ministerial Committee (JMC). There are also accompanying Concordats on Co-ordination of European Policy Issues, Financial Assistance to Industry, and International Relations and Statistics – and some inter-departmental concordats. In the absence of devolution in Northern Ireland in 1999, there was no Executive to participate in their development and Northern Ireland was not covered until 2000.

These documents are liberally sprinkled with assurances that they are not legally binding. Even so, they have implications which do not appear to encourage a quasi-federal approach. The Memorandum of Understanding and the terms of reference of the JMC both restate the power of the UK

Parliament to legislate on any matter, devolved or not. The operation of the JMC has encouraged some to speculate that it is intended to minimise the effects of powers having been devolved. JMC meetings in sectoral format were supposed to have consisted of relevant ministers, but two meetings on health were chaired by the Prime Minister (*Quarterly Report* (QR) 6, February 2001) and the Chancellor of the Exchequer convened a JMC on poverty among young children and the elderly (*Scotsman*, 1 March 2001).

It might have been expected that concern to retain central control would have been most apparent in those areas described by Hadden as the 'prerogatives of the sovereign state'. And, indeed, documents just mentioned also restate the centre's authority and competence on the EU and relations with foreign governments. *The Scotsman* (1 March 2001) suggested that a change to the Foreign Secretary's method of co-ordinating British EU policy (requiring the presence of relevant ministers in the devolved systems) could be construed as intended to bolster central control. However, Northern Ireland's Minister for Finance and Personnel welcomed the change (and the Concordat with the Treasury on public procurement) as an opportunity to increase regional influence on the shaping of overall EU policy (*QR* 7, May 2001).

Relations with other states are treated differently in the provisions for the North-South Ministerial Council (NSMC) and British-Irish Council (BIC) (both explained further in the next section). The Memorandum of Understanding and Concordats exempt these provisions allowing horizontal relations in departure from the normal vertical conventions for external affairs. Both institutions are permitted to consider potential commonalities in EU issues, in the one case as between the two parts of the island and, in the other, as between Ireland, Northern Ireland and each or all of the components of Great Britain. So far, this is far more developed on the north-south basis. The NSMC also has within its remit 'matters of mutual interest within the competence of the two Administrations, North and South' – which, as Hadfield (2001) indicates, could lead to changes in the law in the Republic as a result of a sovereign state having altered its laws on the basis of an agreement with a non-sovereign body. It is this that has re-raised the question of quasi-federalism on the island of Ireland. But, in setting this against legal provisions regulating Northern Ireland and the UK, she suggests that what happens on the island of Ireland will be tempered by the lack of internal legal federalism.

Looking at 'the other island', it should be noted that members of the BIC, which also includes the Isle of Man and the Channel Islands, may enter into bilateral agreements with one another. In theory, it would be possible, therefore, for the non-sovereign bodies, Scotland and Wales, to have an agreement with a 'foreign'[6] government – the Republic of Ireland.

The Memorandum of Understanding thus embodies a clash of concepts of sovereignty (the vertical direction of authority in matters relating to foreign affairs and the European Union and horizontal trans-jurisdictional relations permitted amongst all the devolved units of the UK, collectively and/or bilaterally, with another state). This has not yet been put to the test. Given that legal provisions are not quasi-federal - despite some political aspirations to the contrary – it might be guessed that, if there were a clash, the centre would win out.

The idea that a centrist, and the centre's, view of sovereignty would prevail can also be seen in terms of the withdrawal of devolution. From 1999, political, as opposed to legal analysts, thought that there might be a different nuance in respect of constitutional entrenchment in the case of Northern Ireland (O'Leary in Wilford, 2001). Such a view derives from the fact that Northern Irish devolution rests, not only on domestic legislation, but also on an international agreement between two states, ratified by the UN – implying, therefore, that institutions could be suspended only by intergovernmental negotiation. However, the decision to suspend in February 2000 was taken by the Secretary of State, Peter Mandelson, without the agreement of the Irish Government and, indeed, to its annoyance over both the substantive decision and the process by which it was made. The legal authority of Westminster has been shown in subsequent suspensions but, on these occasions, its exercise seemingly followed closer attention to the complex pattern of intra- and inter-state political relationships.

## Institutions and procedures

Institutions are: the Assembly (including Committees), Executive (and departments), Civic Forum, North-South Ministerial Council (and implementing bodies), British-Irish Council, and the British-Irish Intergovernmental Conference.[7]

## The Assembly

The Assembly has 108 members (Members of the Legislative Assembly – MLAs), elected by Single Transferable Vote proportional representation from Westminster constituencies. MLAs have a Code of Conduct which 'is unexceptional by Westminster standards' (Wilford and Wilson, 2001). There are ten Statutory Committees which 'shadow' the relevant departments, six Standing Committees and provision for the Assembly to establish Ad Hoc Committees when asked by the Secretary of State for its advice on reserved matters.

The Statutory Committees are something of a hybrid of select and standing committees at Westminster. In addition to monitoring and scrutinising, they are also responsible for the committee stage of all primary legislation, approving secondary legislation, advising on the formulation of policy and budgets, and they can initiate legislation. One of the Standing Committees, the Committee of the Centre monitors about half of the functions of the Office of First Minister and Deputy First Minister (OFMDFM) – which has grown enormously.

The Assembly is supposed to work on a cross-community basis. Procedures and practices exist to ensure that Committees reflect party strengths which, by and large, they do (the Northern Ireland Unionist Party (NIUP) and UK Unionist Party (UKUP) boycott the committees). The chairs and deputy chairs, who cannot be drawn from the same party as that of the associated minister, are chosen by the d'Hondt mechanism and other members are agreed by the whips on a proportional basis.

There are cross-community decision-making rules. MLAs register a 'designation of identity – nationalist, unionist or other – for the purpose of measuring cross-community support in Assembly votes' on 'key decisions'. Key decisions, including the election of the First and Deputy First Ministers, the removal of ministers, standing orders and budget allocations, are to be so designated in advance. Other decisions can be made into key decisions if a 'petition of concern' is initiated by at least 30 of the 108 members. Key decisions can only be taken if they secure 'parallel consent' or are passed by a 'weighted majority'. The former requires not only an overall majority, but also majorities among both of the self-designated unionists and nationalists (but, controversially, not 'others'). In the latter a 60 per cent majority is needed with at least 40 per cent of both nationalists and unionists.


*The Executive*

Executive authority is discharged by the First Minister and Deputy First Minister, with the assistance of two junior Ministers in the OFMDFM, and ten Ministers with departmental responsibilities. The Ministers constitute an Executive Committee, presided over by the First Minister and Deputy First Minister, responsible for discussing and agreeing cross-departmental policy issues and priorities amongst executive and legislative policy proposals. They are responsible for agreeing an annual Programme for Government and Budget. This does not mean that the Executive Committee can be likened to a cabinet with collective responsibility – notwithstanding their Pledge of Office.

The Pledge of Office and Code of Conduct for Ministers are 'exceptional by Westminster standards' (Wilford and Wilson, 2001). The Pledge of Office contains no oath of loyalty to the Crown; it commits ministers to exclusively non-violent and democratic means, to the pursuit of equality, to the effective and responsible discharge of their duties, and to compliance with the Code of Conduct.

The Executive Committee's departure from the characteristics of a cabinet of collective responsibility stems partly from the ways its members are chosen and partly because of relationship between the Executive and the Assembly (Wilford and Wilson, 2001). The election, or re-election, of the First Minister and Deputy First Minister by the MLAs must be by parallel consent. Ministers of departments are selected through nomination by each of the four parties in government and the application of the d'Hondt mechanism. This means that the First Minister and Deputy First Minister have very little powers of patronage. The only ministers whom they could sack are those drawn from their own parties.

The system of choosing the First Minister, Deputy First Minister and other Ministers was designed to minimise majoritarianism so that political representatives of both nationalists and unionists could be in government. This was reinforced by the Secretary of State, Mo Mowlam, in a Standing Order on 15 July 1999 requiring that the Executive contain at least three unionists and three nationalists. Given party strengths in the Assembly, the Executive is made up of the pro-agreement UUP, SDLP and SF and the anti-agreement DUP. This means that there is opposition within government and that the 'opposition benches' outside it are occupied by a handful of small parties. On the pro-agreement side are the APNI, the PUP and the NIWC; on the anti-agreement side, there are a number of other unionists. Opposition of a more systematic type lies in the Assembly Committees (Wilford and Wilson, 2001). This means that there may be opposition within parties, depending on whether their representatives are in the Executive or on a Committee. Few of the parties in the Assembly feel that they are a party-of-government; rather that they are a party some of whose members are in government.

The restructuring of departments embodied partisan calculations about appropriate numbers and which would be occupied by which party (Wilson, 2001) and could, therefore, be seen as somewhat arbitrary. But their reconstruction also reflects some acknowledgement – if of a cosmetic type in the early days – of a need to redesign those existing under Direct Rule so as to facilitate 'joined-up government'. They are: Enterprise, Trade and Investment (UUP), Culture, Arts and Leisure (UUP), Environment (UUP), Finance and Personnel (SDLP), Employment and Learning (higher and further education, training) (SDLP), Agriculture and Rural Development (SDLP), Education (schools) (SF), Health, Social Services and Public Safety (SF), Regional Development (DUP), Social Development (DUP).

*Civic Forum*

The Civic Forum was proposed by the NIWC in the talks as a way of bringing civil society into the political arena to ensure that the new arrangements were participatory and inclusive (Fearon, 1999; Woods in Wilson, 2001). The community and voluntary sectors, often primarily female, had maintained 'the fabric of society' throughout the 'troubles' and, in so doing, had acquired an expertise in everyday policy-making that was lacking amongst those whose main preoccupations had been with 'high' constitutional politics. The Agreement states simply that a Civic Forum would be established as a consultative mechanism on social, economic and cultural matters, leaving it to the First and Deputy Ministers to set it up. In February 1999, they announced its composition; a chair, six people nominated by the First and Deputy First Ministers and fifty-four other members, chosen by extra-Assembly nominating bodies, from business, agriculture/fisheries, trades unions, voluntary and community sectors, churches, culture, arts and sport, victims (of the 'troubles'), community relations, and education. The person subsequently appointed to the chair is Chris Gibson, a business leader.

### North-South Ministerial Council (NSMC)

The NSMC has an unsuccessful antecedent in the previously noted Council of Ireland, set up under the Government of Ireland Act 1920. Hopes for, and fears of, a renewed potential for some form of re-unification complicated the securing of agreement in 1998 on the scope of north-south co-operation and the institutional means to it.[8] Nevertheless, a solution was found.

The NSMC in its plenary form comprises the First Minister and Deputy First Minister and the Irish Taoiseach. It also operates in sectoral format with each side represented by appropriate ministers. It has a joint secretariat, appropriately accommodated at Armagh, the ecclesiastical 'capital' of the island for the Roman Catholic Church and the Church of Ireland. The powers and responsibilities of the NSMC are similar to those of the Council of Ministers of the EU: it is supposed to identify matters of common interest of all-island benefit (including EU issues), which are within the competence of both administrations and for which Ministers are accountable, and to take decisions by agreement on policies for implementation separately in each jurisdiction.

The Agreement also refers to the creation of implementing bodies and substantive areas of co-operation. The former were subsequently agreed to be: Waterways Ireland (navigable waterways), Food and Safety Promotion Board, Trade and Business Development (now called InterIrelandTrade), Special EU Programmes Board, Language (Gaelic and Ulster Scots), and Foyle, Carlingford and Irish Lights (including, not only lighthouses, but also commerce, recreation, fisheries, aquaculture, marine tourism). It was also agreed that areas of co-operation should include: animal and plant health, teacher qualifications and exchanges, strategic transport planning, environmental protection, pollution, water quality and waste management, tourism, accident and emergency services and related matters.

### British-Irish Council (BIC)

The BIC, also with a joint secretariat, links the Republic of Ireland, not only with Northern Ireland and the United Kingdom Government, but also with the devolved systems of Scotland and Wales, the Crown Territories of the Isle of Man and the Channel Islands and, if they are established, English regional assemblies. The Agreement specifies summit meetings twice a year and regular sectoral or cross-sectoral meetings amongst relevant ministers. The BIC's role is to exchange ideas and reach agreement on matters of mutual interest. Common policies may be agreed with provision for opt-outs.

A unionist idea, either to off-set the rolling integration dynamic of the NSMC or to reflect the 'human truth' of ties of history and kinship on the two islands (Walker in Wilford, 2001), the concept of the BIC was particularly attractive to those politicians in Scotland wishing to maximise autonomy and to do so in co-operation with the Republic of Ireland. This is not always easy for the Taoiseach. In welcoming the new scope for bilateral relations with Scotland and Wales and describing the BIC as a 'loose confederation' (Meehan in Wilson, 2001), Mr Ahern had to tread a difficult tight rope insofar as he did not want to endanger an unprecedently good relationship with the UK Government by appearing to endorse Scottish or Welsh claims for independence.

### British-Irish Intergovernmental Conference (BIIC)

Outside the BIC structures but related to them, the Agreement proposed a network of parliamentary links upon which the British-Irish Interparliamentary Body has already begun, the first meeting having been held in October 2000. From the executive point of view, the whole 1998 Agreement supersedes the Anglo-Irish Agreement 1985 and its machinery. The 1985 arrangements were seen by unionists as a vehicle for nationalists, able to have an input through the Government of the Republic, which they did not enjoy through the British. The new BIIC is a forum for consultation on matters which are not devolved and is intended to promote 'bilateral co-operation at all levels on all matters of mutual interest' on a more equitable basis than its predecessor. It is notable that the secretariat for the old body, in becoming that of the new one, is no longer housed in a 'bunker' on the edge of Belfast but in an ordinary office in the city. Its new name also reflects the transformation from Anglo-Irish to British-Irish relations, which was, perhaps, most dramatically marked by Tony Blair's speech to the Oireachtas in November 1998 and reactions to it.

### Summing up the arrangements

In summing up the new institutions in Northern Ireland, the then Secretary of State, Peter Mandelson, described the Executive and Assembly as 'a ministry of all the talents, a government of national unity, in reality a compulsory coalition' (Lecture, 'Making Votes Count', 26 June 2000). When considering their performance, one is tempted to see the reality of a compulsory coalition as having almost insurmountable disadvantages. On the other hand, there is also some evidence in 'everyday' politics that 'the talents of the ministry' have some potential – notwithstanding the ongoing crises of 'high politics' – to bed-down into something of a 'government of national unity'.

## Performance

Throughout its short life, the 1998 version of devolution in Northern Ireland has been affected by crises. The legacy of the Brooke-Mayhew talks is that the strands of the Belfast Agreement stand or fall together; that is, if the

Assembly and Executive go, so do the other devolved institutions (but not bodies set up under reserved powers dealing with human rights, equality, policing, etc.).

To begin with, the Assembly was set up in 'shadow mode' until issues relating to the Agreement - primarily decommissioning but also prisoner releases and other innovations that were the responsibility of the UK Government – were resolved. Although no weapons were given up, the Independent Commission on Decommissioning was able to report some progress on the inspection of arms dumps. Thus, the Assembly was inaugurated in 'operational mode' in December 1999 and lasted until February 2000 when the political fallout from a lack of decommissioning meant it was suspended by the Secretary of State. After a statement by the IRA and intense bargaining on other difficult issues, the Assembly was re-established on 29 May 2000 but its fate remained embroiled in intra- and inter-party problems over, not only decommissioning, but also policing, flags, polarisation (as shown in the June General Election), inter- and intra-communal violence in Northern Ireland and attacks on London targets by dissident IRA groups. Perhaps it is, therefore, remarkable that the institutions have functioned as normally as they have.

**Executive and Assembly**

When, at the end of the February-May suspension, the Executive reconvened, on 1 June 2000, the DUP announced that it would not participate in it or in the other Executive institutions – because of its opposition to the presence of SF in government in the absence of decommissioning. It would fill its ministerial posts but holders of the two posts would rotate. And it continued to participate in the Assembly. Soon afterwards, the DUP also announced that its ministers would not be bound by the Pledge of Office – even though, of course, they relied on the obligation to do so when justifying their call for SF exclusion.

The first action of the reconvened Executive and Assembly was to accept the budget, which required cross-community consent. The preceding hiatus meant that the budget had been determined for Northern Ireland by the

Chancellor of the Exchequer and endorsed by the Secretary of State - almost without participation by Northern Irish politicians. The Northern Irish Minister for Finance and Personnel was similarly constrained in the Comprehensive Spending Review.

In the same month the Executive presented to the Assembly the first 'home-grown' Agenda for Government to the Assembly – a sign of what was to become a cross-community and relatively 'joined-up' Programme for Government. This Agenda was operational until a full-blown Programme was agreed and endorsed by the Assembly. It had the consent of DUP ministers who, despite their boycott, had participated in its formation through bilateral meetings with the OFMDFM. Though criticisms of the Agenda were expressed in the Assembly, there was a large degree of consensus in its acceptance (*QR* 4, August 2000).

Public consultations were initiated in the summer on the content of a Programme for Government and a draft was presented to the Assembly on 24 October 2000. Because of pressures arising from a combination of the suspension earlier in the year and the statutory timetable for the Northern Ireland budget (Section 64 Northern Ireland Act 1998), the draft budget was unveiled to the Assembly several days before the draft Programme – on 17 October. Various MLAs noted that this was putting the cart before the horse. Moreover, the late introduction of the budget presented considerable difficulties for proper scrutiny by the Committees in time for approval by 11 December 2000 (*QR* 6, February 2001). Nevertheless, the budget was approved.

Progress on transforming the draft Programme for Government into a final version was slower than expected. A final version, retitled as *Making a Difference*[9], was presented to the Assembly at the end of February and approved in March 2001. Passage through the various stages was not without criticism (*QRs* 5, 6, 7, November 2000, February and May 2001) – for example, that too much of it was more aspirational than concrete and, by anti-agreement parties, that it embodied too much 'north-southery'. Conversely, the DUP commended those bits where its ministers had made commitments – regional development and social development. The APNI opposed endorsement of the final version on the ground that its provisions to deal with deep divisions and inequalities were inadequate, while the DUP – a party in government, unlike APNI – opposed its inclusiveness because the government incorporated 'Sinn Féin/IRA ministers'. However, on 6 March, there was a sufficient majority for cross-community endorsement of a 'key decision'.

Notwithstanding APNI reservations, the Programme for Government has been argued to reflect better the new politics of inclusion and 'joined-up' government than its counterpart in Scotland where such aspirations were allegedly more deeply rooted. The reaching of agreement between the SDLP and the UUP on 'the philosophical underpinnings of policy' was a major achievement in itself. Unlike the Scottish counterpart, it was organised not around objectives for departments but 'entirely around policy goals' (Wilford and Wilson, 2001).

At the beginning of the 2000-01 session, the First Minister and Deputy First Ministers also announced 21 legislative proposals. Added to them were those remaining from a legislative programme announced in the month before the February suspension and not completed after re-establishment in May. Thus, in the 2000-01 session, thirty bills had to be considered by the 'multi-functional' Assembly Committees. By May 2001, eleven bills had been granted Royal Assent.

Discussion of financing devolution has ranged widely. For example, the Programme for Government identified five areas for expenditure under Executive Programme Funds (EPFs), administered by the Executive as a whole rather than by individual departments. This was announced as showing that government could work in a 'joined-up' way but, nevertheless, like the first budget, also provoked concern in the Assembly about lack of time for scrutiny. Secondly, there has been discussion of the Barnett Formula and alternatives. Discussion of UK support for Northern Ireland's expenditure – a much higher per capita rate than in England or Great Britain – brings together some strange bed-fellows since constitutional affiliations do not parallel incipient right-left outlooks and neither can be 'matched' to ideas about Northern Ireland's 'right' to high rates of support versus an escape from dependency. Nor do they readily 'read over' to ideas about how to deal with a backlog of under-investment in infrastructure as well as funding current services, to promote financial discipline and to views about private-finance or other solutions. With respect to tax-varying powers, SDLP party policy favours the same as those in Scotland but only APNI – not in the Executive – supported the Fabian Society (2000) suggestion that Northern Ireland might have the same tax-varying powers as Scotland.

**Assembly Committees**

The responsibilities of Assembly Committees and their relationship to the business of government make for a heavy workload. In addition to the budget, Programme for Government and the legislative programme, each one has initiated enquiries. Their work has been complicated by procedural uncertainties, their reputation was marred when research showed them to be much less transparent than their counterparts in Scotland, and they have had to seek extensions of the committee stages of some bills (*QR* 5, November 2000). But it has been argued that, where there is 'a unanimous committee, led by a redoubtable chair', Committees can exercise a 'clear influence over public policy.' Moreover, liaison amongst the Committees has developed. Under the leadership of the Finance and Personnel Committee, for example, there is an enquiry into public-private partnerships and the private finance initiative. And the Education Committee liases with the Committee of the Centre on the children's commissioner and with the Health Committee on the educational aspects of addressing teenage pregnancy (*QR* 7, May 2001). Together they have generated thirty-three reports on a range of topics. What they have not done – and may be unable to do, given their workload – is to initiate their own legislation (*QR* 6, February 2001).

**Civic Forum (*QRs* 5 and 6, November 2001, February, 2001)**

Though the Civic Forum was accepted by the Deputy First Minister as an example of 'inclusive democracy', this was challenged several times by the DUP chair of the Committee of the Centre and other unionists on the ground (apparently baseless) that the Orange Order had not been consulted over the nomination process and for other alleged defects in its composition. The DUP also complained that it was unnecessary and, therefore, an extravagance. All the same, it met for the first time in October 2000 to agree a programme of work. In February 2001, the First Minister proposed to the Assembly how it would relate to the OFMDFM. It would 'offer its views on such social, economic and cultural matters as are from time to time agreed between the Chairperson of the Forum and the First Minister and Deputy First Minister.' Subject to resource constraints, the Forum would not be prevented from addressing any issue. The Assembly could also invite the Forum to offer views. Despite its difficult beginnings, the Civic Forum exists as envisaged in the First Minister's motion and, from the start, began to examine a number of issues in the draft Programme for Government – poverty, peace-building and life-long learning – where it has 'done good work.'[10]

## Intergovernmental relations

### *NSMC (QRs 4, 6 and 7, August 2000 and February and May 2001)*

The first meeting of the NSMC had to await the full functioning of the Assembly, an inaugural plenary being held on 13 December 1999 and a second in September 2000 – in between which, of course, there had been the February-May suspension. Until a crisis about attendance, provoked by the decommissioning issue, the remarkable thing about 'the north south agenda – so critical in 1974 – was that it quickly became the one thing that was not likely to bring the Belfast Agreement down.' When devolution was restored in May 2000, 'a rash of sectoral-format meetings took place' – fourteen in the period between May and November – covering topics both with and without special implementation bodies. The first was to do with special EU programmes. This was followed by meetings on inland waterways, agriculture and the environment.

However, the NSMC became a victim of the absence of visible signs of decommissioning. Staving off pressure from within his Party to withdraw from government in October 2000, Mr Trimble put a motion to the UUP which included amongst conditions of continued support for participation in government the exclusion of SF from the NSMC until the IRA had engaged substantially with the Independent Commission on Decommissioning. Subsequently, he refused to sign papers nominating SF Minister to attend an NSMC meeting on health. In fact, it went ahead with Bairbre de Brún and the Deputy First Minister, Seamus Mallon (in a deliberate show of support for her rather than the First Minister) – but redefined as a bilateral meeting. She and Minister of Education, Martin McGuiness, applied for judicial review of Mr Trimble's decision which was heard on 15 December and a judgement delivered in February 2001. The ruling accepted the SF case, though it made a distinction between the unlawful withholding of nominations and reaching a conclusion that a potential nominee was unsuitable because he/she had not made an effort to implement the Agreement. Mr Trimble changed the nature of his ban and announced that UUP ministers would not attend plenaries.

In the meantime, with the support of SDLP and the Irish Government, sectoral meetings continued throughout the winter – held as bilaterals. One of these was on transport and attended by the First Minister and Deputy First Minister who had been obliged to take over this responsibility from the DUP Regional Development Minister because of the DUP's policy of non-co-operation. Work has continued since the publication of the judicial ruling. As noted in the Quarterly Reports, the 'continuing work of the north-south bodies [is] 'all the more striking' given the political context and that 'north-south bodies and co-operation have acquired a steady-paced momentum of their own.'

*BIC (QRs 5, 6 and 7, November 2000 and February and May 2001)*

The first, so far only, plenary of the BIC took place in December 1999. Unique in itself, it brought together delegations led by the Prime Minister, the Taoiseach, the first ministers of Scotland, Wales and Northern Ireland, the chief minister of the Isle of Man and representatives of Jersey and Guernsey. Though mostly 'symbolic', agreement was reached on which matters were regarded as urgent and on a corresponding distribution of responsibilities. The Republic of Ireland agreed to take the lead on drugs, Scotland and Wales social inclusion, Northern Ireland transport, Jersey the knowledge economy and the UK the environment. The second plenary was postponed because of the suspension of the institutions in February 2000 and by Donald Dewar's funeral. And it has since become a victim of the dispute over nominations to the NSMC as the plenary was to have dealt with drugs and would have involved the SF health minister. Postponement on the ground that decommissioning, policing and security normalisation needed urgent attention – in order to save the settlement – was regarded by SF as a smokescreen. They saw it as an excuse to avoid the nomination of the health Minister to the BIC as well as the NSMC.

Meanwhile, the BIC has met in sectoral format. In October 2000 environmental issues were discussed when it had been agreed to concentrate on radioactive waste from Sellafield, an issue which is virtually the only problematic area in the good relations between the two Governments (and where Denmark has also declared an interest in acting with the Republic). The Irish Government and the Isle of Man authorities agreed to prepare a paper for the next meeting. The UK Government agreed to lead on the impact of climate change and the Scottish Executive to prepare a paper on initiatives in Scotland on waste management.

In December 2000 it met to deal with transport. In the absence of the DUP the First and Deputy Ministers took over the lead. The meeting set out methods of identifying common interests and priorities, discussed public-private finance and other sources of funding, road and rail safety, access to and from regional and London airports, improved links for peripheral regions, and better road and rail connections with seaports.

*JMC (QRs 4 and 5, August and November 2000)*

The JMC for health met on 5 June 2000. This brought SF Minister Bairbre de Brún and the First Minister to a meeting chaired by the Prime Minister which considered how to improve the running of the National Health Service throughout the UK. However, she declined to attend a second meeting in October, on winter planning and modernisation, on the ground that it had been arranged at too short notice, though there may have been other more political reasons. The JMC met in summit form for the first time in September 2000 in Edinburgh and considered the Memorandum of Understanding and Concordats. Ministers discussed how each polity would take account of the interests of others and stressed the importance of continuing informal dialogue.

*BIIC*

The BIIC also met for the first time in December 1999, chaired jointly by the Prime Minister and Taoiseach and attended by the UK Secretary of State, the Irish Deputy Prime Minister (Tanaiste), and the Ministers for Foreign Affairs and for Justice, Equality and Law Reform. It lived up to its promise to be something completely different from the body it replaced by also including the Northern Irish First Minister and Deputy First Minister. Matters of common interest were identified as immigration, social security, education, drugs, and the EU. However, as a formal body, it has been rather submerged by the necessity of meetings between the two Governments, with or without Northern Irish participation, to deal with the crises that have since plagued the settlement.

# Conclusion: Has devolution made a difference?

While the Programme for Government included items reflecting innovations in Great Britain, such as public-service agreements, the First Minister and Deputy First Minister showed that it also included proposals that would not have emerged under direct rule. These were; free travel for senior citizens, a new programme of support for students[11], the intention to establish a children's commissioner and a greater emphasis on sustainable development and partnership. Though the Programme for Government is notable for its distinctiveness, the Executive's consequent legislative programme has been criticised by APNI and SF for too 'slavishly' following the 'parity principle' of conformity with Westminster legislation (Wilford and Wilson, 2001). To date, save for the abolition of school 'league tables', there are very few examples of entirely 'home-grown' concrete initiatives – though, of course, this will alter once the Programme for Government begins to take effect. It is perhaps noteworthy that one of the initiatives arising from the Programme for Government brought Northern Ireland closer to parity with the Republic of Ireland than Great Britain – the free travel for pensioners on public transport in the north matches that in the south and on north-south journeys.[12]

Foot and mouth disease, while disastrous of course, had a silver lining in Northern Ireland. It provided a notable example of 'joined-up' government and cross-community support in the Assembly and beyond for a government for once showing collective responsibility. Under the leadership of SDLP Minister of Agriculture, Brid Rogers, for the first time for thirty years an issue unrelated to constitutional status took precedence in public concern (Morrow and Wilford, in *QR* 7, May 2001) – or at least almost unrelated, since the DUP accused the south of hiding outbreaks. The action taken showed the capacity of a devolved administration to respond differently (closure of ports to animals from Britain) to what might have been expected under Direct Rule.

The limits, however, to what can be achieved by the devolved Executive can be shown in 'the litmus test' of the health sphere where there are 'grim rates of morbidity and mortality' (*QR* 9, February 2001). As noted, the First Minister and Deputy First Minister stress their promotion of 'joined-up government'. The SF Health Minister has spelled out the extent to which improvements depend on measures beyond the responsibilities of the health services. But a policy taking account of this is inevitably reduced to aspirations when key areas such as macro-economic policy and welfare, with their 'pre-eminent impact on public health' are reserved or excepted powers.

With respect to the Assembly, it can be said that it is working reasonably well (*QRs* 4 and 6, February and May, 2001). Despite the constraints imposed by their workloads and distorted timetables, Statutory Committees are beginning to assert their independence and to become constructive critics in policy and legislative matters – to function as a small 'o' opposition. They have begun to manage agendas in a more 'effective and efficient way' and are increasingly recognised outside the Assembly as 'a useful means to exert indirect influence on departments.' They are also reaching out to their counterparts in Edinburgh, Cardiff, London and Dublin. Moreover, 'although the systematic and co-ordinated scrutiny of the Executive Programme Funds – and, more broadly, the budget itself – remains wanting, there is evidence that inter-committee co-operation is beginning to flourish, in some measure prompted by the finance committee.'

On numerous occasions plenary debate in the Assembly has been the occasion for the playing out of opposition by anti-agreement parties to the presence of SF in government. An example was a vote of no confidence, moved on 8 May as a Petition of Concern by the DUP, in the SF Minister of Education, Martin McGuinness when it was reported that he had admitted - what everyone 'knew' but which had never been explicit - to his involvement in the IRA at the time of Bloody Sunday in 1972. Wilford (*QR* 7, May 2001) suggests, it could be construed that the 'plenary meetings of the Assembly are little more than occasions for ritual abuse' but considers this to be 'somewhat misleading.' It 'is working on a growing number of bills', has 'dealt with a succession of matters relating to the operation of the north-south bodies' and has 'held many debates on diverse matters.'

Despite uncertainty about the sustainability of devolution, the strand one institutions have been working. Those of strand two (north-south) of the Agreement were doing so and, as shown, continue to have a presence in the face of adversity. Only the strand three east-west institutions remains to prove themselves. To sum up:

> Until the underlying instability of political relationships is resolved, devolution in Northern Ireland will remain tentative. In the course of its first complete year, however, the habits of government have become entrenched. There is now a clearly defined political class which has established sufficient consensus to deliver a Programme for Government and begun to tackle change in social and economic policy without collapsing under the weight of sectarian pressure. What is not clear is that working together on practical matters in itself produces any dynamic to ensure that all underlying divisions will be overcome. On the other hand, by creating a system in which every party has a stake, the loss of regional institutions through further constitutional dispute would now be recognised as a serious cost. (Morrow, *QR* 7, May 2001)

## Notes

[1] The phrase, 'Making a Difference', was used by Democratic Dialogue as a title for its unofficial 'Programme for Government' (*QR* 7, May 2001) and was adopted by the Executive. As the Deputy First Minister once said at a consultative meeting on ideas for a programme, organised by Democratic Dialogue, plagiarism was not a 'dirty word' when the OFMDFM was looking for good ideas!

[2] This chapter draws heavily on ongoing research co-ordinated by Robin Wilson of Democratic Dialogue and Rick Wilford of the School of Politics, Queen's University Belfast. Their project is the Northern Ireland branch of a Leverhulme and ESRC funded programme, led by the Constitution Unit, University College, London. Other researchers, including this author, contribute to the *Quarterly Reports* (*QR*) on Northern Ireland. These are available on Democratic Dialogue's web site, as indicated in the bibliography under R. Wilford and R. Wilson, eds. and conts., 2000 and ongoing. When referred to in this text, the citation takes the form of (*QR* No. x, month and year). The chapter also draws on other Democratic Dialogue projects, including a Guide to the Northern Ireland Assembly (Wilson, 2001). The author would like to thank Robin Wilson and Rick Wilford and other contributors to this range of projects for enabling her to write this chapter. Any misinterpretations or mistakes are, of course, hers alone.

[3] B. Hadfield in Wilford, 2001, provides a detailed account of the differences between Scotland and Northern Ireland.

[4] The architect of and persuader for acceptance of the consent principle in the Republic of Ireland was Dr Garret FitzGerald (FitzGerald, 1991).

[5] The Northern Ireland Assembly is precluded from 'dealing with' an excepted matter, while the Scottish Parliament has no competence in respect of a provision that 'relates to reserved matters'. The former replicates the wording of the Northern Ireland Constitution Act 1973 and the latter the Government of Ireland Act 1920 (more dominion-like in conception and subsequent judicial interpretation).

[6] However, under other British law on Ireland, nationality and immigration, Ireland is not a 'foreign' government and nor are its nationals 'foreigners'. When the Republic of Ireland left the Commonwealth, the conventional dichotomy between the UK and Commonwealth (governments and nationals) and 'foreign governments' and 'alien' nationals was conjoined by a third category for the Irish alone, giving them a status similar to that of Commonwealth members (Meehan, E., *Free movement between Ireland and the UK*, Study in Public Policy 4, Dublin: The Policy Institute, 1999).

[7] The Agreement(s) also required the two governments to act. Separate legislation has established a Human Rights Commission and a new (replacing separate commissions for different forms of discrimination/inequality) Equality Commission (which also has a remit for a form of impact assessment under Section 75 of the Northern Ireland Act 1998).

[8] Dropped areas of co-operation were social security/welfare, inland fisheries and urban and rural development (Coakley in Wilson, 2001).

[9] In the context of public scepticism of whether devolution had made a difference (*QR* 7, May 2001).

[10] However, the Civic Forum also attracted the opprobrium of a former SDLP local councillor and columnist on the Irish News – where it was, in turn, defended in subsequent letters.

[11] The Assembly Committee took evidence from Andrew Cubie but came up with a proposal that, to the chagrin of the Executive and its priority for inclusion, was one which, being universal, was effectively more beneficial to middle-class parents (*QR* 6, February 2001).

[12] An example of problems in collective responsibility; Mark Durkan said this was a collective decision by partners in the Executive, minus DUP, while DUP claimed credit for it (*QR* 7, May 2001).

# 3

# The English Question

# The Federal Constitution of England?

## John Tomaney

### The English Question

England has represented a stumbling block when it comes to thinking about a devolved, let alone federal, UK. Because of its size, England, even though generally acknowledging the national traditions and aspirations of the other components especially Scotland, has dominated the UK. At least in part for this reason, unlike in Scotland or Wales there has been little demand for the (re)creation of an English Parliament during the past century. The lack of interest of the English in a parliament of their own helped to scupper initiatives such as 'Home Rule All Round' prior to the First World War. From time to time over the past century or so, commentators have suggested a federal system in which England would form one element alongside Scotland and Wales. But, this solution has generally been rejected as unsustainable. An English Parliament representing a population of 45 million, as compared to Scotland's population of 5 million and Wales' population of 3 million, would overshadow any federal parliament.

At the same time, it is frequently argued that England lacks traditions of regionalism or, as Harvie (1991) puts it, English regionalism is 'the dog that never barked.' It is certainly true that the English political class has shown itself uninterested in the kind of issues that arouse great passions in Scotland. It is sometimes argued that this is because England can boast a '1000 year history' of integrated governance stretching back to the Norman Conquest. In 1885 the celebrated constitutional theorist A. V. Dicey could argue:

Two features have at all times since the Norman Conquest characterised
the political institutions of England [...] The first of these features is the
omnipotence or undisputed supremacy throughout the whole country of the
central government [...] The second, which is closely connected with the
first, is the rule or supremacy of law. (quoted in Weir and Beetham, 1999)

Such a constitutional theory would appear to leave little space for a
federal solution to the English. However, the essentially 'Whiggish' view of
English history, that underpins Dicey's assumptions has been challenged by
modern historiography, which suggests it applies most accurately to the
southern core of the English state. In fact, throughout the Middle Ages,
the English periphery – especially the border regions with Scotland and
Wales – was characterised by a significant measure of political autonomy
based on localised military power. The Tudor period saw a concerted attempt
to remove the political bases of regional autonomy (marcher lordships,
ecclesiastical palatinates) from the English periphery at the same time as it
enforced the union of England and Wales. The centre finally asserted its
domination. Thus Thomas Cromwell, in the Acts of Appeals in 1533
asserted that '[...] this realme of England is an Empire [...] governed by one
Supreme Head and King [...].'

The Tudor period, however, also saw notable attempts to resist the
encroachment of central rule, notably in the North – the Pilgrimage of Grace
and the Rising of the Northern Earls – and in the West – the Cornish Rising
(Calder, 1998, Urwin, 1982). However, it is true that these sources of regional
power were undermined by the end of the seventeenth century at the latest.
The peripheral English regions did, however, retain distinctive cultures and
identities, some of which gained new potency as industrial revolution occurred
in regions distant from the southern heartlands. The new British
historiography, though, would see the incorporation of the English periphery
as part of the broader designs of the English state to dominate the Atlantic
archipelago. One result of this has been that the English have tended to
conflate their own identity with that of the British and have left themselves
ill-equipped to address searching questions about identity thrown up as a
result of devolution, European integration and broader social and economic
changes.

Despite the highly centralised character of the English polity, it was governed on the basis of a 'dual polity' (Bulpitt, 1983), in which some autonomy was ceded over local affairs ('low politics', according to Bulpitt), while the central state concerned itself with 'high politics' (defence, national currency, Empire, etc.). Thus local government did play an important social and economic role in the late nineteenth century and, especially with the growth of the welfare state in the twentieth century, although it generally lacked the constitutional safeguards that are found in federal states. The conduct of 'high politics', though, occurred in close concert with key interests in the City of London. A centralised, almost imperial, political culture based around the House of Commons is a defining feature of the UK, particularly England, which has lacked strong regional institutions in the modern period, despite the growth of the welfare state. As severe economic problems re-emerged in some English regions in the 1960s, and worsened in the 1970s, efforts were made by Labour governments to introduce some regional planning institutions. However, these were weak bodies and remained very much the creatures of central government: they did not survive the election of the Thatcher's Conservative Government in 1979. It is only recently in the modern period that English regionalism has begun to be a serious political force.

In opposition, the Labour Party accumulated a range of ill-specified commitments as far as the English regions were concerned. The 1992 manifesto committed the Party to elected regional government in England, alongside proposed reforms in Scotland, Wales, Northern Ireland and London. However, little detailed policy work was undertaken on the subject, although the statement was enough to stir signs of interest in regions like the North East. Under Tony Blair, Labour drew back from its previous commitments and made a more tentative promise of action 'where there was demonstrable demand.' Meanwhile, John Prescott, the deputy leader, won the Party to the idea of creating Regional Development Agencies, ostensibly to tackle regional inequalities, but also implicitly as a *quid pro quo* for English MPs' acquiescence in the devolution debate.

### New Labour and the English Question

Thus, the English Question – that is, how will England be governed in a devolved, let alone federal UK – was left largely unanswered by New Labour in its first term of office. As Bogdanor (1999) notes, 'England is hardly mentioned in the devolution legislation, and yet England is, in many respects, the key to the success of devolution.' There was a striking absence of proposals concerning England in Labour's initial devolution programme. Much concern was expressed about the possibility of an 'English backlash' to Scottish and Welsh devolution, but to date the attitude of mass opinion in England appears to express benign indifference. There is no guarantee that the English will continue to adopt this attitude, as the wider implications of devolution for the UK become more apparent. For this reason, the English Question continues to be raised and solutions proffered. One solution to the 'English Question' lies in proposals for an English Parliament. This option is now favoured, in one form or another, by the Conservatives. The other option, to which the Labour Party is ambivalently committed, sees the solution to the English Question in some form of regional governments *within* England. This option gets support from the more peripheral regions, especially those that abut Scotland and Wales, which tend to see an English Parliament as just another form of London government.

Although the Government paid comparatively little direct attention to the needs of England and, more especially, its regions in its first term, it did initiate some changes. Within England the Government established eight Regional Development Agencies (RDAs). Each RDA has a board of directors selected from within its respective region. Ministers in London, on the advice of civil servants, however, appoint these boards. The Government has also encouraged the formation of 'regional chambers', primarily from local authority associations, but incorporating interest groups such as business, unions and voluntary organisations. These organisations were only given a consultative role; they have no statutory basis or direct powers; and they, therefore, look very weak compared to the institutions created in Scotland and Wales. The Labour Government announced its intention to legislate for English regional government only where there is demand for it but did notably little itself to stimulate such demand in its first term.

One area where the Government did legislate is in relation to London, where it created an elected mayor and accompanying assembly of 25 members. While the Greater London Authority (GLA) model represents a constitutional innovation, insofar as it introduces the concept of the directly elected mayor, it represented a weak form of devolution. Unlike the Scottish Parliament or Welsh Assembly, the GLA takes over few central government activities; it does not have a single block grant to fund its activities; and it is subject to the veto of the Secretary of State for most of its actions. The mayor has important *responsibilities* in areas such as transport, policing and planning that are of great import to the London public. It is less clear that the mayor has the *powers* necessary to make progress on these issues. The mayor, however, is able to claim a large mandate, and this has proved to be a recipe for tension, especially over transport, between the incumbent mayor, Ken Livingstone and the central government. New Labour's worries here echo those it had in Wales. The Labour party became embroiled in an unseemly squabble in late 1999 making a vain attempt to ensure that its candidate for the post was suitably loyal to the New Labour project.

Historians will judge devolution as one of the lasting legacies of the first Blair Government, but as Tony Wright MP observed, initially at least, the English were 'spectators at the devolutionary feast'. Labour left the English Question largely unanswered in its first term. However, as Labour's first term ended, there were signs that regional question was beginning to move up the Government's agenda. The governance of England was finally becoming an explicit political issue.

### The outlook for England

The high tide of New Labour's engagement with regional question in its first term came with the creation of Regional Development Agencies (RDAs) and the promotion of voluntary local authority led regional chambers in 1997. Both sets of institutions got off to a wobbly start and were pale shadows of what had been proposed by John Prescott's Regional Policy Commission before the election. Labour made no moves on the commitment – in its 1997 manifesto – to legislate for elected regional assemblies ('where there is demand').

But in the run-up to the General Election Labour began to deepen its engagement with the English regions, not the least because of the widening range of political pressures compelling it to do so.

The leading figure in the Government in the promotion of regional policy and regional government was – and remains – the Deputy Prime Minister, John Prescott. The first signs of this deepening engagement were the sound of new voices in the debate. Chief among these was the Chancellor Gordon Brown. In a speech in Manchester early in 2001, the Chancellor made the case for RDAs having greater financial flexibility (albeit within centrally agreed 'outcome targets') and for new mechanisms for holding them to account, both through strengthened regional chambers and new arrangements in the House of Commons. Although, the Chancellor stopped short of raising the prospect of directly elected regional government, his remarks were widely interpreted as laying the ground for just such an eventuality. However, there remained a key problem – Tony Blair, despite his apparent northern connections, appears to have little interest in regionalism!

Irrespective of whether the Chancellor had been converted to regional government, his Manchester speech signalled a new concern with regional policy as a means for achieving the Government's ambition of full employment. Also, in a series of speeches, the then Trade and Industry Secretary, Stephen Byers, made what sounded like an old fashioned Keynesian case for regional policy. Byers called for a widening of the 'winner's circle' beyond the South East of England. An additional new voice in the debate was the former Northern Ireland Secretary, Peter Mandelson. In March 2001 he made a powerful call for a North East regional government. Describing himself as a convert to the cause, he argued that '[...] we cannot achieve economic revitalisation in the North East without modernising the means of delivering our economic policies, and this means renewing the region's political institutions.'

Within this context, the Government acted to strengthen the principal existing bodies. Moves to strengthen RDAs came in the face of criticism – not least from business – that their funding levels were inadequate and too closely tied to nationally determined programmes, which reflected the priorities of Whitehall departments rather than the regions themselves. In his Pre-Budget Report in late 2000, the Chancellor announced extra resources for RDAs (albeit tied to unspecified 'outcome targets') and stated that the Government would create a 'single cross-departmental framework' to address the criticisms about 'departmentalitis' described above. The importance of RDAs in the Government's broader approach to industry policy was further emphasised by the publication of the DTI's White Paper *Enterprise, Skills and Innovation*. It called for a 'bottom-up approach' to enterprise policy. To this end, RDAs were given a leading role in the objective of raising productivity, particularly through the promotion of 'industry clusters'.

RDA chairs were not wholly convinced of the Government's *bona fides* though. Graham Hall, the chair of Yorkshire Forward, went on record to attack the Whitehall cult of centralisation, calling for a radical decentralisation of authority to the regions. Tensions reached a high point in early 2001 when RDA chairs clashed with senior officials in the Department for Environment, Transport and the Regions over the nature of the new funding arrangements. The outcome of the pressure from the regions led to the Chancellor and Deputy Prime Minister jointly announcing that financial freedoms for RDAs would be in place by April 2002. By the time of the General Election, RDA chairs were convinced that the Government was now firmly pushing the regional agenda.

At the same time as he announced the new powers for RDAs, John Prescott also proposed a strengthening of voluntary regional chambers (or 'assemblies', as most prefer to style themselves) drawn from representatives of local and 'social partners'. These voluntary associations had been initially encouraged in order to provide some scrutiny of RDAs. Some chambers took on the role of Regional Planning Conferences from local authorities and more are likely to follow suit. New resources from the Government are likely to see them reinforce their role as regional actors. Indeed there was evidence in 2001 that chambers are beginning to flex their limited muscle. For instance, in the unlikely location of the East of England – an entirely artificial construction with no regional identity or tradition of regional action – the Assembly was the first to run into conflict with its RDA, when it rejected the latter's regional economic strategy. In the South East of England, the Regional

Assembly was the first to come into direct conflict with the Government over the latter's decision to reject the case for a road development on the Kent/ Sussex border. In the East Midlands the Regional Assembly launched an Integrated Regional Strategy, intended to provide a framework for the proliferation of regional strategies that has occurred since 1997. Regionalism, it seems, is breaking out even in the English heartland.

As well as acting to strengthen RDAs and chambers, the Government also enhanced the Government Offices for the Regions (GORs), which were established, ironically, by the last Conservative Government. Until 2001, they included the regional activities of Department for the Environment Transport and the Regions, Department of Trade and Industry and the Department for Education and Employment. In April 2001, responsibilities from the Ministry of Agriculture, Fisheries and Food (now Department for Environment, Food and Rural Affairs), the Department for Culture, Media and Sport and the Home Office were moved into the GORs. At the same time a Regional Co-ordination Unit was established in Whitehall, to ensure the central government initiatives take account of regional contexts.

Taken together these changes amount to a significant strengthening of regional governance in England, by a Government that nonetheless remains ambivalent about devolution. However, these bodies are only the most prominent in what is the currently fractured governance of the English regions. A study by the Centre for Urban and Regional Development Studies at Newcastle University for the North East Chamber showed that over 20 government (or government-sponsored) organisations were involved in the preparation of at least a dozen regional strategies, which affected many aspects of the region's life. Although the RDA, Regional Assembly and especially the Government Office for the Region were heavily involved in the preparation of regional strategies, many other government departments, non-departmental government bodies and other agencies were also involved.

The dominant trend amongst these bodies is toward the creation, or strengthening, of regional structures in order better to assist them to contribute to regional strategy making. This quiet regionalisation of government structures, and simultaneous proliferation of regional strategy making is a relatively unnoticed feature of the governance of the English regions. The senior decision-makers within these organisations work on the assumption that the trend will grow rather than diminish. They welcome the move to regional strategy making, but express frustration about the failure to 'join up' individual strategies and the lack of capacity properly to implement them. In addition there was a surprising acceptance of the need for greater accountability of the existing structure of regional governance. In short, the study revealed both the potential and current limits of existing regionalism (see figure on the next page).

Alongside the evolution of regional structures, the period before the General Election saw the growth of civic regionalism in England. The North East stands out as the leader in this respect. The Campaign for a North East Assembly was formed in 1992 and a North East Constitutional Convention was established under the Bishop of Durham in 1999. Regionalism in the North East draws on a comparatively strong sense of identity and the political campaign is underpinned by a growing cultural awareness. It is fed though by a widely held sense of economic injustice, born of the region's enduring position at the bottom of most lists of social and economic indicators. These factors mean that in the North East, more so than elsewhere, the politics of regionalism is a high profile media issue. In other parts of England, though, campaigns are beginning to emerge. Yorkshire and the North West have active campaigns, while new ones have been established in the West Midlands and the South West. Together these have formed a national lobbying body, the Campaign for the English Regions. The forces producing these are varied, but generally they are bottom-up organisations that are seeking to publicise and broaden the debate. As a result of this activity the issue of devolution is beginning to creep onto the media agenda in each of these regions. To date, though, only in the North East is there evidence that public attitudes support regional government.

In the General Election of 2001 the Government reaffirmed its commitment to elected regional assemblies ('where there is demand'). It also made a big effort to be seen to be responding to regional concerns with John Prescott and Gordon Brown launching a document about the English regions at a pre-election rally in Wakefield. John Prescott used the occasion to promise the publication of a White Paper on regional government after the election.

## Governance of North East England

**Columns:** LOCAL | REGIONAL | CENTRAL

**CENTRAL**
- Home Office
- Department for Environment, Food and Rural Affairs
- Department of Trade and Industry
- Department for Transport, Local Government and the Regions
- Department for Education and Skills
- Department for Work & Pensions
- Cabinet Office
- Department for Culture, Media and Sport
- Department of Health

**REGIONAL**
- VONNE
- A] Environment Agency
  - B] Countryside Agency
  - C] English Nature
  - D] Rural Development Service
  - 2
  - a,b,d
- E] Housing Corporation
  - F] Highways Agency North
  - 3
  - a,b,c,d,e,f
  - e
- Government Office for the North East
- Regional Development Agency (aka One North East)
- 1
- Regional Assembly
- a,b,c,d,e,j
- G] Learning and Skills Development Agency
  - H] Learning and Skills Council
  - 4
  - a,b,h,j,n
- Employment Service
- Co] Communications North East
- I] English Heritage
  - J] Sport England
  - K] Community Fund
  - L] Northern Arts
  - M] Heritage Lottery Fund
  - N] Northumbria Tourist Board
  - O] North East Museums, Libraries & Archives Council
  - 5
  - i,j,k,l,m,n,o
- Social Services Inspectorate
- NHS Executive Northern and Yorkshire

**Regional (strategies/programmes)**
- Regional Rural Development Programme
- Regional Housing Statement
- Sustainable Development Framework
- Regional Planning Guidance (including Regional Transport Strategy)
- Regional Economic Strategy
- Regional Cultural Strategy

**LOCAL**
- Waste
- Police
- Fire and Civil Defence Authorities
- Airports
- Passenger Transport Executive
- Local Authorities
- Health Action Zones
- Community Health Councils
- Trusts
- Health Authorities

**Key**
- —— Funding/Control
- ‑ ‑ ‑ Organisational input into Regional Strategies

The debate around the White Paper is likely to dominate discussion of the English regions in the coming months. However, post-election changes to Whitehall structures complicated the picture. The massive Department for Environment, Transport and the Regions lost responsibility for RDAs, which are now sponsored by DTI, while a new Department for Transport, Local Government and the Regions (DTLR) retains responsibility for other aspects of regional policy. At the same time, a new Office of the Deputy Prime Minister in the Cabinet Office oversees Government Offices, while John Prescott was assigned to chair the new Cabinet committee on the 'nations and regions'. From this milieu a White Paper will be produced. Key actors in these early stages were the Regions Minister, Nick Raynsford (author of the Greater London Authority Act in the last Parliament), Stephen Byers, the Secretary of State at the DTLR and John Prescott. In the minds of ministers it is likely that the GLA looms large as a possible model for the English regions. It is also likely that, even with a following wind, only the North East would have a functioning Assembly by the end of the current Parliament. It also remains to be seen whether the London model would satisfy opinion in the North East. The Government, however, seems serious in its commitment to move forward, with Stephen Byers promising legislation for the 2002 Queen's Speech.

Despite the ambivalence of the Prime Minister, regionalisation is slowly (and quietly for the most part) becoming the order of the day in England. This is throwing up new challenges for public and private sector organisations. Many organisations exhibit only the first glimmer of a dawning realisation of the scale of current and possible future developments. Whatever the misgivings of New Labour, the English Question seems increasingly to demand an answer.

### A federal England?

While England has represented a stumbling block in the search for a devolved solution to the governance of the United Kingdom, recent developments suggest that the importance of these questions may finally be dawning on the English. It is becoming increasingly evident that any such solution is likely to involve a regional dimension. The present Government is overseeing a quiet regionalisation throughout England, not out of a strong political or ideological commitment, but because such structures are a practical requirement of governing a complex and diverse country the size of England. Civic regionalism, however, is growing at an uneven pace. It is strongest by far in the North East England, but it is also growing in other parts of the English periphery (including the South West) and even stirring in the southern heartlands. The growth of regionalism in the North East is conditioned, in some measure, by its proximity to Scotland, as well as the relative strength of its identity. If the regionalisation of England is to be driven in the way that is anticipated by the Government it is likely to be an uneven process, with some parts of England seeing devolved government before others. The process is likely to produce a scenario of 'quasi-federalism' (Hazell, 1999), rather than the clear division of powers that would be expected under an orthodox federal constitution.

At the heart of the political future of England are questions about its identity. As noted earlier, the political identity of England has hardly been a subject for discussion. It is hardly surprising, therefore, that the most profound questions about the future of England and its relationship with the other nations in a devolved UK should first be asked in the periphery, rather than in London and 'the Home Counties'. The debate about a devolved England is simultaneously a debate about improved governance and the search for a new, more pluralistic conception of English identity.

# The Greater London Authority
## A new local authority for London or England's first regional government

### Alex Bax

In his speech launching the Greater London Authority, Ken Livingstone MP, the first directly elected Mayor of London, said that he saw the GLA 'blazing a trail' for regional government for England.[1] He predicted that over the next fifteen years more and more powers would be devolved to the Greater London Authority (GLA), and that other English regions would watch closely the lead given by London.

The voluntary regional assemblies and the members of the Regional Development Agencies around the country are calling for the next steps towards democratically elected English regional government to be speeded up. At the same time, however, the Labour party nationally seems to have lost some of its earlier enthusiasm for English regional government. There was no mention of regional legislation in the post-election Queen's Speech though a White Paper is apparently promised for publication before the end of 2001. Is the Greater London Authority (GLA) 'blazing a trail' for the English regions, or has it been established to address problems that are specific and particular to London? And does the early establishment of the GLA mean that 'the problem of London'[2] has already been solved as far as English regional devolution is concerned.[3]

The establishment of the GLA fulfilled a long-standing Labour Party commitment to return some form of city-wide government to greater London.

Seen as a replacement for the GLC, the GLA does not fit neatly into debates about regional government or devolution. Is the GLA a revived upper tier of local government for the UK's largest Metropolitan area, or one of the first steps towards the regionalisation of England – part of a coherent New Labour project of devolution and constitutional reform, or both? Certainly the Mayor of London has taken to referring to the GLA as regional government.

Debates about the nature of sub-national government in London have been more extended and intense than in other parts of England due partly to the capital's size and dominance in national affairs, but also to the number of times national governments have intervened to tamper with the structure of London's government over the last one hundred and fifty years. Perhaps the GLA is better understood as yet one more attempt by central government to solve the particular difficulties that the British state has always had in dealing with the government of its capital city. This chapter describes the genesis of the new arrangements for the government of London and begins to consider how far the GLA can be described as an early example of English regional government.

The Greater London Authority Act 1999 is apparently the largest single piece of legislation passed by the UK Parliament since the Act of India paved the way for Indian independence in 1949. This simple fact signifies the complexity of the government of London. Before describing the institutions this latest London Government Act created it is worth taking a brief look at some of the GLA's predecessors.

The first serious institution formed during the modern era to address London-wide problems was the Metropolitan Board of Works, created by Parliament in 1855, specifically to address London's sanitary problems. As with all subsequent institutions of London government, by 1889 the Metropolitan Board of Works had been given numerous additional functions. In that year it was replaced by the London County Council (LCC), almost as an afterthought in legislation reforming the English Counties. The LCC became a powerful and successful multi-purpose authority responsible for most local authority services covering the area that is now known as inner London. However, the continuing growth of London, particularly the dramatic expansion of suburban London between the wars meant that by 1945 the LCC actually only governed about half the population living within the urban area known as London. Pressure for reform grew during the 1950s and in 1957 the government of the day established a Royal Commission on Local Government in London (the Herbert Commission). The Commission reported in 1960, recommending the establishment of a Council for Greater London with jurisdiction over more or less the entire contiguous built up area. Subject to one or two amendments, the boundaries recommended by Herbert, and the general division of services recommended by Herbert, were brought into being in 1965 with the creation of the Greater London Council and the 33 London boroughs (Herbert had actually recommended that there should be 50 London boroughs beneath the GLC).[4] The boundaries for Greater London established some forty years ago by a Royal Commission on *local* government in London have now become the boundaries for the new strategic, (and possibly regional) authority for the capital city.

Given its abolition only 22 years later, the GLC could be judged as an unsuccessful attempt to address the problem of London's government. On the other hand, if longevity is any recommendation, the 33 London boroughs might be judged as having 'succeeded remarkably well.' From the start the GLC was hobbled by an unhelpful and unclear separation of functions between it, the boroughs and the national government. In retrospect, many of the services it was responsible for are today seen as models of good practice, 'but it was singularly unsuccessful at building a sense of community within its boundaries.'[5] The London boroughs were also larger, and stronger, than Herbert had recommended.

Growing dissatisfaction with the performance of the GLC led a Conservative administration in County Hall to set up in 1977 an independent inquiry chaired by Sir Frank Marshall. This inquiry was to examine the relationship between the GLC, central and local government and to review the distribution of powers and functions between them. Marshall conducted his inquiry against the background of a wider debate about regional devolution.

With the benefit of hindsight, Marshall's never implemented report seems extremely prescient in its prescribed solution for London government.

At the beginning of his report Marshall noted that the GLC was 'effectively set up as a type of regional authority, for which there was no precedent.'[6] Marshall gave 'much thought to the question of what is 'strategic' and whether there is a place within London government for a 'strategic' authority'. He noted that all those who wanted the GLC to opt out of their business said it should concentrate on strategy, but no one had defined what strategy meant. 'Strategy' is a key term for the GLA but it has not been given a general definition in either the GLA Act or the Green or White Papers that preceded it. Marshall's definition of strategy in the context of strategic Metropolitan government is:

> 'The setting of broad objectives in the wider public interest for the welfare of the Metropolitan community, coupled with the oversight of policies and the overall control of resources necessary to achieve them.'

The GLA seems remarkably close to the 'strategic/executive role' that Marshall proposed except that the GLA does not have many powers to intervene in borough affairs, which Marshall saw as necessary for this kind of organisation.

Addressing planning issues, Marshall recognised that a regional level authority for London and the South East (i. e. some kind of authority covering the whole region for planning purposes), was politically unrealistic given the size and dominance of London and the South East in the UK as a whole. So Marshall suggested a 'regional or Metropolitan corporate planning and directing authority'. But this could not happen in London alone. Against the background of possible devolution to Scotland and Wales he advocated eight regional strategic authorities for England, each with revenue raising powers and major resource allocation responsibilities. Logically this would have left central government with the role of allocating nationally raised revenues between regions and leaving them to decide how to spend the money in their region. Marshall accepted that the achievement of this regional aim would be 'a long-term goal' and that such a solution would need 'to be applied nation-wide or not at all; and this pre-supposes a re-organisation of the whole structure of local government.' It is surely no coincidence how closely many elements of the GLA fit with Marshall's prescriptions. The GLA has been set up to be 'strategic'. The services it runs are operated by arms length executive agencies to which the GLA (effectively the Mayor) allocates resources and for some of which the Mayor sets strategic priorities. The current Government has tended to avoid using the word 'regional' in documents about the GLA, although at the launch of the Green Paper in July 1997 John Prescott explicitly linked developments in London with the question of English regional devolution:

> 'It is almost a forerunner to any decision we make on regional government. [...] When we look at the structures for the regions of England we will look at this. If the lessons are good we will certainly draw [on them] for other regions.'[7]

Marshall provides a reasoned justification for a city-wide government not dissimilar to what has now been put in place, though I am sure he would see the many fetters on the new GLA's financial independence as severe limitations on his model. Marshall clearly saw such an authority as necessarily part of a new tier of English regional government. Marshall provided a blueprint for an Authority which, due to the Thatcher intervention in London government, had to wait twenty years to be implemented.

O'Leary has described the abolition of the GLC as a 'Nietzschean folly', irrational when viewed from any reasonable policy evaluation framework. Abolition was a 'by-product of intergovernmental conflicts.'[8] Having taken the decision to abolish, the Conservatives came up with a number of post-hoc justifications for their actions. The Thatcher Government was not interested in regional government as a form or concept. However, London did not fall apart over night in the absence of city-wide government, but under the post 1986 arrangements: 'Many important metropolitan government functions are left to the whim of voluntary or near voluntary joint arrangements.' The lack of city-wide government 'proved the catalyst for partnerships [...] but they are not a substitute for effective governmental action.' London needed another tier of government because of the lack of co-ordination in the middle, 'London is a city with much government but little political power.'[9] (Tony Travers' diagram of the government of London in the early 1990s is reproduced as Fig. 1 on the next page.)

Short of recognising the folly of abolition, later Conservative governments made efforts to improve London governance (through the London Pride initiative, the encouragement of business partnerships like

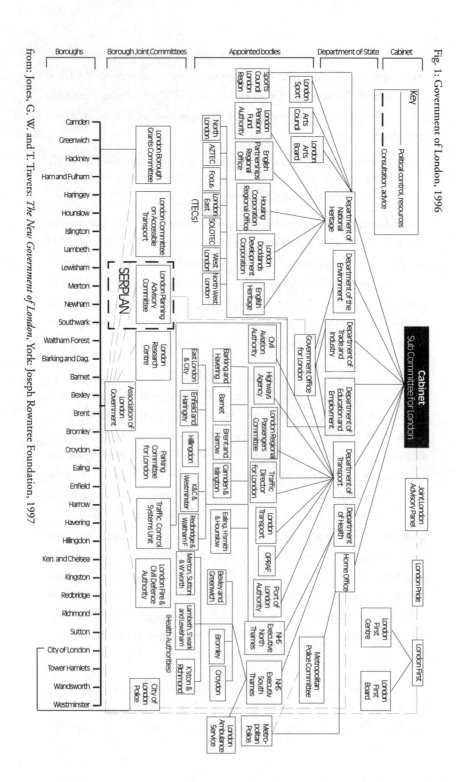

Fig. 1: Government of London, 1996

from: Jones, G. W. and T. Travers: *The New Government of London*, York: Joseph Rowntree Foundation, 1997

London First, the establishment of a Minister for London and creation of the Government Office for London). As the Labour Party began work on preparing its manifesto for the 1997 general election the issue of London's governance was back on the political agenda. Lack of co-ordination and accountability were the two headline issues for London government. Labour's national discussion of regional government recognised these two factors, but the main focus in the English regions was for new institutions to address perceived regional economic imbalances.

In a way London presented Labour with an easier task than the regions. London had an empty space at the strategic level waiting to be filled. Jack Straw MP said in 1995 'One thing we are clear about in England, you cannot establish regional assemblies as well as having shire counties and districts underneath them.'[10] London presented New Labour with 33 unitary authorities and therefore a new intermediate tier could be, and has been, re-inserted.

**Creating the Greater London Authority**

In 1996 the Labour Party published 'The Road to the Manifesto: a Voice for London'. It sought views on how London should be governed and set out the Labour view of the main problems with London's government: lack of co-ordination and lack of a coherent voice. 'That is why a Labour government will set up a directly elected London-wide strategic authority to bring together and augment the energy, talent and commitment of Londoners from all walks of life – all working together for a city to be really proud of.'

The document was primarily concerned with the allocation of functions – what precise 'strategic' roles should be given to a new authority? However, it did ask for views about boundaries. Three proposals were made: the GLC's old boundary; a 'linear city' extending along the river; or extending Greater London to the M25 and beyond. The document recognised that, 'to take London's boundary beyond the M25 would be to establish a regional government covering London and much of the South East with a population much greater than that of Scotland and Wales combined. We do not think this is sensible.'

Discussing the potential boundaries for the new authority it said that 'the present [the GLC] boundaries broadly make sense and are now familiar. To adopt the present boundaries would be straightforward and would avoid delay and expense.' This is the longest discussion about boundaries in any Labour Party or official document leading to the GLA's establishment, though one can detect tacit recognition that a truly *regional* government for London would have boundaries beyond those of the GLC (and now GLA).

Lines of accountability and areas of responsibility were to be clearly defined between the three proposed tiers: local government, central government and the new intermediate tier, the GLA. The new authority would work in partnership with London's 33 boroughs, but be directly elected and therefore separately accountable to the people. The document did not relate the proposed new authority to any other constitutional reforms, it simply said it would be 'new', 'city-wide' and 'strategic'.

Labour's 1997 General Election manifesto contained a straightforward commitment to bring back a strategic authority for London to 'take responsibility for London-wide issues.' The next paragraph dealt with the 'regions of England' offering them a slow track, 'on-demand' approach to regional government. Unitary authorities would need to be the dominant form of local government of the lower tier before regions could be established. Apart from the fact that they are dealt with consecutively in the text, the 1997 manifesto made no link between the reform of London government and the introduction of regional government across England.

Following their May 1997 election victory Labour quickly produced a Green Paper on London's government. It contains a brief justification for bringing back a third tier of government for London: to give institutional recognition to London's sense of identity; to address a perceived democratic deficit (unaccountable quangos) and to bring decision making closer to the people, 'bridging the gap between community level government and national government.' One paragraph addresses London's role and relationship with the rest of the United Kingdom, stating that there are 'strong reciprocal links with the rest of the UK, Europe and the World.' But there is no mention of the wider South East region. This is interesting given that the DETR was simultaneously working on proposals for RDAs. Speaking in the House of Commons John Prescott explicitly linked the London proposals to the Government's wider devolutionary programme:

'We are committed to moving, with the consent of local people, to directly elected regional government in England. That complements devolution in Scotland and Wales and the creation of a Greater London Assembly.'[11]

The Green Paper proposed a new form of government for London. It was to build on private and voluntary partnerships, sub-regional partnerships and the achievements of the London boroughs since GLC abolition. The Green Paper set out ten key criteria to underpin the new authority including 'strategic: concerned with strategy, thinking and planning for London, particularly at a pan-London and sub-regional level.' It is noticeable that unaccompanied use of the word regional is avoided (the word or phrase 'sub-regional' is, however, scattered throughout the Green Paper). Under the heading 'a voice for London' the Green Paper mentions some key roles including fostering economic competitiveness, encouraging inward investment, leading civic projects and 'defending its [London's] interests here and in Europe.' The Green Paper deals with the boundary issue in just two lines, which simply confirm the GLC boundary.

Between publication of the London Green Paper in July 1997 and the White Paper the following spring a study called *The Greater London Authority: principles and organisational structure* was produced by IPPR and KPMG. Holtham and O'Brien were the principal authors but amongst others the study's steering group included Andrew Adonis from the Downing Street policy unit. In contrast to the London Green Paper the study consistently and unashamedly describes the GLA as a tier of regional government. There is an unambiguous statement that 'a London strategic authority will [...] be England's first experiment in regional democracy.' In more detail:

'The GLA should be clearly identifiable as a regional tier of government in three senses: there should be a decentralisation of powers, resources and responsibilities from central government (for example in land use planning); and an extra decision making capacity should be created to fill an identifiable gap in existing governance mechanisms (such as in our recommendations on a public health function); and the electoral mandate of the local tier should be respected. [...] A regional authority would improve the representativeness and

efficiency of governance by rationalising and bringing a democratic dimension
to existing arrangements.'

These improvements were explicitly stated as being applicable to all
English regions.

The study endorsed the Government's view that the GLA's boundary
should be the GLC's old boundary, because of the complexity and political
difficulty of changing it. A city-region of London and the South East would
be just too big, too distant from local authorities to bridge the gap between
them and government. The study suggested a separate South East region. In
the event, of course, Government has quietly and expediently cut the former
South East region in two.

Under a heading 'Plugging the gap' the study defined the main gaps in
London government as being the lack of co-ordination, accountability and
'joined-up-ness' in the tangled middle ground of London government. The
new authority would explicitly address these three issues. The study adopted
Marshall's definition of strategic, a term not defined for the GLA anywhere
else. All GLA service management responsibilities should be devolved to
arms length agencies. Finally, the study endorsed the principle of subsidiarity
and the need for regional government across England. The word regional is
used regularly throughout the report with proposals for a 'regional land use
plan', a 'regional housing strategy' and an ability to set 'clear regional goals'
for public health. It is interesting to contrast the formal response to the
Green Paper made by the Association of London Government (the political
association of the 33 London boroughs) in its document *Capital Choices*.
Perhaps reflecting borough wariness of a strong and clearly defined regional
authority for London, it uses the word 'regional' only once.

The White Paper setting out detailed proposals for the GLA was
published in early 1998. In his Foreword, John Prescott again links the reform
of London government with the Labour Government's wider programme of
constitutional reforms for 'democratic renewal'. However, the proposals for
London are 'tailor-made', emphasising London's special role in Britain. Prescott
was not the only Government Minister to present the GLA as part of a wider
project of constitutional reform. The Lord Chancellor set out the

Government's constitutional programme in December 1997. He described the Government's 'coherent' but pragmatic 'overall prescription for change'. Lord Irving listed four main elements of the programme for institutional change: devolution, London, regional government in England, and reform of local government. Lord Irving said that the Government was 'not promoting a federal style uniform devolution of powers, but differential devolution to different parts of the United Kingdom.'

The White Paper proposed an American style executive Mayor with a scrutinising Assembly. It set out the division of powers between Mayor and Assembly. All executive powers were to rest with the Mayor. The Mayor was to be given varying levels of control over four arms length executive agencies. He would have power of appointment, resource allocation and strategic powers over Transport for London and the London Development Agency; and resource allocation, and limited powers of appointment over the Fire Authority and a new Metropolitan Police Authority. The Mayor would be required to publish eight strategies: transport, economic development, spatial development, culture, municipal waste, ambient noise, air quality and biodiversity. Several of these strategies would exert significant power over the London boroughs. Because of his powerful democratic mandate, the Mayor would be able to wield influence over many areas outside his direct control. A subsequent example of this influencing role is the strategic partnership that has been established between the Mayor and the London Region of the NHS, though what direct influence over health services this arrangement will deliver remains to be seen. Finally, the GLA (effectively the Mayor) was the first English sub-national authority to be given an effective general power of competence. The Mayor would, however, have no responsibilities for education, social services or (except through his planning powers) housing which would remain with the boroughs, along with many other services. Fig. 2 (on the next page) shows a picture of London government today.

There were few changes between White and Green Papers. Except that the Mayor's Spatial Development Strategy (christened by the Mayor the new 'London Plan') will have to conform to Regional Planning Guidance for the South East[12] the relationship between London and the wider region is not

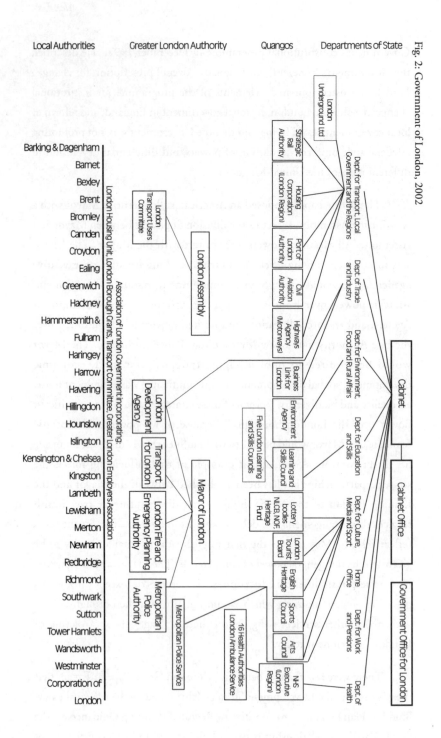

Fig. 2: Government of London, 2002

Local Authorities    Greater London Authority    Quangos    Departments of State

defined. One change between Green and White Papers was the decision to re-draw the boundary of the Metropolitan Police District so as to exclude some areas to the north and east of the Greater London boundary that had previously been covered by the Met. Perhaps indicative of just how difficult it is for governments to re-draw significant political boundaries, this is the one place in the whole process where an existing boundary was changed.[13]

The GLA Act implemented all the main proposals contained in the White Paper. The GLA assumed its powers, following Ken Livingstone's victory in the first mayoral elections, on 3 July 2000.

Definitions of regional government generally agree that to answer to the name an institution needs resource allocation responsibilities. On the face of it the GLA appears to have a large budget and this may suggest that the Mayor has significant resource allocation powers. The first year's budget was nearly £3 billion for the GLA and its four functional bodies. A proportion of the Mayor's budget is raised through a precept on the local Council Tax but he remains overwhelmingly dependent on central government grant. Government set tight spending guidelines for police and fire services; and the London Development Agency's budget comes direct from central government. The Mayor does have a certain amount of revenue raising freedom with the Transport for London budget, in that he can vary the levels of fares (of course only on London busses until the Government concludes whatever arrangements it can for the discredited private partnership initiative on the London Underground). He has one new revenue raising opportunity - congestion charging – but any money raised can only be spent on transport.

Whilst £3 billion may sound like a significant amount, in fact it represents only about ten percent of identifiable public expenditure in London. Despite the contrast with the English regions, where RDA expenditure accounts for only about one per cent of public spending,[14] this is still far from what might be reasonably expected for the resource allocating powers of a strategic regional authority. The Mayor has been demonstrating his role as a voice for London arguing for additional resources for the capital, and would undoubtedly argue that the democratically elected regional authority for London should be able to control and distribute additional resources.

It is still too early to assess the GLA's place in the new British constitutional settlement. Its relationship with the Government's other constitutional reforms – devolution, English RDAs and local government modernisation – remains unclear. During the passage of the GLA Act a research paper produced by the House of Commons Library suggested 'that ministers regard London governance as distinct from devolution, regionalism or local government.'

From GLC to GLA debate about London government focused largely on the 'restoration' of democratic strategic government rather than proposing that London become a test bed for English regional devolution. So what kind of institution is the GLA, how much is it re-formed local government and how much regional devolution? Clearly it is a multi-purpose, democratic authority with characteristics common to both local and regional governments. It is not concerned with the distributional, often more local, side of government: services like education, health or benefits. However, the Mayor does have some direct powers over London's 33 local authorities.

In functional terms one might expect a regional authority's powers and responsibilities to be devolved from above. On this basis the GLA would be considered as an example of devolution. However, many of the GLA's executive functions either were previously, or in any other city would have been, the natural preserve of a city hall. The GLA has not received the kinds of service responsibilities that a city government could expect to have. However, there are two specific areas that take the GLA beyond other English cities or local authorities: the Mayor's strategic planning responsibilities (the Spatial Development Strategy and his power to intervene in local borough planning decisions) and his control of the powers and budgets of the London Development Agency. (In this respect actively campaigning English regions would like to emulate the GLA). In both cases the GLA's powers to set policy or vary the distribution of resources are constrained by legislation and statutory guidance,[15] but nevertheless, the GLA is an embodiment of devolution, however limited, and represents a step towards the resource allocating role, advocated by Marshall and seen as one of the key functions of a regional tier government.

The GLA's boundary has been in existence for 35 years, but Londoners' ability to identify with it must still be open to question. Even if the majority of Londoners do in part identify themselves with the city, getting them to identify with the Mayor and Assembly will be hard, because of the sheer scale of London, the continuing complexity of its government, and perhaps the weakness of the Mayor's powers. Even with the high profile mayoral contest, turnout in the GLA election was only just over 34 per cent. The Mayor's drawn out battle with the Government over the future of the London Underground has served continuously to remind Londoners of the Mayor's existence, while at the same time giving an example of just how much power remains with central government.

So the GLA is only a first step. The diagram (Fig. 2, p. 114) shows just how many bodies remain accountable to central government, and therefore how many areas of influence the Mayor of London might hope to convert into direct power: for example through taking control of learning and skills or regional sport and arts bodies. Also, for the GLA to be truly regional, functional questions remain about its boundary. In terms of scale London within the GLA boundary is big enough to be a region (or a nation) by itself; however, the boundary drawn by the Local Government Act 1963 was an attempt to encompass a continuous urban area, not a region. This brings us back to the 'problem of London'. London is clearly the metropolis at the heart of the South East region of England, but it is politically impossible for the Government to give institutional form to this reality by creating what would be a region of perhaps 18 million inhabitants and thirty to forty per cent of UK GDP. In order to balance the interests of the rest of the UK, London must remain divided from the South East.

Vernon Bogdanor suggests that 'the London mayor and authority will be part of a weak upper tier of local government rather than an embryonic regional authority. In providing for a mayor and authority in London the Government took a conscious decision against devolution.'[16] So, while the Mayor and at least some in Government are happy to see the GLA as 'blazing a trail' for English regional government, at least one leading commentator sees it as more likely to get in the way. The GLA is 'trail blazing' but on questionable boundaries with inadequate powers or control over resources.

Compared to previous incarnations of London government the GLA does have a more avowedly strategic role. The Mayor does not have the powers to interfere in many day-to-day 'distributional' services; but does have some significant strategic powers, which will influence the long-term direction of the city and the region. The Mayor is a far more powerful figure than the leaders of the two new neighbouring regions. As the new South East and Eastern Regions move along the proffered 'slow track' towards regional government, perhaps the logic of their current boundaries will be questioned again.

So what of the other tiers of London government: the 33 'strong' local authorities and central government's continued extensive responsibilities? The Government Office for London (GOL) has not been disbanded, indeed Government recently decided to give GOL, not the GLA, responsibility for delivering the new National Strategy for Neighbourhood Renewal, not exactly a ringing endorsement of the new strategic authority it has established for London (or perhaps the Mayor who was elected!). Predictable tension between the Mayor, with a duty to consider the needs of the whole city, and the individual municipalities was illustrated by the Mayor's decision to cease membership of the municipal Association of London Government (ALG) only six months after joining it, citing obvious conflict of interest in GLA membership of a borough funded lobbying organisation. 'The ALG performs a very precise function in representing and organising the work of the boroughs. But this function is quite distinct from the needs of the GLA, which is a layer of regional government rather than local government.'[17]

Nevertheless, the GLA, led by the Mayor with significant transport, policing and economic development responsibilities has become the more dominant regional level player. The office of Mayor gives the organisation a strong urban and metropolitan municipal feeling, but on the other hand London also has an 'Assembly', as does Wales. We must wait to see whether Mayor Livingstone can enhance the autonomy and power of the GLA, and begin to gain for London's new authority some of the powers granted to the Welsh Assembly, as Tony Travers has proposed in an article in a special London supplement of the New Statesman, or whether 'the problem of London' will overwhelm its latest solution, and perhaps campaigns for English regional devolution as a whole.

## Notes

[1] The author's personal recollection of the Mayor's inauguration speech at Tate Modern, 3 July 2000

[2] 'The problem of London' being defined as the long recognised economic and demographic size and dominance of London within the British state, therefore making lop-sided any regional based efforts at devolution.

[3] Garside, P. and M. Hebbert, *British Regionalism 1900-2000*, p. 10

[4] Royal Commission on Local Government in Greater London, 1957-60, Report, Cmd. 1164, HMSO, London 1960

[5] Hebbert, M., *London, more by fortune than design*, p. 114

[6] *The Marshall Inquiry on Greater London. Report to the Greater London Council by Sir Frank Marshall MA, LLB*. GLC, 1978, p. 7 (The Marshall Inquiry)

[7] Reported on the *Local Government Chronicle* web site 1.8.97

[8] O'Leary, B., 'Why was the GLC abolished?' *International Journal of Urban and Regional Research*, Vol. 11, 193 - 217, p. 203

[9] Jones, G. and T. Travers, *The New Government of London*, p. 28

[10] Quoted in Bogdanor, V., *Devolution*, p. 270

[11] Rt. Hon John Prescott MP speaking in the House of Commons on the RDA White Paper, *Building Partnerships for Prosperity*, quoted in V. Bogdanor, *Devolution*, p. 272

[12] *A Mayor and Assembly for London*, Section 5.61

[13] Section 323 of the *Greater London Authority Act 1999* amends the Local Government Act 1963 so that 'The Metropolitan Police District shall consist of Greater London.'

[14] Morgan, K., 'The new territorial politics: rivalry and justice in post-devolution Britain', in: *Regional Studies*, Vol. 35.4, 2001, pp. 343-348.

[15] See for example, *The Town and Country Planning (London Spatial Development Strategy) Regulations 2000*, DETR, Statutory Instrument, 2000 No. 1491 and *The Town and Country Planning (Mayor of London) Order 2000*, DETR, Statutory Instrument 2000 No. 1493

[16] Bogdanor, V., *Devolution*, p. 274-5

[17] GLA Press Release, April 2001 (http:www.london.gov.uk/news/2001)

# Decentralisation, Devolution or Deconcentration
## Alternative views of the modernisation agenda

### Baron Isherwood

### Introduction

This is a personal account of the development of one aspect of regional devolution, namely the 'transfer' of regeneration responsibilities from Government Offices to Regional Development Agencies. The word is in quotes because, despite impressions at the time Development Agencies were being formed, the regeneration of our towns and cities is now more of a split responsibility than it was prior to the establishment of RDAs, requiring considerably more administrative effort to overcome the effects of fragmentation than had been expected when dedicated regeneration agencies had first been proposed. Whether this is part of a deliberately induced creative tension designed to force regional stakeholders to work together more collaboratively, or whether it is a reflection of the fact that the institutional arrangements, functions, roles and responsibilities of the different agencies had not been thought through, requires more analytical insight and background into this aspect of regionalism than is open to me.

In the process of moving from being a Director of Regeneration and Strategy in a Government Office, to the Director of Regeneration of a Regional Development Agency, one is of course cut off from old files, relevant papers, reports that may now have been forgotten, and the dates of key events. And with the passing of time perhaps perceptions of events were simply wrong, or that however close one felt to these developments at the time, it may not have been sufficiently near the centre of things. Decisions get taken at the heart of government that are sometimes only dimly glimpsed by those working 'down the line', at the periphery of the government machine. So this is in no sense an authoritative version of events surrounding the slow shift that appears to have taken place over the last few years from a highly centralised administration with regional outposts, through increased de-concentration of functions and institutions with a stronger regional presence, to the beginnings of more devolved decision-making at regional level.

### Regional Offices in a central administration

Once upon a time it appeared a good thing, within a Civil Service career, before a 'sound' spell in Finance or Personnel became an essential stepping-stone to success, to have worked in a Regional Office of one of those Departments that had a regional presence. In Headquarters there were reportedly people who were close to the heart of policy-making, who had also been close to the delivery of that policy at a local level, and who presumably brought that knowledge into the development of policy. Regional Office activity appeared to offer 'hands on' experience in dealing with real problems of deprivation, poor housing, the need for reclamation of derelict land and buildings, local but significant planning issues, and also regional transport and industrial policy delivery. The over-riding 'mission' of Regional Offices was indeed to deliver national policy. They were formally no more than regional outposts of a highly centralised administration, in which power and decision-making resided at the centre. While not exactly 'post boxes', the arrangement perpetuated the culture of administration by well-written submissions to Ministers, preferably directed through policy divisions, of course.

Informally Regional Offices had the advantage of offering a fair amount of autonomy within broad policy parameters. To a large extent this was implicitly understood by the Centre as a reflection of the fact that a broad framework cannot deal with individual local circumstances (for example, when Salford Quays was first being planned, the only tools available were the Urban

Programme and Derelict Land Grant, and some invention was necessary), and partly explicitly encouraged on the basis that if the Regional Offices were to act as the eyes and ears of Government in the regions, their members were expected to 'go native' to a certain extent. While becoming too much of an 'enthusiast' was firmly discouraged, especially in relation to the display of 'bleeding stumps' of local conditions, judicious finessing of centre-local relationships, was accepted. It may only have been a pale reflection of that ability to deal with ambiguity so valued by the centre, but it had the effect, culturally, of welding the Regional Offices into the central administration.

Even so, such autonomy was largely exercised within fairly firmly defined policy 'silos' – for example in several Regional Offices of DOE, 'housing' and 'urban affairs' came under different Regional Controllers. The evolution to an integrated approach to regeneration came relatively slowly, and probably was more advanced at the local level than at the centre. When it became clear that the regeneration of the Hulme estate in Manchester, which suffered not only from spalling concrete, infestation by vermin and poor insulation, but also from very high levels of social deprivation and crime, the heartfelt minute detailing the need for an integrated and comprehensive approach that incorporated social as well as housing regeneration led to the response from those at the heart of the policy machine – 'there is a limit to the extent to which policy can be designed by reference to conditions on the ground.' However, it should not be assumed that such a comment implies a closed mind – from the upper levels of the Civil Service it might just as easily have been an ironic understatement of the writer's own frustrations at putting together a policy that made sense, both to Ministers and in relation to local circumstances. One can never tell, particularly from the regional level perspective. But whatever the motivation, policy did not change quickly.

**Initial moves to deconcentration**

In time an integrated approach to regeneration did emerge, partly as a reflection of the limitations of the land and property focused Urban Development Corporation approach, partly because the more 'technical' issues of dealing with these aspects of regeneration and physical development were 'deconcentrated' from Regional Offices and English Estates to English Partnerships, and partly because it was the only approach that made sense when faced with the 'multi-faceted' nature of urban problems and urban deprivation. It took Ministerial changes to shift policy to this extent, but the Regional Offices were very much to the fore in the development of the all-embracing City Challenge experiment, by which integrated and comprehensive regeneration was delivered indirectly through separately established companies, and readily took on the mantra of 'finding local solutions to local problems.' A fair amount of experience was subsequently gained in developing and working with local partnerships in the pursuit not only of City Challenge redevelopments, which embraced a good mix of physical regeneration and social improvements, but also in exploiting the subsequent Single Regeneration Budget. It was introduced, more or less synonymously with the creation of combined Government Offices, formed from the amalgamation of the Regional Offices of the Departments of the Environment and Transport, Trade and Industry, and Education and Employment. Those Regional Offices had previously come together infrequently. So-called 'Regional Boards' of regionalised Departments and Agencies occasionally met, but with no remit, there was no result, and attendance lapsed. City Action Teams were formed from a few Regional Offices in a few places to pursue limited small-scale development activities, but otherwise Regional Offices followed separate and rarely interlocking agendas of their parent Departments.

The Single Regeneration Budget, and the creation of the many and varied local regeneration partnerships created to access its funds, was at the time seem as an increase in deconcentration – the concept was familiar from the French use of the term in the early 1990s, although the apparent degree of responsibility given to the Prefets, let alone the quality of accommodation of French Prefetures, seemed far in advance of that enjoyed by the Regional Offices. The great merit, as far as regional civil servants were concerned, was that it recognised the need for regional Civil Servants to think outside the box. They felt just a little less constrained by the Vote Managers and Finance Desks at the Centre, and began to take seriously the implicit message that they were there to implement policy in a combined way to improve the overall quality of life in regional towns and cities rather than simply to disseminate central policy, or organise ministerial visits and photo-calls.

**Decentralisation?**

Unfortunately, while deconcentration to regeneration agencies appeared to become quickly part of the regional institutional framework the push to decentralisation that accompanied it (as Government Offices sought greater responsibility in deciding their own priorities) was seen by parts of Headquarters' Departments as something of a threat, rather than as an opportunity to provide a unified approach to regional issues. Unlike the single Cabinet Office responsibility that now pertains for Government Offices, in their initial days they were 'run' by a triumvirate of senior officials from each of the three departments. They had to answer to three Permanent Secretaries, while their newly appointed over-arching Regional Directors (whose enhanced status was not recognised in terms of enhanced pay or influence) were asked to weld together a unified Regional Office from those different departments, with their different cultures and at least three different sets of pay and conditions.

It quickly became clear the Senior Management Teams within the new Government Offices that clarity of purpose was not one of the features of the new regime. One of the Departments was avoiding playing the regional game. Indeed, the first attempt to develop a separate regional strategic view on economic and social pressures and possibilities was stillborn as the deliberately cautious draft documents were regarded as insufficiently distinctive to warrant development. Strengthening regionalism was evidently not to be a matter for Government Offices – such a fundamental shift could not come from within the system. It required a political initiative from within the region and from Europe to begin to develop a regional identity as well as the pressure to create regional institutions (see below).

One minor effect of this was that Government Offices were no longer seen as being advocates for their region in Whitehall, as had been the case for quite some time, but were to regard themselves as 'the voice of Government in the regions'. From the perspective of the Government Offices themselves, it felt that their function of acting as an intermediary, which had hitherto been useful on many occasions, was no longer as valued as it had been.

While some regretted the loss of influence resulting from this difference in interpretation of the Government Offices role, it was understandable given the developments in the regions themselves.  For example, spurred on by the European Commission's requirement that European Regional Development Funds (ERDF) could only be distributed on the basis of an agreed Regional Strategic Framework, the North West Chamber had begun to form, and evolve an agreed approach to regional issues albeit one that appeared to be based on a recognition of proportionate shares of ERDF rather than the identification of pan-regional priorities or major growth opportunities.  Conflicts between the Government Office, being the regional voice of a fiercely anti-regional central government, and European Commission officials who would have preferred to deal directly with regional government, became the background against which Programme Monitoring Committees met to agree the financing of projects.  While the conflicts livened up otherwise very tedious and largely procedurally based meetings, it did seem regrettable that the moves that had been made to finance regeneration activities on a programme basis should be undermined by an inability to align European Funds on the same basis – projects, on a first come first served basis, were required to dominate.  An integrated approach to the development of comprehensive approaches to local strategies seemed as distant as ever.

**First moves towards devolution?**

The change of government in 1997 to one with a very different regional agenda appeared to offer the prospect of not only maintaining a holistic approach to regeneration, but of allowing a regional identity to develop, and regional autonomy to be exercised, in pursuing regional objectives. However difficult the birth of the Scottish and Welsh Assemblies, they had happened, and something similar for the English regions no longer appeared impossible. The new Regional Development Agencies, established with the remit of reducing regional disparities in income levels, not only within England but raising incomes to those of European averages, was the first step.

By far the largest proportion of RDA funding came from the Government Offices' Single Regeneration Budget (SRB), which was passed over in its entirety to the RDAs. Nonetheless, the development of policy on RDAs took place, at least from the perspective of one in a Government Office involved peripherally in some of the discussions, without considering the implications on Government Offices themselves or in relation to other institutions having a regional presence. Raising such issues at the various meetings that took place between Government Offices and the Policy Units within Whitehall establishing the RDAs, seemed to be rather bad form. Recollections of the previous line taken on whether it was possible to recognise conditions 'on the ground' lightened the frustrations of attempting to influence centralised policy making. Under the pressure of policy development, the need for announcements, legislative timetable etc., it must indeed be difficult to think through all the angles in advance. But here was a major change in the machinery of government (the RDAs) coming very soon after another very significant, but more incremental change (the Government Offices), alongside the development of an independent regional chamber. What was to be the relationship between these decentralised institutions?

**Political geography of decentralisation**

Rumours were rife. At one stage it was thought that the RDAs would supplant the Government Offices. An influential European Commission official had said that the Commission regarded the RDAs as being the potential Ministries of Finance of a future regional government, whose current embodiment was the regional chamber. With the departure of the SRB funds and staff into the RDA, along with the loss of some DTI staff into the competitiveness side of the RDAs, and the collapse of the DfEE component of the Government Offices following the development of Local Learning and Skills Councils, there was a suggestion that the Government Offices themselves could be abolished. Apart from dealing with housing matters at a local level, there was little else within the Government Office that needed to be dealt with within the region – planning for example is a largely quasi-judicial matter in which, although local knowledge might be important, local contacts and local lobbying would be prejudicial to a consideration of the evidence on strict land use planning criteria. There was a view that planning work could be de-regionalised.

Alternatively, if Government Offices were to continue to exist, there was logic in giving them a 'sponsorship' role for RDAs, ensuring that links to Ministers and the policy-making machine would be routed through Government Offices. This had worked reasonably well in relation to Urban Development Corporations. Although there was always a temptation to go direct to the seat of power in London, and for Chairmen to open only the doors that Chairmen can open with Ministers, fairly good relationships had been established in most cases, with both Government Offices and the Development Corporations working co-operatively together on agreed and productive Corporate Strategies. However, it was by no means clear that this would be acceptable to the policy-making machine, which would not want to delegate its influence and powers over RDAs as quickly as the Government Offices would wish. It would be equally unacceptable to Chairmen and Chief Executives to think that organisations that represented the whole of a region (albeit appointed by a Secretary of State) should relate to the Centre only through an appointed Civil Servant. The fact that some Regional Directors had applied to be Chief Executives of RDAs because 'that is where the action is', a route and reason followed by some of their own senior staff, only reinforced the position of RDAs relative to Government Offices.

At the working level, a number of trilateral meetings between the Government Office, the RDAs and the Chamber were attempted to make the undefined relationship work, come what may. As with most trilateral arrangements, they were not a success. Remits were unclear, agendas were still being formed, and political attitudes being developed. The need for greater clarity in the relationship between these organisations was a subject of several discussions, possibly even papers, within the Civil Service, but the situation did not appear to change while there was an imperative to establish the RDAs themselves, select the Boards and the senior staff, and maintain their inherited programmes. Indeed, it was the inherited programmes that drove their activities in the initial period following their establishment, and the Government Offices found themselves only peripherally involved in relatively low-level matters of sponsorship of the RDAs – the real lines of communication were between the RDA operating divisions and the Departmental policy divisions.

The coincidence of timing between establishing the first RDA Corporate Plans and the Comprehensive Spending Review 2000 perhaps made this inevitable, but it was compounded by further directions, requirements, and continuous demands for data and improvements to processes that seemed to weaken regional relationships rather than strengthen them. In the field of regeneration, the links between the sponsorship branch of DETR previously dealing with English Partnership (EP), and the Land and Property sections of the RDA's which had taken on EP regional staff, were particularly strong, effectively by-passing the Government Offices. The weaknesses in the previous management arrangements between EP and DETR, exposed by audit examinations, required immediate and full responses by the RDAs. By one means or another the centre seemed to be saying – 'don't think you're going very far down this devolution road.'

**The centre strikes back**

The position of Government Offices was, of course, eventually comprehensively tackled by the Policy and Innovation Unit.[1] The exhaustive analysis, which was surprisingly self-critical of Whitehall departments and attitudes, came rather late in the day. No doubt there were subtle and political reasons for this. But at the regional level the lack of vision on the part of Whitehall of what regions ought to look like, which organisations were required to deliver policies effectively, and what the relationships between the various functions of the various organisations ought to be, was puzzling. 'Reaching Out' as the study itself noted '[...] took place at a difficult moment – too late to affect the decision to establish RDAs and designated Chambers, but too soon to have a full appreciation of their performance.' (para 3.30) Nevertheless, the Report does establish a rationale to differentiate between RDA and GOR functions:

'[...] the main factor which should determine whether to allocate functions to RDAs should be the closeness of links to the production of a strategy for the region and the delivery of programmes for which they are responsible. RDAs' functions should be concentrated around those activities where prioritisation and planning is needed at the regional level, as distinct from the role of supporting and evaluating local performance, or representing the views of government, which should be the function of Government Offices.' (conclusion 34)

Similarly, the Report concludes that

'[...] the key distinction between RDAs and GORs is that RDAs should concentrate mainly on what needs to be prioritised and planned at the regional level, as well as delivering programmes and co-ordination to support that aim, while GORs provide a leading role in relation to co-ordinating and integrating the actions of government players in the region.'

It adds that

'[...] GORs also provide a monitoring, supportive and advisory role to the local tier in relation to Government policy, and an effective upward channel of communication, as part of Government, to Whitehall.' (para 3.75)

While superficially attractive, this does not in fact provide sufficient distinction between the RDAs and the GORs to allow for a helpful delineation of roles and responsibilities. For example, as the Report recognises, there is a particular issue in connection with the relationship between Regional Strategies and Social Exclusion. (paras 3.118-3.126) Having inherited the SRB programme, which had evolved from the broad based City Challenge model of regeneration to focus more on social exclusion issues, and was being spread very thinly, it may be right to question whether the RDAs operating primarily at a regional strategic level ought, as has in fact happened, to begin to concentrate more on the economic development issues facing a region than on the detailed local social exclusion issues. There are in practice two difficulties with this. The first is that the number of truly regional projects that can be devised at a regional scale to improve regional competitiveness is very limited. With the exception of major flagship schemes (such as a large scale infrastructure projects, whether in relation to transport, information and communication technology, the science base, or major industrial inward investment) economic prosperity must be built up from a large number of individual and local actions in which both economic and social exclusion are addressed. The second issue is that to limit the capacity of one of the key delivery agencies in a region to address an integrated regeneration agenda reduces its effectiveness in making contributions to local, sub-regional, and hence regional competitiveness and prosperity.

**A creative tension?**

Thus in regeneration alone (similar areas of ambiguity are to be found in relation to Strategic Planning Guidance, skill development, and the encouragement and development of enterprise), the situation post-RDA and post-Government Office refocusing, remains 'fuzzy'. The following separation of responsibilities would be relatively clear. On the one hand the RDAs could operate to implement policies on economic competitiveness and regeneration. Their focus would be on delivery. The Government Office on the other hand could be dedicated to the promotion of policy, the development of cross-cutting advice and co-ordination of other government departments' contributions, and the monitoring and evaluation of policy. But in fact each organisation effectively tries to do something that the other is also attempting.

Both the RDAs and the Government Offices attempt to deliver regeneration, neither quite believing in the distinction between social and economic regeneration. Although regeneration is written into the RDAs remit, it is also the responsibility of the Government Offices, being affected through the New Deal for Communities, and now Local Strategic Partnerships, especially those in receipt of the Neighbourhood Renewal Fund (NRF). Even an apparently natural inclination to use RDA funds to complement NRF in the most deprived wards has led to some interesting reactions, along the lines of 'but that is what we are doing', and if RDAs were to do that, it could be seen as 'an implicit criticism on the level of resources allocated through the NRF'. The silos remain standing. Housing also remains with the Government Office and as housing is an essential part of the regeneration of many northern towns in particular, that too will have to integrate somehow with the economic regeneration efforts of RDAs. Yet housing is excluded from the RDAs' remit. Also the national regeneration agency, English Partnerships, continues to hold land and to seek development opportunities on sites that are predominantly of local, rather than of national or even regional significance.

Moreover, while the RDA is indeed responsible for an overall Regional Strategy, which in the case of some regions goes rather wider than an economic strategy in order to attempt to integrate social and environmental concerns, the Government Office too is eventually responsible for the over-arching Land Use Planning Strategy contained in Regional Planning Guidance (although that is initially drafted by the Regional Assembly). The development of relationships is a key element of RDA activity, for without effective partnerships the larger part of its Regional Strategy will not be able to be delivered; but the Government Office too is responsible for the accreditation of Local Strategic Partnerships and the maintenance of other relationships in the region. In relation to monitoring and evaluation, the RDA arguably has the more onerous task in that only if it meets its agreed targets (one of which is a very firm target on reducing social deprivation and the 'housing on brownfield land' target, as well as its economic targets) will it receive resources for further work; while the Government Office has been asked to monitor schemes, even small scale and property schemes, which the RDA also monitors routinely for development control and auditing purposes.

While none of this intimate inter-meshing completely inhibits work on regeneration and other activities, it requires a level of 'n-dimensional' chess playing that makes one wonder whether matters could not be organised more straightforwardly. In parenthesis, it does however, offer a useful alternative definition of deconcentration – one certainly needs to concentrate on so many peripheral as well as mainstream activities and partners, that achieving full focus on any one objective is made rather more difficult than seems strictly necessary.

### Devolution within regions

One way in which some RDAs are attempting to simplify the model is indeed to attempt to operate at a more strategic level, in regeneration terms. The sub-region appears to be an appropriate level at which Regional Development Agencies can operate effectively. Sub-regional partnerships and alliances, identifying common and cross-boundary issues in the areas of economic development and infrastructure development are beginning to be formed, in recognition of the ineffectiveness of purely local approaches to job creation, skill improvement and development of the knowledge economy. One RDA has decided to devote 80 per cent of its budget to its sub-regional partnerships on the basis of simple proportional shares in relation to population numbers.

The informal institutional arrangements which are being developed impose considerable challenges on the large number of partners required to form them, and on the intellectual competence of those required to draw up the sub-regional strategies. Local identity expressed through local authorities, remains extremely strong and coalitions between them are not easily developed. For example, in the face of competition over economic development of particular sites – it has been difficult to gain agreement over the selection of truly regionally significant strategic sites. And while there is recognition of the fact that local job creation schemes can never address structural imbalances in labour markets which operate at a larger scale, there appears to be little readiness yet to embrace the idea of the city-region, with all that it implies about the loss of local sovereignty. At the intellectual level, sub-regional strategies will not only have to sit under the over-arching Regional Strategies (which are due for review very shortly), but they will need to sit alongside a relatively large number of strategies that have been produced since the establishment of the RDAs. From the relatively recent position when a few sheets of A4 were regarded as too great a challenge to national policies, there has been a vast growth in the number of documents produced setting out strategic improvements to regional prosperity, competitiveness, and the quality of life.[2] As well as needing to be consistent laterally, sub-regional strategies will need also to cover those emerging from Local Strategic Partnerships, which themselves may be built up from Community Plans.

The RDAs will need to work out mechanisms to engage with both levels of partnerships. And they will need to decide upon the style with which they do so. All the RDAs appear to have decided not to operate a bidding round along the lines of the Single Regeneration Budget which, when administered by the Government Offices, led in many peoples' minds to a 'beauty parade' in which there was insufficient transparency and accountability for the decisions taken by regional officials. The RDAs see themselves not as administrators of national schemes, but as advocates and proponents of regional priorities, and will want to work closely alongside sub-regional partnerships as they produce their Strategies. At the Local Strategic Partnership level, RDAs will need to be selective, not least because of the requirement on them to hit their targets on deprivation, urban renaissance, and reclamation of brownfield land (in the regeneration area at least). This implies that in taking forward local priorities, the RDAs will be but one of many other partners pursuing Local Strategic Partnerships strategies. While they will no doubt be intent on maintaining an integrated approach to social, economic and environmental regeneration, RDAs are likely to look increasingly to other partners to provide the bending of mainstream resources that will deal with social and possibly some elements of environmental regeneration, concentrating themselves more on economic aspects of regeneration. Quite how this is going to be achieved has also been the subject of long debates and serious concerns over the loss of the potential social exclusion element from the RDAs portfolio, on the part of RDA Boards and executives. Ideas are being discussed in various consultative meetings with regional stakeholders and partners. The beginnings of a new agenda are emerging from the Treasury involving ideas from America on developing competitive inner cities, paying particular attention to the needs of indigenous and ethnic minority businesses and establishing the networks and conditions that will enable them to thrive in the belief that the most effective way to tackle social exclusion is by finding a solution to economic exclusion. These ideas are all in the process of evolution.


**Conclusion**

While it is dangerous to impose too neat a pattern on events over the last 10-15 years at a regional level, particularly from a regional perspective, it is possible to discern a movement from the main regional institutions being merely regional outposts of an overwhelmingly centralised administration, through deconcentration via the creation of a number of agencies, to the present position of a somewhat confused degree of decentralisation, in which regional agencies and regional representatives of national agencies explore regional issues. A full devolution of administrative functions to the regional level remains some way off (although there are interesting dimensions of devolution within regions).

Regional Offices of central government departments were there to implement national policies, and brought with them a strong element of control from the centre, the traffic being almost entirely one-way – centre-out, top-down – with the regions bringing very little influence to bear on the development of national policies or priorities. That control was mirrored, at least to a large extent in regeneration activities, by the control exercised primarily by local authorities on economic development activities.

Very few other players were involved until other agencies such as English Partnerships, the Highways Agencies, Urban Development Corporations, City Challenge Companies, Training and Enterprise Councils, and Business Links, were created. These all embodied a much greater deconcentration of activity than had previously been the case under a centralised administration. That deconcentration continues through Single Regeneration Budget partnerships, and the Small Business Service and the Local Learning and Skills Councils (LLSC). Originally the RDAs had felt the SBS and LLSC ought to come under their remit, but they have now recognised the new political requirement to influence and persuade rather than to control and direct.

The RDAs are a definite step towards greater decentralisation. It is not, of course, complete because they still report to a Secretary of State at the centre, and are required to meet targets set centrally, and have a remit that restricts them from developing wholly relevant regional policies (for example, through their equivocal relationship with Regional Planning Guidance and the lack of any direct influence over housing issues). Nevertheless, they do have a greater degree of autonomy than was enjoyed by Government Offices. This autonomy is exercised by their Boards, subject mainly to the quality of the argument that they can parade in support of their policies and priorities. There is a period of uncertainty ahead as sponsorship passes from one central department of state to another, but adaptation and flexibility has long been one of the regional attributes, allowing progress to be made in the face of a sometimes disturbing indifference to regional conditions.

As yet, full devolution of powers to the regions has not been achieved. At least from a regional perspective one can only feel that the process is underway, reinforced for example by the Government's decisions to endow each of the regional assemblies with resources to scrutinise the strategies and policies of the RDAs. The evolution of regionally relevant ideas, and regionally relevant deconcentrated and decentralised institutions to implement them, may eventually appear in retrospect as essential elements in the move to a devolved and mature approach to regional issues.

.

*Notes*

[1] Reaching Out: The Role of Central Government at Regional and Local Level

[2] In the North West alone the following documents have been produced since 1998: A Strategy Towards 2020; Strategy Economic Baseline Report & Labour Market Assessment; England's NW – A Strategy Towards 2020 & Regional Planning Guidance Review – Spatial Implications of the NW Regional Strategy; Regional Strategy Update 2000; A Strategy Towards 2020 Consultation Report; A Strategy Towards 2020 Sustainable Development Appraisal; A Strategy Towards 2020 Indicators and Targets; Regional Strategy Annual Report 2001; Innovation Strategy; Skills Strategy – The Right Angle on Skills NW England; NW Transport Priorities Strategy; European Strategy Group; Regional International Trade Strategy 2001/2005.

# Sub-national Government in England
## Local authorities and the regional agenda

## Stanley Henig

The earlier chapter by John Tomaney demonstrates the relative lack of salience of regional government in England until relatively recently. It is perhaps not surprising that local authorities showed the greatest interest. Historically they have been the sole on-going manifestation of sub-national government in England. A series of re-organisations in the 1970s, 80s and 90s served to demonstrate local government's total constitutional subordination to (the whims of) central government. If anything the totality of those changes left behind a system of local government with limited historic resonance and with its functional effectiveness all too often impeded by territorial boundaries which failed to recognise the complexity and over-lapping nature of issues requiring settlement at sub-national level. Administrative deconcentration – particularly the establishment and development of Government Offices for the Regions (GORs) – also drew attention to a significant democratic deficit. In dealing with central government local authorities can always use the good offices of MPs: this is much less the case where decisions are effectively being made at GOR level.

The linkage between local and regional government was underlined by the establishment of two Royal Commissions appointed during the 1960s – Redcliffe-Maud on Local Government and Crowther/Kilbrandon on the Constitution. These remain a major source, perhaps even the intellectual inspiration, for a good deal of subsequent discussion.

Redcliffe-Maud's report was published in 1969 and it offered a conceptual framework seemingly universally applicable to any tier of governance, albeit one which has usually been ignored by subsequent governments. It posed a key question – 'What is, and what ought to be, the purpose which local government serves.' The very first paragraph of the report offered a basis for constructing the answer: 'The pattern and character of local government must be such as to enable it to do four things: to perform efficiently a wide range of [...] tasks [...] to attract and hold the interest of its citizens; to develop enough inherent strength to deal with national authorities; and to adapt itself to the [...] process of change.'[1] It is by no means clear that any of the myriad reforms of local government over the next thirty years took much account of either the question or the answer.

The Crowther/Kilbrandon Commission was appointed by the then Labour government at around the time when Redcliffe-Maud was completing its work. Its remit was to consider the whole gamut of sub-Westminster government – actual and potential. However, the political impetus for its creation arose from the slowly gathering head of steam for some kind of devolution to Scotland and Wales. Crowther/Kilbrandon's analysis of different types of devolution is highly complex, but the final majority report clearly decoupled the concept of regional government in England from the devolution regimes proposed for Scotland and Wales. Whilst the latter were to be based on directly elected assemblies, a system of regional co-ordinating and advisory councils would be established in England. These would be 'partly indirectly elected by the local authorities and partly nominated.' The proposed organic link between the two tiers of sub-national government gives salience to a key reason underlying the opposition of most members of the Commission to directly elected regional assemblies in England – 'the reorganisation of local government outside London in two tiers with only forty-five authorities [...] in the top tier, has left no room for directly elected regional authorities.'[2] Despite the abolition of many of those authorities in the succeeding twenty-five years this argument still resonates, especially with members of the surviving 'top tier authorities.'

The dynamic of party politics can lead to bizarre juxtapositions. Although the Conservative Party has always been committed to the concepts of the unity of the United Kingdom and the sovereignty of the Queen in Parliament, the party has not historically been associated with the notion of pervasive, ever increasing centralisation. It is perhaps hardly surprising that successive Conservative governments between 1979 and 1997 sought to remove devolution from the political agenda. However they also introduced an apparently unending series of changes to local government – all designed to make it far more subservient to central government. The upper tier authorities in Metropolitan areas were simply swept away; immensely tough financial regimes imposed; and the Banham re-organisation in the 90s focused entirely on boundaries with the Redcliffe-Maude principles totally ignored. By the mid-1990s Labour, having lost four successive general elections, had become the overwhelmingly dominant party in local government in natural opposition to the Treasury regime of ever harsher financial controls and the accompanying centralisation. It was equally natural for Labour to champion devolution as an additional curb on apparently all-powerful Conservative central governments. Use of the terminology 'New Labour' could hardly conceal the 'etatist' tradition of commitment to strong central government as the key means of controlling the economy and driving through social reforms. But the incoming Labour Government of 1997 was now also committed to reinvigorating local government and promoting national and regional devolution.

Between 1992 and 1997 the Banham re-organisation had helped focus interest amongst local authorities on possible regional developments. There was an initial assumption that Banham would result in the general establishment of a uniform system of all-purpose authorities, implying the total removal of the 'upper tier' as had already happened in the metropolitan areas and in both Scotland and Wales. In the welter of paper produced by the Banham Commission, it is hard to discern any coherent philosophy whilst the methodology of touring the country in search of evidence and opinion inevitably set authority against authority. County Councils were unsurprisingly hostile to their own abolition. Where those councils were Labour controlled there was an interesting twist to the argument. Recognising that the Labour Party was, at least in theory, in favour of all purpose authorities, those County Councils argued that their abolition should be part of a package which would include the creation of regional authorities. Clearly this did not always exclude the possibility that new regions might in some cases be identical to old counties! On the other hand there was tacit support throughout local government for the proposition that a new regional tier should suck power down from central government and not upwards from existing local authorities.

In the mid-1990s loose groupings of local authorities began to appear in a number of regions. Collaboration between different types of local authority reflected the creation at national level of a single Local Government Association (LGA). This could be considered as a very belated response to the suggestion by Redcliffe-Maud that 'what local government needs is a single powerful, association to look after its interests and speak for it.' The LGA, large and potentially diffuse, needed itself to generate some kind of regional organisation as a basis for, and an arm of, its activities: certainly this was a further impetus for developments. Although there was some disappointment in the English regions that the priorities of the incoming Labour Government seemed focused on Scotland, Wales and London (plus Northern Ireland for very different reasons), Regional Development Agencies (RDAs) were established throughout England and there was an invitation to create what were to be termed regional chambers. These would receive reports from the RDAs to which they could also give some rather vague strategic direction. In many cases the new chambers, sometimes renaming themselves as regional assemblies, grew fairly naturally out of pre-existing local authority regional associations. However, since they were also required to bring in the private and voluntary sectors (one third of the membership) they actually bear an almost uncanny resemblance to the provincial councils suggested by Redcliffe-Maud and the regional councils proposed by Crowther/Kilbrandon. Perhaps there is rather more continuity between the thinking on structural issues between the 'old' and 'new' Labour governments than protagonists of either might care to admit!

Local government can certainly claim to be the handmaiden or mid-wife for the initial tentative steps towards regional government in England. The future relationship will be profoundly affected by the answers to a number of recurring questions. A first factor concerns the structure of local government itself. The Banham commission did not produce a uniform structure: it created a significant number of new all-purpose authorities but many shire areas retained a two-tier structure. The Government has little enthusiasm for re-opening this particular controversy, especially if it sets one Labour controlled authority against another. From a cynical point of view this could begin to change if during its second national term of office Labour start to lose significant ground in local government as a whole. Restructuring of local government, presumably involving the final removal of the 'upper tier' would be politically easier if the remaining shire counties were not Labour controlled. So long as the present patchwork quilt of local government remains in place, the creation of directly elected regional assemblies would bring about a situation in which part of the population would be 'governed' by three tiers of sub-national authority.

The second factor reflects the nature of the 2001 general election campaign and re-awakens the older tradition of Labour as an 'etatist' party wanting to use the power of central government as a vehicle for reform and improvement of a range of services affecting people's lives. Labour's commitment to a wholesale improvement of health and education and other public services does not rest easily with the concept of regional priorities. There is a public perception, reinforced by the media, that people should not lose out on quality and provision of these services as a result of geography or postcode. The implication is that regional autonomy might have to be limited to what could be termed 'non-essential' sectors – hardly an adequate basis for establishing a formally recognised new tier of government based on direct election. Resolution of the conundrum is likely to take time and could ensure that further regional developments in England do not become a priority for Labour's second term.

During the five years of New Labour Government since 1997 local authorities have sought to influence, if not to control, the regional agenda in England. This has manifested itself in three different ways. First, all RDAs include a 'quota of local councillors. Second, two thirds of members of the regional chambers or assemblies are drawn from local authorities.' Third, in the absence of an established tier of regional government, local authorities have sought with some success through the LGA and its regional groupings to dominate the appointment of members of the Committee of the Regions of the European Union. The implications of this last go beyond the confines of this chapter and, even to some extent, beyond the scope of the book. However, the others are important indicators of the ongoing relationship between local and regional governance and they need to be looked at in some detail.

At this stage in their development the RDAs are regionally based, but for the most part centrally accountable. Regional chambers/assemblies receive reports and can offer some strategic direction, but this hardly makes the RDAs accountable to them. The complex relationship of RDAs with Government Offices for the Regions is examined elsewhere in this book. Funding is from central government allocations and there is no suggestion that this might in the future come at least in part either from regional taxation or by direct subventions from local government. There was an immediate tussle between central government and local authority dominated regional associations over the process of appointment of chairs and members of the agencies. The inevitable outcome was that central government would control the process and make the actual appointments. However, the region could put forward a nomination for the post of Chairman. This certainly happened in the North West where Lord Thomas was appointed. It was also agreed that three or four members of each RDA would be elected local councillors – present or past. Nominations could come from individuals or from individual local authorities, but the appointment would be made by the Secretary of State for the Department for Environment, Transport and Regions (DETR) and subsequently the Department for Transport, Local Government and Regions (DTLR).

It may be worth noting the essentially pragmatic nature of these arrangements. Devolution for the English regions would seem to suggest directed elected assemblies: RDAs would be the executive arm, presumably with much clearer lines of accountability to those assemblies. There would clearly be an argument for a different appointment procedure. Would or should they include elected members and if from local authorities within the region, then why not from a future directly elected regional assembly? In the absence of such an assembly there is a compelling logic behind the ambition of politicians, especially those who are beginning to operate at regional level, to seek membership of the RDA. However, if directly elected assemblies are finally established, they will be the natural regional locus for politicians. The most obvious power to be devolved to an assembly would be that of holding the RDA to account. At one level it is hard to see why any particular number of places would need to be reserved for elected regional or local politicians. On the other hand there is inherent illogicality in a system in which the RDAs are appointed by central government whilst being accountable to a regional assembly. Having said which, it can be noted that there are places on the London Development Agency reserved for Assembly members.

Prior to 1997 the private and voluntary sectors had little formal involvement, or much interest, in the nascent regional associations. This changed rapidly once the Government had established RDAs and laid down ground rules for the recognition of regional chambers. The requirement of a 70:30 ratio of local government to private and voluntary sectors and the perceived need to involve all local authorities has, in many cases, made for very large chambers/assemblies. The different sizes of local authority (measured in population terms this could hypothetically range from populations of less than 80,000 to over a million) raised potential issues about voting – a problem in practice normally ignored or catered for by a system of weighting. Another problem was that Labour's dominance in local government in some parts of the country necessitated bringing in additional members if there were to be any reasonable political balance. It is interesting in this respect to compare the South East Regional Assembly (SERA) with the directly elected Greater London Assembly. The former has a total of 111 members, whilst the latter has only 25. Two thirds of the 111 are local authority representatives; 60 per cent of the 25 are also members of a borough council (see table on the next page). The powers of the GLA are hardly considerable: those of the SERA are very much less!

It has been suggested that the Government foresees directly elected regional assemblies as similar to the London model. Election would be by proportional representation and assembly size would reflect population. If the Government maintains this view post regional referenda, then it seems unlikely that any assembly would have more than 25 members. In this context it may be worth noting that the smallest of the existing regional chambers - Yorkshire and Humberside - has 24 local authority members. On this basis there is no way in which all districts could hope to have any kind of direct

**Local authority members of regional chambers[3]**

| Regional Chamber | Mode of Selection | Weighted Voting | Overlap of chamber membership with membership of regional LGA* |
|---|---|---|---|
| East Midlands Regional Assembly | At least 1 representative selected by each local authority | No, top up members according to council size | 57% (37/65) |
| East of England Regional Assembly | Members of the Executive Committee of the regional LGA | No | 100% (28/28) |
| North East Regional Assembly | At least 1 representative selected by each local authority | No, 2 representatives from each County, Metropolitan or Unitary Council, 1 from each District Council. 9 co-opted top-up members to ensure political balance | 73% (32/44) |
| North West Regional Assembly | At least 1 representative selected by each local authority | Yes | 100% (56/56) |
| South East Regional Assembly | 1 representative selected by each local authority | Yes, according to the system used by the central LGA | (various LGAs, not matching the boundaries of the assembly) |
| South West Regional Assembly | 2 representatives selected by each local authority | No, top-up members to ensure political balance | 76% (63/83) |
| West Midlands Regional Assembly | At least 1 representative selected by each local authority | No, top-up members according to council size and to ensure political balance | 68% (46/68) |
| Yorkshire and Humberside Regional Assembly | Leaders' Group of regional LGA | No | 100% (24/24) |

* local authority members who are also regional LGA members/ total number of local authority members

representation in a regional assembly and this would seemingly preclude any umbilical link between local and regional government.

This may to some extent already be colouring attitudes amongst local authorities towards directly elected regional assemblies. However, it is only one factor – geography and party politics both play a strong role. In general support for regional government is strongest in the North and weakest in the South. The Labour and Liberal Democrat parties are officially favourable, whilst in both cases acknowledging the need to take account of differing local and regional needs and views. The Conservative Party remains generally, although not totally uniformly, hostile. The local authorities, which constitute two thirds of the regional chambers/assemblies, reflect these differing views. There is consequently strong support for the formal establishment of directly elected regional government amongst local authorities, and, consequently, in the assemblies of the three northern regions – North East, North West and Yorkshire and Humberside. It is, though, worth noting the existence of one significant boundary problem. Cumbria has been placed in the North West region, even though opinion in four of its six districts prefers identification with the North East. The problem might ultimately be resolved by a local government reform involving the abolition of Cumbria County Council.

Opinion in the three central regions – East of England, East Midlands and West Midlands – is much more divided, although the key factors seem to vary. The boundaries of the East of England region are somewhat artificial as well as lacking in historic salience. Conservatives are significantly represented in local government in the region, so that political party rivalry is one defining factor. There is some evidence that for major local government players in the East Midlands, the preservation of the umbilical link between local and regional government is seen as particularly valuable. Debate in the West Midlands has been influenced by the dominance of Birmingham where there is some support for both the city mayor model in local government and the concept of the city region.

The Conservatives are most strongly entrenched in the two southernmost regions where the debate is also influenced by proximity to the capital. The two regions have little public recognition or resonance, whilst the boundaries between and around them are little more than lines on a map. The allocation of Milton Keynes to the South East seems quite arbitrary; the dividing line between South East and South West is artificial; there is significant regional sentiment at the furthest extremity in Cornwall, but for the county as a separate region in its own right rather than part of the South West.

In conclusion five years of Labour's modernisation plans have undoubtedly changed the perspectives of local authorities and their leading councillors. More than ever before they are involved with the regional arena. The authorities are brought together through both the regional chambers/ assemblies and the regional branches of the LGA. Because there is much overlap between the two, some leading councillors are able to aspire to a significant regional role. So long as the Government insists that the lock for directly elected regional assemblies will rest in separate referenda, local authorities and local politicians will play a major role in determining progress.

*Notes*

[1] Royal Commission on Local Government in England, London: HMSO, 1969.

[2] Royal Commission on the Constitution, London: HMSO, 1973.

[3] Table compiled by Ulrike Rüb.

# The New English Regional Agenda and Europe

## Ines Newman

### Introduction

This chapter seeks to outline the current regional agenda in England and some of the tensions in its evolution. In particular it argues that regionalism in England has been more about government administrative decentralisation than devolution and that regional democracy and accountability over national decisions that impact on regions remain weak. The chapter outlines some of the implications of this for policy makers at local and regional level who are involved in the European Union – either in attempts to influence EU policy development or in terms of implementing existing EU policies and programmes. It suggests that the regional agenda in England is unstable and incremental and questions whether there is currently political support for a comprehensive regional constitutional settlement. It suggests that an attempt to create such a settlement at this stage could result in weak, unstable regional structures. It concludes by arguing that the key task is building political support for a strong regional voice that can legitimately represent the region in Europe but can also evolve towards a clearer constitutional structure through what is bound to be a messy, gradual process of devolution.

### Background to the current regional settlement

The constitutional agenda for the English regions was laid out in 1995 by Jack Straw in the consultation document *A Choice for England* (Labour Party,

1995). This paper proposed a strategic authority for London and regional assemblies using the same boundaries as the integrated Government Offices for the Regions. The latter had been established by the Conservative government in April 1994 in the light of pressure for a regional tier and a regional programme as a framework for EU Structural Funds and following criticism from the audit commission of the 'patchwork quilt' of regeneration initiatives (audit commission, 1989). Jack Straw's paper committed the party to the proposal that regional assemblies were to be created only after successful referenda. In the meantime regional chambers of local authority councillors would co-ordinate economic and other strategies.

A year later the Regional Policy Commission (1995) published the Millan report. The main recommendation was that '[...] RDAs be established, separate from the Regional Chambers, but responsible to the chambers and acting as their executive arm in the area of economic development.'

After the general election in May 1997, it became clear that (with commitments to a Scottish Parliament, a Welsh Assembly, a new Greater London Authority and a constitutional settlement in Northern Ireland) Prescott and his colleagues were only going to be given time for one simple Parliamentary Bill on English regions. The constitutional reform necessary for paving the way for assemblies was dropped for the lifetime of the 1997-2001 Parliament. The Regional Development Agencies Act was passed, establishing quangos responsible to central government, with regional chambers given a consultative and scrutiny role in relation to RDAs. While this Act was pushed through by the DETR ministers, it met considerable opposition from the DfEE and DTI. The final funding and powers of the RDAs therefore reflected their DETR base. Far from creating an executive economic development agency responsible to the chamber, the government had created quangos with weak ability to operate directly in financial and commercial markets and limited influence on the private sector.

The period leading to the general election in June 2001 and the post election settlement saw some attempt to deal with this institutional mess. The RDAs' budgets were reformed. They were given new performance targets by the government and moved to become the responsibility of the Department of Trade and Industry. For the first time they started to look like the economic agencies envisaged in the Millan report. The co-ordiation role of the Government Offices for the Regions was strengthened through the new regional co-ordination unit in the Cabinet Office. The regional chambers were strengthened through a new £15m fund over three years and a promised White Paper on regional assemblies for the autumn of 2001. But this tripartite arrangement for the English regions of government offices, RDAs and regional chambers remains complex and unstable. The three institutions are looked at in more depth below to highlight some of the tensions.

### The Government Offices – devolution or prefectures

As mentioned above, the Government Offices for the Regions (GORs) had been set up in 1994 by the Conservative Government partly as a response to the European Commission's agenda. There has been considerable debate as to whether this reform reflects the development of a 'Europe of the Regions' or is a strengthening of central control over local and regional agendas. Atkinson and Wilks-Heeg (2000) in a useful summary of the competing interpretations argue that, while European integration is strengthening the position of sub-national government, the regions have little influence over the development of the institutional framework of the EU. They also suggest that the regional offices have been developed as gatekeepers for Whitehall rather than support for locally based regional actors. Indeed the European Union has played only a limited role in the constitutional design of regional government in France, Germany, Spain and Italy: domestic factors were the primary driving force. On balance there is no hard evidence that the creation of the regional offices has led to a 'hollowing out of the state'. This can be illustrated by looking at the recent reforms to the regional offices. It is perhaps significant that they are now increasingly being referred to as Government Offices rather than Government Offices for the Regions.

In 2000, a Cabinet Office report (Performance Innovation Unit (PIU), 2000) focused attention on the role of GORs. The offices had been set up in 1994 with civil servants from the DETR, DfEE and DTI. Co-ordination in Whitehall was almost non existent. The GORs submitted plans annually and they were were then disaggregated as the DTI, DfEE and DETR negotiated their GOR element separately with the Treasury. All this did not make for 'joined-up' Government! Furthermore the report was clear about the problem of too many area initiatives:

'Department's programmes targeted at particular local areas are poorly co-ordinated and waste scarce local capacity: they do not always work well with mainstream programmes. Progress on delivering the Government's priorities is being slowed down as a result. [...] in general, the regional tier of central Government is highly fragmented, is not able to deal with cross-cutting issues well and does not have sufficient influence over the centre on policy design and implementation.'

The PIU report argued that GORs would provide the best focus for co-ordinating central government action and representing central government at regional level. It did not see this role being played by regionally controlled institutions. The report called for the GORs to have a strongly enhanced role and to be regarded as the leading element of central government in the region in relation to issues with a cross-cutting dimension. Their role was seen as:

• influencing the way bids are presented to ensure they accord with government priorities

• encouraging local and regional players to address cross-cutting issues and work to common goals, and co-ordinating central government input on these issues

• providing information and technical support to local and regional players and back into government departments

• representing the views of government to regional and local partners and the media

• influencing central government departments to take significant account of local and regional circumstances, and the wider impact of their policies and programmes, in policy formulation

• evaluating and monitoring broad strategies and performance of local and sub-local players in the region

• the delivery of programmes for individual departments.

To move forward in this enhanced role, the PIU recommended that the existing Government Office Management Board, Government Office Central Unit and Interdepartmental Support Unit for Area Based Initiatives, be replaced by a new regional co-ordinating unit. The Government moved quickly on this recommendation. The original unit was at first physically located in the DETR although separate within it. Since the election the unit has been moved to the cabinet office. The unit has its own funds, covering the running costs of GORs as well as any cross-cutting programme expenditure budgets run by the GORs. This means that the staff and budgets in GORs are now the responsibility of one central unit rather than the three parent departments.

The PIU report contained a series of recommendations to ensure strong central co-ordination and joined-up working:

• The unit will develop, in conjunction with other relevant departments, a set of precise cross-cutting objectives and targets for the GORs against which their performance will be evaluated. These will be regarded as Public Service Agreements (PSA) and will based on a mixture of outcomes and processes.

• Before any new or extended initiative or the creation of any new Departmental outreach function is decided on, there will be a double key arrangement under which the co-ordinating unit and the GORs are consulted systematically in advance. The Department bringing forward the new area based initiative or change in mainstream programme will have to make a case and look at its relationship with mainstream programmes in their own and other departments and outline the flexibilities included in the scheme.

• The unit will provide a reporting line upwards for GOR regional directors and will provide an access point for them to influence central government policy.

• The unit will bring forward proposals and oversee arrangements in GORs for financial flexibilities in programme expenditure to encourage joined-up governance.

• The unit will ensure that all departments using GORs have satisfactory service level agreements and that these are clearly related to GORs' overall objectives in their PSA.

• The unit will research and disseminate best practice.

The report also argued for a significantly wider departmental presence in GORs. It argued that what is now the new Department for Environment, Food and Rural Affairs, should have their staff involved in policy formulation and implementation on rural development and structural funds integrated into the GOR framework. It asked the Department of Health to report progress on co-terminosity to the Cabinet Office in 2002. It also called for additional staff in GORs with knowledge of health and social care; and for the number of home office staff working in GORs to increase relative to the centre in order that they could monitor the performance of local crime and disorder partnerships. It also argues that all other departments need to consider the case for closer integration and staff secondments.

This radical reform of government regional administration is very important and more joined-up administration has been widely welcomed. However it is no coincidence that the report mentions the French prefecture system favourably. What the government is moving towards, in this report, is effective decentralised government administration rather than devolution. The report fails to discuss the role of the regional chamber or grapple with the issues of local and regional accountability. It moves from a situation where funds are allocated on formula, based on need, towards allocation on the basis of GOR assessment plans – a model where the GORs would take a 'leading role in 'signing-off' commitments by Government, having reached an agreed strategy with local authorities and their partners.' Ultimately this reform of central government will only bring local and regional benefits if it is matched by a strengthening of local and regional democracy. Regional capacity building requires resources and greater partnership between central and local/regional institutions. This is not the focus of the PIU report or current government reforms of the GORs.

**The advance of the quango state – The RDAs and other regional quangos**

From 1 April 1999 eight RDAs became operational. They have boards of directors, appointed by the Secretary of State. Some 4 of the 12 or so directors have a local authority background. The majority and the chairs are from the private sector. The ninth RDA, the London Development Agency, is accountable to the new Mayor in London and became operational with the Mayor's office on 1 July 2000.

The key role of the RDAs is to develop and implement the economic strategy for their region. They were asked to produce the first economic strategy by October 1999 and there has been criticism that these rushed strategies failed to integrate competitiveness with social inclusion and sustainability.

The RDAs are also responsible for regeneration, including: the administration of the regional functions of English Partnership, the work of the Rural Development Commission and the expenditure that was committed under the Single Regeneration Budget (SRB). The funds available to the RDAs to promote local area regeneration (£671m in 1999/2000) were 55 times greater than those for promoting regional competitiveness or attracting inward investment (£21.1m). Many other agencies and partnerships also have a role in regeneration. 'At the last count there were over 50 different challenge fund schemes managed by 12 departments or agencies allocating nearly £4 billion alongside 30 action zones and other initiatives established since New Labour came to office.' (Mawson, in Dungey and Newman, 2000, p. 43).

This situation was clearly untenable in the long run. The Government's continual changes of priorities for the RDAs weaken their ability to deliver on their strategies. It is significant that the spending review 2000 allocated a further £500m to RDAs to be spent flexibly between 2000/ 1 - 2003/4 with all their budgets merging into a single pot from April 2002. The flexibility in this single pot will increase over time as expenditure committed under seven year SRB programmes (which ceased in 2001) declines. After the June 2001 election, governance of the RDAs was transferred to the DTI. While this rationalisation is logical, given the role of RDAs as economic agencies, it does weaken their focus on social inclusion and reinforce their private sector dominated quango role. Effectively funds that were allocated to regeneration, in which social inclusion was emphasised, have now been transferred to the DTI to be spent on economic development. It is significant that the Secretary of State, Patricia Hewitt, in her first press release on the RDAs after the election (DTI, July 2001) announced that individual performance targets will be negotiated with each RDA. These will focus on economic output indicators (start-ups, jobs created and retained, numbers trained) and brownfield land development (rather than social and environmental outcomes). She also stated that the number of board members with business experience is to be increased.

Meanwhile the earlier reluctance of the DTI and DfEE to release key economic budgets, such as those for regional selective assistance, business links and Training and Enterprise Councils (TECs) to the RDAs, has led to a proliferation of quangos at the regional level. The DfEE has redirected the TEC budgets, together with the further education budget, into a new Learning and Skills Council. This has 47 local delivery and policy-making arms. At the same time the DTI reorganised the Business Links budget into a new executive agency – the Small Business Service, with 47 local franchises. There are also the new Connexions services bringing together the careers service and youth service into an enhanced support service for young people. Each RDA now has several of these new organisations in their area. Finally, RDAs were given 'a leading role' on European structural funds. This issue is looked at in more detail below but it is clear that, in performing this role, their position in relation to the GORs who lead on administration remains unclear. Under the Commission rules a quango can not be responsible for administrating structural funds. The role of the RDA in relation to all these areas remains very weak and there is bound to be institutional competition as to who is responsible for small business support, regional skills strategies or EU single programming documents.

This growth of a fragmented and regional state with limited local accountability has presented a strong argument for elected regional assemblies and reform of quangos to open them up to local influence and scrutiny. The regional chambers, outside London, are currently the only body trying to plug this democratic deficit but, as argued below, they struggle to perform this function adequately.

### The democratic region? The regional chambers

The Regional Development Agencies Act contained provision for the Secretary of State to designate appropriate bodies as regional chambers. These chambers have a legal right to be consulted on the RDAs' economic strategies and on their business plans. The chambers are meant to contain around 70 per cent local authority members and 30 per cent other regional stakeholders.

All regions outside London now have designated regional chambers. These vary in size and composition. For example, the Regional Chamber for Yorkshire and Humberside has representation from each local authority. These 22 members form the Leaders Group on the Regional Assembly, identical with the local government grouping for the region founded in 1996 that brought together the regional planning conference, the Yorkshire and Humberside Regional Association and the region's European Office. It also has 13 partner representatives from the CBI, the Chambers of Commerce, the TUC, Further and Higher Education, the regional forum for voluntary and community organisations, the rural community councils, the environment agencies, the health sector, the faith communities, the regional cultural consortium and an ethnic minority representative.

The chambers were originally set up with no central government financial support. This was widely criticised:

'It is surely a matter for concern that the government is able to find some £18m per annum to finance the administration of the Scottish Parliament and £15m to fund the Greater London Authority election yet it cannot offset some of the costs which local government is incurring in voluntarily running the chambers nor can it provide adequate support to other regional stakeholders to enable them to participate in the new governance structures which central government is keen to see.' (Mawson, in Dungey and Newman, 2000, p. 40)

The government responded to this criticism in March 2001 and announced a £15m fund over the next three years to 'empower' the chambers (DETR, 2001). £1m of this is to be used for project specific bids in year one, so there is around £500,000 per chamber per year for the period 2001/2-2003/4. Although a significant improvement, the funding remains limited. Staffing is also limited, varying, early in 2001, from 3 to 20 staff. The draft guidance on the regional accountability fund suggested that the money was used to increase the capacity to scrutinise the RDAs. It did not suggest that chambers have a role in scrutinising GORs and this was confirmed in the final guidance. To scrutinise GORs they would need Government co-operation and this has not yet been forthcoming. Ministers have also so far refused to appear before the elected GLA to account for policy. Meanwhile the chambers' formal powers of scrutiny and consultation in relation to RDAs are still weak. Essentially voluntary, they cannot go further than the collective will of the region's authorities.

Having said this, chambers are a very important partnership organisation at the regional level and the main way currently of ensuring some local and regional democratic accountability at the regional level. In the long run they could provide a base for directly elected regional assemblies. The more progressive chambers are working hard to create open and accessible regional bodies, with inclusive consultation and capacity building mechanisms. Most of them work in a consensual way with RDAs and GORs, and several have concordats for working together. There has been only one known example of a chamber refusing to agree a regional economic strategy. In the East of England the RDA made changes to their regional economic strategy following comments from the local chamber but the disagreement was kept behind closed doors and achieved through private negotiation rather than open conflict.

As a regional partnership body, they are also expanding their role. The chambers have been encouraged, through Planning Policy Guidance note 11, to take over responsibility for developing Regional Planning Guidance. This has happened in the Eastern Region but in some other regions this function has remained with the local government conference. In the West Midlands, for example, there is a strong local government association and a feeling that only elected representatives should be involved in such decisions without the strong private sector representation in the chamber exerting an influence. Conflict in this area could grow, as RDAs become stronger, private sector, economic growth, driven organisations. Consensus within the chambers, and even more with the local authority associations, may then be harder to achieve.

Several chambers also see their role as developing overarching regional strategies covering wider issues such as health and sustainability. One of the problems of the current regional agenda is that there are a number of regional strategies (e.g. regional planning guidance, regional economic strategies, regional skills strategies, EU regional programming strategies, regional sustainability frameworks, regional cultural strategies, health improvement programmes), produced by different organisations, all of which are meant to be compatible and none of which has precedence over the other. A directly elected regional assembly could establish a more corporate approach to regional strategic planning across the full range of policy fields (see Roberts, 2000). In the meantime the chamber has a key role in establishing the overarching regionalism and spatial strategy and ensuring coherence in the regional agenda. Yorkshire and Humberside's *Advancing Together* and East Midlands' *Integrated Regional Strategy* are both attempts to fulfil this role.

The forthcoming White Paper will pave the way for elected regional assemblies. Chambers are likely to play a key role through regional conventions in building democratic support for a 'yes' vote in a referendum. However the earliest possible date for referenda is likely to be 2003/4, so chambers will have to fill the democratic deficit for several more years. It is also clear that the support for elected regional assemblies is stronger in regions like the North East and Yorkshire and Humberside than the South East or Eastern Region. If these regions are to depend on chambers for the foreseeable future it has been suggested that the chambers are put on a statutory footing and are given a stronger role by developing a schedule of quangos or bodies that could be statutorily required to consult them and which the chambers could hold to account. Sandford and McQuail (2001) also argue that if Ministers were to appear before chambers to give an account of their actions this would shift the balance of power and the boundaries of the debate. If the chambers had a recognised role to hold the GORs to account and if directors of GORs appeared regularly in front of chamber scrutiny committees, this would have a similar impact. It remains to be seen how the chambers develop their current partnerships with the other regional institutions and at the same time increase the accountability of these institutions to the region. This dual policy is easier to achieve when there is no conflict but the growing business domination of the RDAs suggests that differences are likely to develop in the future.

**The implications of the current English regional settlement for European issues**

The European agenda has in the past partly driven the regional agenda in England. The current regional position can be seen either as an institutional mess or more positively as presenting a number of learning opportunities to regional partners and stakeholders as we gradually evolve to greater devolution and the establishment of directly elected regional assemblies. Professor Peter Roberts has argued that this learning experience is 'similar in nature to the positive experience of the early and mid-1990s when partners worked together to produce the Structural Funds Single Programming Documents.' (Roberts, 2000)

The European dimension remains critical to the regional debate. It has important implications in terms of democratic accountability in both directions (from MEPs and members of the Committee of the Region back to the regions and from the regions to Europe) and in terms of programme implementation. These aspects are looked at below.

**The role of the MEP**

The democratic deficit at regional level, described above, leaves the MEP as the only directly elected representative of the English regions. There has been much criticism of the proportional representation system adopted in the UK to elect MEPs but the system has at least aligned constituencies with regional boundaries and this gives MEPs a new role. The nature of this role still needs to be defined, representatives need to grapple with how they want to see it evolve. As Richard Howitt MEP says:

> 'Is the MEP a policy-maker within the region? - almost all of us have been consultees of RDAs in the new Regional Economic Strategies. Or do we want to be given the received wisdom of the region, and then seek to deliver outside? Should MEPs have a formal role in the new structures either as voting partners or as accountable rapporteurs? Or should we maintain an informal role, as behind-the-scenes catalysts to make regionalism work? Are we lobbyist or lobbied? In practice, the lines will be blurred, but there are questions all involved in the new regionalism should ask, not leave to the MEPs themselves.' (Howitt in Dungey and Newman, 2000)

Howitt points to the Scandinavian model of participative democracy in the regions, which has brought together government representatives, local representatives in the regions and MEPs to co-ordinate European programmes and policy. This approach shows how regionalism in England could develop bringing together all the tiers, from local to European, in accountable and constructive dialogue.

## The Committee of the Regions

The Committee of the Regions' (CoR) aim is to influence EU policy formulation and legislation that affects sub-national government. There are 24 full members from the UK who, by law, have to be elected representatives when nominated, although this is not required by EU treaties. The members are nominated by the government in consultation with the local government associations, but they do not necessarily resign their position if they cease to be a councillor. They, therefore, currently have no direct regional accountability and substitute members can come from other regions. This process has been subject to much criticism and it has been argued that CoR representatives should be elected from regional local government associations, with due regard for fair representation by party and by type of authority, and that they should resign if they cease to be an elected local councillor. They should then report back on their activities to the regional local government associations.

The creation of regional chambers and stronger regional local government associations has now given the CoR members a regional forum to which they can report on their work. Potentially this has strengthened their position. But closer working relationships between CoR members and the emerging regional institutions in England will also depend, in the long run, on the support these structures can offer to the CoR members. Currently, when an English CoR member is responsible for an opinion (the rapporteur), they have to turn for support to the Local Government International Bureau (LGIB). The designated chambers now have secretariats but most of these are under-resourced, even with the new £15m empowerment fund. Better resourcing for regional chambers and local government regional associations will not only make them more effective but will also allow the

CoR members to be briefed on the local and regional effects of EU policy, directives and regulations.

### European structural fund programme strategies

The White Paper *Building Partnership for Prosperity* (December 1997) states 'The structural funds, and other forms of European funding, will continue to play an important role in regional competitiveness and social policy in the English regions. [...] the government intends that RDAs should take a leading role in the new programme in the English regions [...].' The RDAs were given a 'leading role' on European structural funds in the Regional Development Agencies Act.

The lead in developing regional structural fund strategies had rested with the GORs. They had established programme monitoring committees for each programme, which commented on the regional strategies, allocated funds according to agreed criteria for each programme and monitored progress. These programme committees were partnership committees with key stakeholders represented. *Agenda 2000* (European Commission, 1997) introduced new structural fund programmes for 2000-2006. New regional Single Programming Documents (SPDs) for Objectives 1 and 2, together with a Regional Programme for Objective 3, had to be produced. RDA regional strategies cover the whole region whilst Objective1 SPDs cover defined areas (e.g. Merseyside in the North West). Objective 2 areas are often a patchwork quilt within a region. Programmes for Objective 3, which cover the whole region, are more specifically labour market focused and will link as much to the work of the Learning and Skills Councils as to the regional economic strategy. The rapidly produced regional economic strategies have not provided clear direction for the SPDs and in reality the RDAs have not been able to play a leadership role as they have not had the staff or expertise to do so. The SDPs were developed by the GORs with the programme committees.

There is evidence of the three regional institutions working together. The Commission has made it clear that it expects the RDAs' regional economic strategies to be consistent with the single programming documents and RDAs and chambers have been consulted and their strategies referred to in drawing up the SDPs. Several of the regional chambers have offices in Brussels and three have European sub-panels. Sandford (2001) argues that the business of obtaining EU structural funds concentrated the minds within the chambers and brought an 'outbreak of regional harmony'. The RDAs are represented on the programme committees: they contribute to strategy papers, annual reviews and are trying to develop as a focal point of contact for partners for strategic issues. Some RDAs are now seeking to establish their leadership role. In the North East, One North East has taken the lead in establishing a co-ordinating committee between the 3 programming committees for the 3 objectives. This is usefully bringing together the fragmented European strategies with those involved in taking forward the regional economic strategy.

The concern about the European programmes is that the 'institutional mess' is creating a vacuum, in which civil servants at the GOR gain considerable influence on the distribution of European funds with limited local and regional accountability. This is less of a concern in Objective 1 areas where often powerful, sub-regional partnerships, which involve representatives from local authorities and the local voluntary and community sector, have significant influence on the SPD. However for Objective 2 areas, scattered through a region, it remains a problem. Some regional chambers are attempting to fill the gap working with their RDA. The regional local authority associations, and hence the chambers which they dominate, have wide experience of working on European issues. Success in integrating approaches and developing a shared understanding of regional priorities will require the RDAs to work closely with the chambers as 'partners' rather than 'leaders' on European issues.

Meanwhile the PIU report, mentioned earlier, when criticising the fragmentation of area initiatives and calling for stronger, more co-ordinated GORs, also discussed the difficulties caused by separate European programmes. It suggested that the Government should look at aligning UK area programmes (i.e. allowing them to run on a January-December basis) with European programmes and that they should bring together the monitoring frameworks. This would reduce the administrative costs and increase the flexibility for the programme managers. No progress has yet been made on these important suggestions. In bringing together the regional institutions and their strategies, it will also be vital to rationalise all the programmes and their auditing and management procedures.

**Other EU related issues at the regional level**

RDAs will need to consider how to address the impact of other EU issues on the development of the regional economy. Three examples are given below.

There is the key issue of sustainability. The UK strategy for sustainable development *A Better Quality of Life* called for each region to have a high level Regional Sustainable Development Framework by the end of 2000. Furthermore, the RDAs and regional planning bodies are required by government to assess how their strategies will contribute to sustainable development and consequently they have carried out sustainability appraisals. All this has to fit into the EU's Sixth Environmental Action Programme. Yet despite all these calls for integration, the regional economic strategies 'demonstrate only patchy commitment to sustainable development.' (Brooke, in Dungey and Newman, 2000)

With the rural and urban white papers, the need for integration is further highlighted. Both of these have been influenced by European policy (e.g. the URBAN programme, the reform of the common agricultural policy, Agenda 2000 and the environmental programmes). It is important for Europe to have a clear understanding of the impact of its policies on the English regions. Similarly UK policy in this area should complement European initiatives and develop in ways that allow the different priorities of different areas to influence what is done in each region.

The Treaty of Amsterdam included a new employment chapter that led to the establishment of an annual National Employment Action Programme being agreed between each Member State and the European Commission. This is meant to have a strong regional focus yet it remains a central government document that has not been developed in a participative way with local and regional players. This remains an area of concern, especially with the growing north/south divide.

There are many other European issues where there is an English regional interest. However lobbying on European issues remains at an early stage and is not helped by the fragmentation between the three regional institutions. However it is clear from all the discussion in this chapter that their position would be strengthened by democratic regional institutions.

## Conclusion

All the issues discussed above illustrate the need for far more co-ordinated regional institutions that provide a clear voice for local authorities and the regions at European level.

This chapter has argued that the current situation is not satisfactory. On the one hand there are the RDAs, which are being given a shifting brief by central government and are likely to have their future funds tied to clear central government performance targets. As private sector led quangos, they lack the legitimacy to bring together all regional strategies into a coherent framework. But they also lack the executive powers or clarity of purpose to fully deliver on their regional economic strategies. On the other hand there are the GORs, which are being strengthened as arms of regional administration but which lack local and regional accountability. There is a danger that they become judge and jury of local authority and regional programmes that would then reflect national priorities rather than those determined more locally. Finally there are the MEPs and COR members. The former are democratically elected on a regional basis but their role remains to be clarified. The latter are only partly seen as regional representatives and have little or no regional support.

The hope remains that the regional local government associations and the voluntary chambers can promote the new regional agenda and build up support for elected regional assemblies. The London model, where the London Development Agency is the executive arm of the GLA as recommended in the Millan report, and where civil servants delivering London programmes have now been transferred to the Mayor's office, provides part of a more coherent and effective model. A democratic regional tier could also take over a range of quangos from Learning and Skills Councils to strategic health authorities. There is much to be done before the rest of England moves towards devolved directly elected regional government. Not only must the political parties be convinced of the need for devolution but support also needs to be built for such institutions among the electorate. This is not an easy task for under-resourced regional chambers. It will require the development of much more inclusive, open and transparent policy making at the regional level. It will also require the consolidation of partnership working among the existing regional institutions and capacity building of regional stakeholders (especially the voluntary and community sector) so they are able to take local views to the regional stage and onto the National and European level.

To try and impose a constitutional settlement in the current environment is likely to lead to the centralised state continuing to dominate. There is a danger that the democratic regional tier will be given a very limited co-ordination role that will make it appear like a talking shop. Such a body would command little political support and there would be the danger of considerable voter apathy. On this basis it would be in no position forcibly to represent regional interests in Europe. Gradual regionalism has the disadvantage that it makes it easier to suck up powers from local authorities than to devolve partially government powers. This is hardly devolution and must be guarded against. But gradual devolution has the advantage that if you can show that it works more people are likely to support further moves to build up the regional tier. It is no accident that the North East, next to Scotland, is the strongest supporter of directly elected assemblies. A favourable referendum in this region is likely to evoke a domino effect.

So there is a lot to be done to move towards a more rational division of power and a more stable relationship between the tiers of government. However, the prize for effective democratic regional government is better policy-making at all levels from the neighbourhood to the European arena. It is a prize worth striving for by all of us – from the MEP to the local councillor.

# 4

# A Federal State in a
# Federal Europe?

# Managing Federalism
*A comparative overview*

## Wilfried Swenden

## Introduction

In the contemporary world, federalism assumes an ever-greater importance. The word 'federalism' is brought forward in relation to the future development of the United Kingdom; it is used to describe some institutional features of the European Union and it is thought of as a suitable way to contain nationalism in multinational polities which are slowly democratising such as Indonesia or Nigeria. It is not possible in a single chapter to describe in detail the specific features of each of the world's federal systems. Instead, the comparative analysis is restricted to federal countries with a level of socio-economic development or a political tradition that resembles that of the United Kingdom, namely Australia, Belgium, Canada, Germany, Spain, Switzerland and the United States.

I will first attempt to define federalism and to illustrate its difference with devolution and confederalism. Subsequently, I will show that despite the relatively limited number of federations under review, federal states differ significantly from one another. Differences in the distribution of competencies between the federal (central) and regional governments or in the institutional arrangements associated with federalism are looked at first. Subsequently, I shall elaborate on the rigidity of federal constitutions and discuss the role which constitutional courts are playing in adjusting the federal-regional balance. Differences in the character of intergovernmental relations and the degree of fiscal autonomy of the federal and regional levels of government are looked at next. Finally, I consider the presence and strength of regional parties and the extent to which parties with a federation-wide following feature strong regional party wings. Variety in federal states leads to the conclusion that asking whether federalism makes a difference for public policy-making is the wrong question. Rather, one should ask whether differences in federal structures (or federal design) may be helpful in explaining divergent policy outcomes.

## Federalism: a vaguely defined concept

The study of federalism is problematic insofar as social scientists have not agreed on a common definition. This disagreement partly results from the great variety in federal systems. Each federal system reflects the national or historical context in which it is embedded. For instance, although federalism requires the distribution of a set of competencies to the central (federal) and regional levels of government, there is no exact blueprint as to which competencies should be assigned to the central and which to the regional level of government. In Australia the railway system is operated by each of the states (regions) separately, but by the federal government in Germany and Belgium. In addition, federalism is in essence a dynamic process: each federal system has evolved over time to take stock of the latest social developments and to reflect changes in public opinion. For instance, because the emergence of the welfare state followed the creation of several federal countries, the question which level should be made responsible for the provision of crucial welfare services (health care, education, and pensions) was not adequately dealt with.[1] Insofar as public opinion demanded the universal provision of welfare services, a greater role for the federal government was accepted. Sometimes such changes to the federal balance were articulated in an amended federal constitution, sometimes the judges of a constitutional court widely interpreted the constitutional powers of the federal government.

The inherently dynamic and original character of each federal system means that theorists of federalism have only agreed about two characteristics that all federal systems have in common: the presence of two or more distinct layers of government with autonomous policy-making powers allocated to each layer of government. I would argue that democracy is also a necessary condition for federalism (the presence of directly elected legislators and executives is essential in facilitating the possibility of differently coloured legislatures and executives controlling different levels of government).

On this basis, a federation can be defined as a political system that is characterised by:

- the presence of at least two layers of government;
- each with directly and democratically elected representative institutions;
- the attribution of a significant amount of legislative and/or executive competencies to both layers of government;
- the division of competencies is set out in a written constitution which cannot be amended without some sort of involvement of both layers of government;
- a constitutional court interprets the constitution and ensures that neither level of government illegitimately encroaches upon the competencies of the other level. It also prevents one or several regions from acting against the interests of the other regions;
- mechanisms are at hand to ensure that the interests of the regions are safeguarded at the federal level, either via intergovernmental conferences bringing together policy representatives of both levels of government or via the presence of a sufficiently powerful second chamber.

It follows that the following countries can be perceived as federal: Argentina, Australia, Austria, Belgium, Brazil, Canada, Germany, India, Spain, Switzerland and the United States of America.

If the regions of a particular state arrangement possess more powers vis-à-vis the centre than necessary on the basis of the above criteria one may possibly consider this a *confederal* arrangement.[2] Conversely, if the regions of a particular state arrangement have significantly fewer powers vis-à-vis the centre than required on the basis of the above criteria, one may possibly consider this a *regionalised* or *devolved* arrangement.

More specifically, a confederation is to be distinguished from a federation by the following characteristics. First, the member states (not regions) of a confederal arrangement retain their full sovereignty after they have signed a confederation treaty (not a constitution). As a consequence, unlike the regions of a federal state the member states of a confederation are recognised as subjects of international law. Second, each member state of a confederal arrangement has a free right of secession. Third, the confederation treaty cannot be changed without the consent of each of the member states (unanimity instead of majority-rule). By comparison, in a federation, the constitution binds the federal and regional governments and cannot be changed without the consent of both (the federal government and a majority of the regions). Finally, decisions taken by a confederal government only enter into force if they have received the prior consent of the executives or legislatures of the member states concerned whereas decisions taken by a federal government have direct and immediate effect upon all of the federation's inhabitants.

Federalism can be distinguished from devolution as it is practised in the United Kingdom in the following two respects. First, in a federal setting the autonomy of the regions is only constrained by the provisions of a federal constitution, the amendment of which requires the participation of the regions as well as the federal level of government. In the case of devolution competencies are devolved to a regional level of government at the discretion of the central government. Since the decision to devolve powers to Scotland, Wales and Northern Ireland was laid down in primary legislation enacted by the Westminster parliament, a decision to *recentralise* all or some powers can be taken without the approval of the regional government or the region's population. Recent British experience with devolution has shown that the central government can temporarily suspend the powers of the Northern Irish assembly and executive, albeit with the consent of the Northern Irish Prime Minister and a majority of his cabinet. Such a decision would be more difficult to take if the UK possessed a written constitution which required changing first, or if amending the legislation could only result from a preceding referendum in the affected region, as was the case when powers were first devolved. It follows from the absence of a written constitution that there is no constitutional court to watch over the rules dividing competence either.

Second, a case can be made that the scope of competencies assigned to the regional level of government is much larger in a federal state than is the case at present in Britain. For instance, whereas the Scottish government has only very little tax raising autonomy, and the Welsh government lacks even this, the German or American regions have a far greater say in setting tax rates, either by participating in federal tax legislation via the intergovernmental circuit or a federal second chamber, or by raising their own taxes. In addition, the embryonic state of Britain's devolution process has also meant that the intergovernmental mechanisms are not yet as strongly developed as in most federations. The absence of a powerful and territorially composed second chamber adds to the strength of this observation.

Nonetheless, devolution could lead towards more decentralisation and possibly even federalism. Despite the absence of a federal constitution, the British government is not likely to take away the limited autonomy it conferred upon Scotland and Wales, particularly because such an act could not be legitimised on the same political grounds that served to suspend devolution in Northern Ireland. Furthermore, the Scottish and Welsh regional governments may grow more assertive in time: to the extent that their actions receive the support of a majority of regional public opinion, such assertiveness may be translated into a demand for the transfer of more legislative or executive powers. A British government may feel tempted to give in to such demands as a means of safeguarding its public support in the region concerned.

# Variations in federal systems

In the previous section I have attempted to identify common features in federal systems: I will now seek to highlight the variety among federal states. Precisely because federal systems vary substantially, it cannot be said that federalism as such produces specific policy outcomes. On some occasions two federal polities may be further apart on specific policy issues than a federal and a non-federal polity. It follows that (1) the federal/non-federal divide should not be thought of as a dichotomy, but as a continuum instead; (2) it is very difficult to single out federalism as an independent variable influencing policy outcomes.

## Centralised vs. decentralised federalism

The first distinction relates to the genesis of contemporary federal systems. Some federations have been the result of a 'coming-together' of previously autonomous countries (or, in the Australian case, British colonies).[3] The commonalty of an external threat, growing trade-relations or the sharing of a common language or constitutional heritage has frequently facilitated this coming-together process. The purest examples are the American, Australian and Swiss federations, the latter notwithstanding the presence of two major religions and four languages. Even so, Switzerland and America emerged as confederations first and in both countries a civil war was needed to shape or consolidate a federal state structure.

But federalism as it exists today may be most appealing as a possible device for 'holding-together' a multi-national polity. In some federal states powers have been devolved from the central to newly created regional levels of government with the purpose of accommodating religious or linguistic concerns. For instance, Belgium and Spain have evolved from unitary states into (quasi-) federal states in less than three decades. Even though Canada emerged as the result of a coming-together of several regions it can be argued that federalism has been the only viable means of holding-together this multi-national polity. In the concluding section I will assess this argument in more detail, but first I turn to the question of how competencies have been constitutionally divided between federal and regional levels of government and whether the coming-together or holding-together genesis of some federations has played any relevance in this respect.

## The constitutional distribution of powers and the role of the constitutional courts

### *The consequences of bringing vs. holding together*

Since federalism is based on the allocation of different competencies to different levels of government, the principle of allocation must be enshrined in a written constitution. The coming-together or holding-together type of federalism is of some relevance insofar as federations of the first type usually stipulate which competencies should be assigned to the newly created federal level, leaving the residue to the states (the so called residual powers). This holds for instance for the US, Swiss and Australian constitutions, but also to the more recent German and Austrian constitutions. By comparison, if federalism results from a devolution process, the federal level of government is most likely to sum up the competencies which should be attributed to the newly created regions, leaving the residue to the centre, a principle that holds for the Belgian and Spanish constitutions.

The pattern just described cannot be universally applied. In Canada for instance, the constitution lists which powers are exclusively allocated to the central and which to the regional levels of government, leaving the residue with the centre. The German and Austrian constitutions are peculiar in that they list powers which are subject to so-called 'framework' or 'concurrent' legislation. The first type of legislation implies that the federal government sets the global legislative framework within which the regions can enact more detailed legislation. The second type of legislation means that one level of government (usually the regional government) can legislate in certain matters, but only for as long as the other level of government refrains from passing laws within the constitutionally stipulated fields. It is said that the constitutionally assigned level of government with an explicit right to legislate (most likely the federal government) is given 'paramountcy': concurring regional bills that contradict the provisions of newly enacted federal legislation are invalidated. The principles of framework and concurrent legislation have been increasingly criticised in Germany and Austria since the federal governments of both countries have become more assertive in narrowly circumscribing federal framework bills and in practising their right of legislative paramountcy. For instance, there is scarcely an area left in the 24 subject-areas listed under Article 74 of the German constitution in which the federal government has not taken up its right to legislate.

### *Federal constitutions: the flexibility vs. rigidity of federal constitutions and the scope for judicial review*

Federations vary in the degree of detail in which the competence dividing rules are constitutionally spelled out. Generally speaking, the degree of detail of a constitution is related to two factors. First, the more recent a constitution, the more detailed its provisions are likely to be. When the United States was created, the structure of society was relatively simple and neither the federal nor the state governments were particularly involved in providing health care or social welfare services. By comparison, when Belgium and Spain made their first steps towards federalisation in 1970 and 1978 respectively, society had become more complex.

Second, the American, Australian and Swiss constitutions were primarily designed 'to frame the structures of government and to protect citizens' rights', whereas the German, Austrian, Belgian and Spanish constitutions were primarily conceived as 'detailed state codes', breaking with past constitutional experience.[4] The German, Austrian and Spanish constitutions contain in-built guarantees preventing a return to dictatorial or authoritarian forms of government. The transformation of the relatively short unitary Belgian constitution into a federal constitution necessitated the enumeration of a detailed catalogue of regional responsibilities. As a result, the Belgian constitution has become long and complex.

Obviously, the more detailed a constitution, the narrower the scope for broad judicial interpretations (judicial review). But also, the more the philosophy underpinning the drafting of a constitution is to provide a detailed state code, the more easily the constitution should be amendable as to reflect societal changes or changes to the federal-regional balance as accurately as possible. It is no coincidence that the American and Australian Constitutional Courts have played a considerable role in altering the federal-regional balance, but also that these constitutions have proved more cumbersome to amend. The only country that does not seem to fit this pattern is Switzerland: the role of the Swiss constitutional court is limited notwithstanding the high institutional threshold for constitutional change. In Switzerland, the people, by means of a referendum, decide on how far a federal government can go in extending its federal powers and encroaching upon regional rights instead. Conversely, the German, Austrian and Belgian constitutional courts have played a more modest role in changing the federal-regional balance, but constitutional amendments in these countries have been easier to implement. Spain does not seem to fit this pattern, insofar as the constitutional court played a crucial role in defining the responsibilities of the federation and newly created autonomous communities.

## Judicial review

Notwithstanding the difficulties of enacting constitutional change in the US and Australia, de facto constitutional change has been made possible by the constitutional courts. For instance, in the US, Franklin Roosevelt's New Deal and Johnson's 'Great Society' involved enacting federal welfare legislation that encroached upon previously held state rights. Either the Supreme Court justified this by widely interpreting the federally allocated power of inter-state commerce or the judges leaned on the power of the federal legislator to 'provide for the common defence and general welfare of the United States.' Alternatively, the judges invoked the federal government's power to 'make all laws which shall be necessary and proper for carrying into execution the foregoing powers' or narrowed down the breadth of the residual power clause (as indicated above in the American and Australian cases the residual power is allocated to the regions).

Whereas constitutional change has become more difficult to implement in Canada, the Judicial Committee of the London Privy Council, and since 1950 the Canadian Supreme Court, have played a considerable role in altering the federal-regional balance. Generally speaking, their judgements have strengthened the role of the provinces – the Canadian federation, when it was created in 1867 counted as the most centralised of its time. Since 1982, the Supreme Court's role has further increased because it must also watch over the compliance of federal and provincial law with the provisions of a Charter of Rights and Freedoms (modelled after the US Bill of Rights).

Compared to the Australian, American and Canadian courts the German federal court (*Bundesverfassungsgericht*) has been less active in altering federal-regional relations. The constitutionally prescribed 'equalisation clause' (uniformity of living conditions for all German citizens) has been widely interpreted, but in other areas the latitude of judicial interpretations has never been as large and contradictory as in America or Australia. The same applies to the Belgian Constitutional Court. It does not yet have the power to check all federal or regional bills against their compliance with all constitutional articles, but it can check whether such bills comply with a few constitutionally enshrined fundamental rights and freedoms and with the so called rules dividing competence between the federation and the component parts. Because these rules are extremely detailed in their provisions, the breadth of constitutional interpretations has been relatively limited.

Precisely because the Spanish federation has taken on a highly asymmetric form (some regions have been given more legislative powers than others), the Constitutional Court has played a significant role in interpreting the breadth of the various autonomy statutes (treaties between the federal government and the regions) establishing or extending regional powers. The most important ruling of the Constitutional Court to date concerns its rejection in 1983 of a federal law seeking to reduce the powers already granted to some regions and requiring federal consent for regionally enacted laws. Generally speaking, the Court's rulings have consolidated or even strengthened the political autonomy of the regional and local governments.

### Constitutional amendments

The more detailed a constitution, the easier it should be to amend. Even so, in any federation, the regions are involved in constitutional amendment procedures. The most difficult formulae require the adoption of constitutional amendments by a popular referendum. The Australian constitution has been successfully amended only eight times in its century long history whereas of *200* proposals for constitutional change which were put to a vote in Switzerland between 1848 and 1996, nearly 75 per cent (145) obtained the required majorities (a majority of voters nation-wide and a majority of cantons). The main reason why constitutional change has been more successful in Switzerland is that unlike in Australia, proposals for constitutional change have emerged from the grassroots in a bottom-up process.

Procedures, which prescribe the adoption of constitutional amendments by both chambers of a federal bicameral legislature and a substantial share of the regional legislatures, should normally lead to more constitutional amendments (USA, Canada). Yet, in the course of two centuries the American constitution has been amended less than thirty times. Although amendments to the US Constitution are initiated by the federal legislature, they require the consent of three quarters of the state legislatures or a similar share of state conventions. The Canadian Constitution Act (1982) which transferred the power to alter the Canadian constitution from the Westminster parliament to Canada contains several formulae for constitutional change. Amendments to the federal-regional balance follow nearly as rigid a procedure as in the United States: they normally require the consent of the federal parliament and two-thirds of the legislatures of the provinces containing at least half of the federation's population. However, the Meech Lake (April 1987) and Charlottetown Agreements (August 1992), which amongst other things proposed the recognition of Quebec as a 'distinct society', required the consent of the federal parliament and *all* of the Canadian provincial legislatures. To overcome critiques condemning the elitist character in which the Meech Lake Agreement was brought about (a federal-regional Prime Minister's conference), the Charlottetown Agreement emerged from intense federal-provincial public consultations and was put to a nation-wide referendum. Even so, the Agreement failed in seven out of ten provinces.

The most flexible amendment procedure only requires consent by a bicameral federal legislature, albeit frequently with special majorities. The federal principle is safeguarded by provision for the representation of territorial interests in the second chamber. The German constitution has been successfully amended on about fifty occasions since 1949. Major alterations in the federal-regional balance, for instance the fiscal reforms of 1966-1969, were laid down in the constitution. This is made possible because constitutional amendments only require the consent of two-third of the votes in both federal legislative houses.[5] Since the leading members of the regional executives compose the second chamber the input of the regional levels of government has been secured.

## Similarities and variations in the distribution of competencies

### Economic theory of federalism

The previous paragraphs asserted the important role of the federal constitution as a 'power-map' allocating the competencies of the federal or regional levels of government. Yet, so far I have not analysed *why* and *which* competencies have been attributed to either level of government. Since federations vary considerably I can only sketch a general pattern, leaning on the economic theory of federalism.[6] According to the economic theory of federalism, the so-called stabilisation and redistribution functions should be assigned to the federal policy level, whereas the regional policy levels should be entrusted with the allocation of most public services.

The *stabilisation* function implies that policies guaranteeing the monetary and economic union of the federation (inter-regional commerce, the protection of free movement of labour, capital, goods) should be in federal hands. A co-ordinating federal role helps to keep the public budgets and inflation under control and to minimise the effects of so-called asymmetric shocks, which may hit certain regions harder than others. Unrelated to the economic theory of federalism, but logically ensuing from recognition of the federal state as a sovereign entity, the federal policy level is also entrusted with the *foreign affairs and defence* powers. However, whether the regions should possess treaty-making powers in areas that fall within the scope of their domestic competencies or whether they should receive the right of representation in supranational or international bodies is a contentious issue. This is particularly the case in the regions of federal states in the EU, many of which find themselves insufficiently protected against the potential impact of EU primary and secondary legislation.

*Redistribution* is of course particularly important to federations that aspire to provide public services of a comparable standard throughout their territory. Such countries (Germany and Australia are the foremost examples) put most tax-raising powers in federal hands, as well as all legislation seeking to redistribute money to that purpose. By retaining most fiscal powers in federal hands, inter-regional tax competition can be avoided.

Finally, the actual *provision* – not necessarily the financing – of public services (for instance public transport, but also health care, policing and education) is usually left to the regions. It is argued that they can more effectively respond to local needs.

## *Legislative vs. administrative federalism*

Federations vary not only in the type and scope of competencies they have attributed to the federal and regional policy levels, but also in the way they allocate legislative and implementing authority. For instance, in the United States, Australia, Belgium, Canada and Spain the policy levels possessing a legislative competence in a certain subject-area *usually* also implement the legislation concerned. Put differently, the level with the 'right to decide' also possesses the 'right to act'.[7] For instance, federal tax offices also administer taxes levied by the US government. This general pattern contrasts with the so-called Germanic federations (Germany, Austria or to a more limited degree Switzerland), where most of the legislation is enacted at the federal level but the regions (or in Switzerland also municipalities) are made responsible for their implementation. In these cases the 'right to decide' and 'the right to act' are attributed to two different levels of government: effective co-ordination requires co-operation between those levels through intergovernmental bodies.

This kind of federalism, by conferring most legislative authority at the federal level, inevitably reduces the scope for individual regional strategies.

## *Symmetric vs. asymmetric federalism*

In most federations, all regions have received the same policy autonomy. However, Spain and Belgium are sometimes referred to as *asymmetric* federations because in both countries some regions have been given more policy autonomy than others. Although the Spanish constitution envisages symmetry, the historic regions of Catalonia, the Basque Country and Galicia (and later also Andalucia) took on regional autonomy faster than the other regions. In addition, the 17 so-called 'Autonomous Communities' do not share identical legislative and executive powers. For instance, the historic regions have gained considerably more autonomy in their educational, policing and health policies than most of the other regions. The powers of each of the regions are defined in bilateral agreements between the federation and the Autonomous Communities and require the consent of the federal parliament and the assembly of the region concerned.

Belgium has also developed an asymmetric form of government, but not to the same extent as Spain. Belgian federalism has a *territorial* (the creation of three regions, Flanders, Wallonia and Brussels) and a *personal* component (the presence of three language communities, the Dutch, French and German-speaking communities). Each of the three language communities was given a particular set of legislative competencies (mainly culture and education). The same applies to the regions which, amongst other things, received legislative and executive powers in the field of regional economic planning, agriculture, the environment and town and country planning. Since 1995, all regions have directly elected legislatures and executives. The asymmetry in Belgium results from (1) the merger of community and regional institutions at the Flemish side of the country, resulting in the creation of one 'Flemish Community' (2) the somewhat weaker regional autonomy of Brussels as compared to the other two regions, given its role as a federal and international capital and (3) the non-recognition of Brussels as a community (providing it with a bilingual statute instead) and of the German-speaking community as a region.[8] With the exception of the statute of Brussels, the powers attributed to each of the regions and communities are comparable. Therefore, the asymmetry in Belgium is not as pronounced as it is in Spain.

**Fiscal federalism**

Policies cannot be implemented without supporting fiscal means. The power of the regions within a federation is strongly correlated with their degree of fiscal autonomy. Three aspects are worth looking at. The first aspect concerns the share of total public expenditure which is made by the regions (the spending autonomy of the regions); the second aspect pertains to the share of regional expenditure which is financed out of autonomously raised taxes (the tax-raising autonomy of the regions). Other things being equal the former are a proxy to measure the degree in which the regions have 'a right to act' whereas the latter are a better measurement for the extent to which regions have 'a right to decide'. The final aspect considers the character of fiscal equalisation schemes: how many equalisation payments are made and how large and to what extent is fiscal equalisation a matter between the regions (horizontal equalisation), the federation (vertical equalisation) or both?

### Spending autonomy of the regions

Distribution of public expenditures in eight federal democracies (in per cent)

| Federal Country | Central Government | Regional Government | Local Government |
|---|---|---|---|
| Australia | 59 | 36 | 05 |
| Austria | 69 | 14 | 17 |
| Belgium | 52 | 37 | 11 |
| Canada | 42 | 41 | 17 |
| Germany | 59 | 24 | 17 |
| Spain | 70 | 19 | 11 |
| Switzerland | 31 | 40 | 29 |
| USA | 53 | 26 | 21 |

Source: IMF, Government Statistics (1999), except for Switzerland (Linder, W., *Swiss Democracy. Possible Solutions to Conflict in Multicultural Societies,* London: Macmillan, 1998, 2nd ed., p. 63) and Belgium (Moesen, W. and V. van Rompuy, *Openbare Financiën,* Leuven: Acco, 1994, p.320).

The above table provides an overview of the distribution of public expenditures made by the central, regional and local levels of government for each of the federal countries that are discussed in this chapter. A considerable variation in regional spending patterns can be observed. The spending autonomy of the Austrian and Spanish regions is considerably lower for instance than the spending autonomy of the Australian, Belgian and particularly Swiss and Canadian regions. On this basis Austrian and Spanish federalism count as relatively centralised whereas Swiss and Canadian federalism are strikingly decentralised. As argued before, since the Canadian social security system counts as one of the most decentralised, a considerable share of public expenditure is made at the regional level. In line with local traditions the Swiss municipalities possess considerable spending autonomy as well. It may be assumed that the further devolution of regional powers in Spain will increase the overall spending levels of the regions.


## Raising autonomy of the regions

Perhaps of greater relevance than a region's spending autonomy is its share of regionally spent expenditure that is based on autonomously raised taxes. The more a region relies on the federal government for the provision of its revenues, the higher the likelihood that it will be politically dependent on the federal government (for instance, because the federal government could attach conditions to the money it provides). From a regional perspective the arguments for autonomous tax-raising powers are not only political but also economic in character. Earlier I raised some arguments supporting a predominant federal role in setting the most important tax rates (economic and monetary union, avoidance of tax-competition). Dismissing such a view, a different group of economists (more strongly adhering to neo-liberal theories) argue that if the revenue which the regions can properly spend is based on regionally raised taxes, they will behave more responsibly, partly because democratic accountability is enhanced. In addition, just as the regions of a federation may have different preferences as far as the provision of public goods is concerned, so their views on the most appropriate tax policies may diverge. Finally, these economists argue that the dispersion of tax policies facilitates inter-regional competition and ultimately will lead to the most efficient use of public money.

The United States, Switzerland and to a lesser degree Canada follow this pattern. Excluding shared federal-regional expenditures – for instance, programmes involving the regional administration of federal social welfare – the amount of regional taxes as a percentage of all regional expenditure in the United States rose to 77.9 per cent in 1994. According to IMF statistics the Canadian provincial taxes raise 66.7 per cent of all regional expenditure. Although the German and Swiss federations have been described as administrative in character, the administration of Swiss federal policies frequently occurs on the basis of regionally raised taxes. In 1994 the Swiss cantons collected 40 per cent of all public revenue, a high enough share to cover most of their expenditures and roughly 10 per cent higher than what the federal government raised and spent.

By comparison, only 18 per cent of the money, which the German regions spent in 1995, can be linked to autonomously raised taxes. Although such a share is rather low, a case could be made that the German regions, via their representation in the federal second chamber, participate in federal tax legislation pertaining to all taxes, the revenue of which partly accrues to them. However, since the *Bundesrat* represents the collective interests of all, or at least a group of regions strong enough to gain a majority of seats in the second chamber, it seems to me that one cannot consider these so-called shared federal-regional taxes as autonomously raised. Particularly striking is the low tax-raising autonomy of the Belgian and Spanish regions. In 1997 the Belgian regions raised only 6 per cent of what they spent. Yet, given the absence of federation-wide parties a low regional tax-raising autonomy has not been as harmful to the political autonomy of the Belgian regions as may be thought. Similarly, only 14.5 per cent of the revenue which the Spanish Autonomous Communities spent in 1994 can be considered as own source revenues. Moreover, more than 75 per cent of these so-called revenues come from borrowing, making the tax-raising autonomy of the Spanish regions even more limited than that of the Belgian. As in Belgium, a considerable rise in tax-raising powers of the regions is currently being discussed, and, as was the case with the regionalisation process itself, the Catalans, Galicians and Andalucians are likely to be the first beneficiaries. The Basques already possess considerably more raising autonomy than the other Autonomous Communities.

### Mechanisms of fiscal equalisation

It should not come as a surprise that as a result of the inter-regional socio-economic disparities characterising most federations, average regional per capita tax-revenues differ significantly from one region to another. Put differently, the American states may collect roughly 80 per cent of the revenue they spend, but that percentage is likely to be considerably higher in California than it is in Arkansas. Tax revenues may be lower in a certain region, for instance because the average per capita income is relatively low, because a relatively high share of the population is unemployed or because the region lacks a considerable number of capital intensive enterprises. At the same time, the regional per capita expenses are likely to be high in such a region, for instance because more unemployment support must be paid out, programmes to re-educate people must be set up or fiscal incentives to attract new businesses must be launched. Hence, without any support of the federal government or the relatively affluent regions, the relatively poor regions are likely to run considerable budget deficits and see their most promising people flock to more affluent regions.

If most of the taxes are raised and collected by the federal government, the federal government may assess the fiscal needs of each of the regions before distributing the tax-receipts, instead of simply allocating the money on the basis of what each of the regions may have contributed to the entirety of tax-revenues. Alternatively, the regions themselves could work out formulae to redistribute tax-revenues which they have properly raised as a means of equalising inter-regional disparities. Equalisation payments, which are primarily the domain of the federal government, are referred to as vertical equalisation payments. By comparison, equalisation payments, which predominantly lean on inter-regional co-operation (inter-state transfers), are described as horizontal equalisation payments. The scope of this chapter does not allow for a detailed overview of fiscal equalisation mechanisms in each of the federations concerned, but a brief analysis is offered for the two federations with the best elaborated equalisation mechanisms, Germany and Australia, and for the federation with the weakest developed fiscal equalisation mechanism: the United States.

As suggested, the level of equalisation payments made is linked to the socio-economic disparities between the regions of a federation. In addition, the more the public and political parties assess differences in regional tax-revenue power as unjust, the more likely the federal government or regions are to intervene to mitigate the inequalities. Germany and Australia are two strong examples of federal countries in which public opinion has generally endorsed strong equalisation policies.

In Australia, a so-called Grants Commission calculates 'per capita relativities for determining the allocation of general revenue grants to the states' with the purpose of delivering social services of comparable standards throughout Australia. The Australian equalisation schemes not only aspire to equalise state revenue imbalances, but also state expenditure imbalances.

Unlike Australia, German equalisation takes place on the revenue side only. However, in Germany equalisation payments are made with the purpose of ensuring that the 'living conditions throughout the federation are equivalent.' The German system of equalisation payments is increasingly criticised for three reasons. First, German unification has drastically increased the cost of equalisation payments. Second, the fiscal equalisation schemes are perceived as extremely complex, involving considerable federal-regional and inter-regional redistribution. Finally, some observers argue that the German equalisation payments have led to 'excessive' redistribution policies: the average per capita fiscal power of the weakest regions may be considerably higher after the equalisation payments have been made than the average per capita taxation power of the strongest regions prior to equalisation. Hence there has recently been a judgement by the Federal Constitutional Court forcing the federation and regions to work out an alternative scheme by 2004.

Given the situation in Germany, it should not come as a surprise that representatives of the relatively affluent German regions look enviously at the United States. The American regions not only have a higher tax-raising autonomy, but the American public as a whole seems to accept higher inter-regional disparities in taxation power. Although Germany and the United States are not hindered by the presence of several regionally concentrated linguistic communities, Americans more easily 'vote with their feet', hence move to the regions which provide the best public services and employment opportunities. Unlike the German *Länder*, the American states are not actively involved in horizontal fiscal equalisation programmes: fiscal equalisation is the domain of the federal government. In the United States, federal payments to the states (grants) primarily aim to assist the states in carrying out federally regulated social security programmes: in this sense, they cannot be perceived as equalisation payments in the strict sense of the word. This is not to deny the predominant role that the federal government has assumed in the construction of highways and in providing support for the needy (AFDC – Aid to Families with Dependent Children – or Medicaid), areas in which the states and municipalities carry most of the responsibility. For instance, depending on the fiscal strength of the states, 50 to 80 per cent of the state's expenditures on AFDC or Medicaid are financed through federal grants. On most occasions federal grants are conditional, hence cannot be used freely to finance other state expenditures (or tax-cuts). Increasingly the role of the states in the distribution process is being undermined, as grants are no longer allocated to states as such, but to persons on the basis of individual need instead.

## Mechanisms of intergovernmental or federal-regional relations

It should not come as a surprise that even in federations, which provide for a fairly strict demarcation of federal-regional responsibilities, well-articulated mechanisms for intergovernmental relations are frequently needed. Sometimes interests may overlap, for instance when two regions are involved in constructing a road, possibly with federal fiscal aid, or when a federal minister of social affairs proposes to raise the minimum retirement age of state school teachers, thus affecting the policy agenda of the regional ministers of education. Evidently, the necessity for intergovernmental co-ordination is particularly high in Germany, Austria and to a lesser degree Switzerland. In these federations the federal government cannot implement its policies without the co-operation of the regions. In Switzerland, the policy autonomy of the regions is further enhanced, not only as a result of the region's considerable fiscal autonomy, but also because the regions could mobilise their electors to call a referendum on a federal bill which they do not wish to implement. Conversely, the regions require the legislative authorisation of the federal government before they can pursue many of their policies.

Federations not only vary in the intensity, but also in the character of their intergovernmental relations. Of all federations that are discussed in this chapter, only the United States has a presidential structure of government. In a presidential system, the head of the executive (president) and legislators are separately elected and usually serve different terms: the president cannot dissolve the legislature and with the exception of impeachment, the legislature cannot normally sack the president. As a result, the legislature can develop into a relatively autonomous policy-making actor and can play a significant role in co-ordinating intergovernmental relations. In the United States, the autonomy of Congress (and the state legislatures) is further enhanced as a result of the selection of party candidates through state-wide (not nation-wide) primaries. Neither the executive branch (president or governors), nor the federal party machines exert considerable influence on the nomination of representatives or senators. Therefore, intergovernmental relations in the United States involve the legislative as much as the executive branch of government. The US Senate plays a specific role in this respect: the relaxed party discipline in that chamber and the procedural rules allowing a single senator to block the closure of debate ensure that the voices of senators are well heard. Given the provision of equal state representation, the voice of a senator representing a small state is given more than proportional attention.

The pattern of intergovernmental relations is different in federations that have adopted a parliamentary model. In parliamentary systems the executive cannot survive without the support of a legislative majority, but the executive can prematurely dissolve the legislature. Executive and legislature are fused: the leading members of the executive branch are normally elected as members of parliament in the first place. Consequently, the roles of executive leader, party leader and legislator coincide. Since most legislators in a parliamentary regime aspire to a prominent position in cabinet (executive) parliamentarianism leads to a concentration of political power within the executive. Additionally parliamentarianism gives rise to a more pronounced dichotomy between the party (parties) in the executive (government) and the party (parties) in opposition than is the case in a presidential regime. Precisely because the executive requires a legislative majority for its survival, parliamentary parties tend to be better organised and employ a larger variety of disciplinary mechanisms than presidential parties. As a result, intergovernmental relations in parliamentary federations are primarily *inter-*

*executive* relations, leaving only a residual role to the federal and regional legislatures. Put differently, parliamentary federations are *executive* federations.[9]

The above has important consequences for the potential role of a legislative second chamber as an articulator of regional interests in federal law-making. First, in a parliamentary federation the second chamber tends to be considerably weaker than in a presidential federation, and, unlike the lower house, it is deprived of executive making or breaking powers. On these grounds alone, all but two parliamentary second chambers are too weak to act as suitable regional interest articulators. Even the German *Bundesrat* and the Australian Senate, which are sufficiently powerful, are weaker than the lower house since they are excluded from the making or breaking of, respectively, a German or Australian federal government. Evidently, the same restrictions do not apply to the American Senate: since the president is not dependent on a legislative majority for his survival, two equally powerful and differently composed chambers do not raise a problem of political accountability.

Second, unless the second chamber of a parliamentary federation brings together the leading regional political elites it is not likely to play a significant role in intergovernmental relations. As argued above, the members of the regional executives count as the most relevant regional party elites. In practice, the German *Bundesrat* is the only second chamber that is composed of members of the regional executives. Therefore it is the only parliamentary second chamber which has played a considerable role in intergovernmental relations. Although the Australian Senate is more powerful than the German *Bundesrat*, Australian senators can be more easily accommodated within the bicameral party group meetings and are less independent of the federal and regional party elites.

Most parliamentary federations have established alternative intergovernmental mechanisms that better suit the pattern of 'executive federalism' and compensate for the absence of a strong or effective federal second chamber. Prominent examples are the regular Prime Minister's Conferences in Canada and Australia, the Council of Australian Governments, Interministerial Conferences in Belgium, meetings between the leaders of the

Spanish federal government and heads of the Autonomous Communities, etc. Although meetings which take place at a ministerial level are the most visible, they are usually preceded and followed up by frequent gatherings of federal or regional civil servants. Even in Germany, numerous intergovernmental meetings at the ministerial or sub-ministerial level have developed. This is the case notwithstanding the presence of the *Bundesrat*: the federal second chamber only operates at the *apex* of a dense network of administrative bodies orchestrating federal-regional and interregional relations.

## Federalism and political parties

Federalism cannot be understood without considering the role of political parties and the position of regional and federal party elites within the party organisational structures. Since federalism implies the presence of regional government structures with directly elected legislatures and executives, the possibility of having different parties controlling different levels of government is a real one. Two aspects are of particular importance. First, the potential impact of regionally concentrated parties on federal-regional relations, second the strength of the regional party branches of federation-wide parties, which means that they cannot be easily compared to parties with a national following in countries with a unitary state structure.

### *Regional parties*

Spain, Canada, Germany, Australia and Belgium feature parties with a disproportionate following in one or several of the regions. Indeed the extent to which the success of regionally concentrated parties reflects a demand for more regional autonomy is considerable. For instance, one could think of parties with a strong regional following but which are willing to work the federal system in exchange for more regional autonomy. Other parties may play the 'federal game' but ultimately aspire to secession in the medium or long term. Finally, some regional parties could be considered as anti-system parties, arguing for immediate secession of a region concerned, not necessarily by democratic means. In the next paragraphs, examples are given for each type of these so-called regional parties. The extent to which regionalist parties can make their voice heard depends on their potential to control or take part in regional (coalition) governments and on whether or not their support is needed for providing a federal government with a legislative majority.

Spain features examples of at least two types of regional parties. The Catalan Nationalists *(Convergència i Unió*, CiU*)*, the Basque Nationalist Party (PNV), the more radical *Euskal Herritarck* (EH, formerly *Herri Batasuna*) and the *Bloque Nacionalista* only campaign within Catalonia, the Basque Country (PNV and EH) and Galicia respectively. Yet the Catalan and Basque Nationalist parties (CiU and PNV) have been willing to support a federal minority government in exchange for more regional autonomy. In 1993, the then Social-Democratic federal minority government relied on the support of the CiU; when it was replaced by a centre-right minority government (Partido Popular), the CiU, now joined by the PNV, proved equally willing to support the federal government. By comparison, HB, which is linked to the Basque terrorist movement ETA, aspires to the independence of a Basque state, and therefore can be classified as anti-system.

In Canada, the support of the *Bloc/Parti Québecois* (PQ) is confined to the province of Quebec, where the party is in government. Unlike the CiU or PNV in Spain, the Bloc aspires to political secession of Quebec from the rest of Canada, but so long as the Quebec electorate has not endorsed a similar position by referendum, the party is willing to maximise Quebec territorial interests within the Canadian federation. Since the Reform Party (currently transformed into the Alliance party by forging links with the Progressive Conservatives) is particularly strong in the West, it is pleading for better representation of the Western provinces in the federal constitution and against asymmetrical federalism conferring a special status upon Quebec.

In Germany two significant regional parties exist: the first, the Bavarian Christian-Social Union (CSU, is strongly affiliated with the federal Christian-Democrats (CDU) with which it forms a joint party group in the federal parliament and elects a common Chancellor-candidate. In turn, the CDU does not put up candidates for regional elections in Bavaria, the sole prerogative of the CSU. The second is the successor party of the former Eastern German

Communists: the PDS. Its main electoral support is confined to the 'new regions' where it acts as a coalition partner in the regional governments of Saxony-Anhalt, Mecklenburg-Vorpommern and most recently Berlin. Similarly, in Australia, the support of the National Party is almost exclusively concentrated within the rural areas of Queensland, Victoria and New South Wales. At the federal parliamentary level the Nationals are in an almost permanent coalition with the Liberals, whereas depending on its electoral strength, the Nationals may decide to compete against the Liberals or to put up joint Liberal-National party candidates at federal or regional elections. Hence neither the Australian or German regionalist parties put the continuation of the federation in question, and with the exception of the PDS all have had experience in federal government.

Perhaps it comes as a surprise that notwithstanding the variety of linguistic communities and the presence of two major confessions, all of the major Swiss parties have a federation-wide electoral appeal. Part of the explanation is that most of the issues that dominate Swiss politics (with the possible exception of further European integration) do not divide the Swiss along linguistic lines.

### *The regional structure of nation-wide parties in a federal state*

With the exception of Belgium, a majority of electors in federal states cast a vote for parties that are not concentrated within a particular region. Federation-wide parties are frequently made up of powerful regional party branches. In this respect the federal party leaders must take into account the views of the regional branches, on which they may be dependent for their selection and campaign money. A distinction must be made between federation-wide parties in a presidential regime and similar parties in a parliamentary system. For the reasons listed in the previous section, parties in a presidential federation are not normally as well organised and as strongly disciplined as parties in a parliamentary federation. Therefore, representatives of the same party representing different regions may easily reflect different tendencies. For instance, in the United States, the Southern Democrats for long have had more in common with the Northern Republicans than with the Northern

Democrats. The region-wide selection of candidates (primaries, even for the presidential candidates) and the election of the American legislatures and executive offices by the first-past-the-post system have contributed to the internal heterogeneity of American parties.

Since with the exception of the United States and Switzerland all of the federations that are discussed in this chapter feature parliamentary systems of government, the organisational structure of parliamentary parties warrants special attention. Because parliamentary systems require considerable party unity, federal party leaders will seek to maximise the level of party discipline, but their capacity to do depends on many factors.

First, notwithstanding their nation-wide appeal some parties may still perform better in one region than in another. For instance, in Germany the Social Democrats have traditionally performed well in the largest region, North-Rhine Westphalia, but badly in the second largest, Bavaria. As a result, the German party system is not simply the aggregate of 16 regional party systems; in the light of regional differences, the Bavarian branch of the Social-Democratic party may take different views on federal party matters from the North-Rhine Westphalian party branch.

Second, countries using a majoritarian electoral system (first-past-the-post or the alternative vote) are likely to have fewer, but less disciplined political parties (a factor that also contributes to the loose party organisation in the United States). Federation-wide parties, which are elected accordingly, may display regionalist factions. By comparison party discipline will be easier to obtain when elections are held by proportional representation: regionalist tendencies may be expressed by a separate party and insofar as closed-party lists have been used for the election of delegates, dissenting party members can be easily sanctioned by placing them lower on the party list.

Third, regional differences of opinion are easily reflected within the organisational structure of federation-wide parliamentary parties. Analysts of political parties, federal and non-federal alike, usually distinguish between *the party organisation* or extra-parliamentary party and the *party-in-office* or parliamentary party. The party organisation refers to the apparatus that selects candidates, organises party platforms (conferences) and electoral campaigns. At the apex of the party organisation stands the party executive, a body bringing together the main party leaders. The parliamentary party refers to all public office holders of a party, starting for instance with a member of a local council, running up to the prime minister or leader of the opposition in Parliament. There is a considerable overlap of membership between the party organisation and the parliamentary party. For instance, the Prime Minister or opposition leader is almost always a member ex officio of the party executive.

In a federation featuring federation-wide parties, the mixture of positions between the party-in-office and the party organisation is further complemented by an intermingling of positions between the *regional* and *federal* branches of the party. The regional party branches are frequently responsible for selecting candidates for regional and federal office alike, perhaps leaving only a co-ordinating role for the federal party machines. The regional party branches may contribute most to the party's finances and may finance most electoral campaigns. The regional party branches each have their own party assemblies (conferences) and executive. From here party activists are recruited to the federal party assembly (conference) and executive. Unsurprisingly, a regional premier or leader of the opposition is usually a member of the regional party executive, and often a member ex officio of the federal party conference. In Germany the most prominent premiers or regional opposition leaders are likely to occupy a seat in the federal party executive as well, making the party executive an important body of intergovernmental or federal-regional co-operation between leading party officeholders. In sum, the external unity of a federal party may mask considerable internal disunity following divergent views of regional party leaders. In a federal state, the party elites must take into account the performance of their party at the regional level and related therewith the demands imposed by the regional party leaders, who may well play a significant role in the federal party machines.

# Comparative federalism: problems, significance and lessons for devolution

The above analysis has shed some light on the meaning of federalism in eight contemporary Western democracies. Federal states are to be distinguished from non-federal states in that, in addition to local government structures, an intermediate or regional level of government is clothed with considerable policy autonomy. Significantly, federalism is a mechanism to disperse political power: important competencies fall beyond the scope of the federal government or cannot be shaped without the active Cupertino of the regions. The political dispersal is reflected within the structure of political parties possessing a nation-wide appeal: the regional party wings are well developed and the regional party leaders must be reckoned with.

The rationale of federalism varies from state to state. The most classic examples are the so-called 'coming-together' federations, of which the United States, Switzerland and Australia are the most prominent examples. A case could be made that Germany and Austria re-instated federalism in their post-war constitutions as a means for preventing the rise of a new dictatorship: by deconcentrating political power multiple checks and balances were incorporated.[10] In addition, federalism in these countries has often enabled politicians to operate first at the regional level. For instance, in Germany the Greens first entered regional coalition governments in the eighties but did not participate in a federal government until 1998. Finally, the plural Belgian and Spanish states have devolved powers to increasingly powerful regional levels of government with the purpose of containing rising demands for more regional autonomy. Indeed, political scientists have not come up with equally suitable alternatives to federalism as a means for containing territorially concentrated nationalism within the framework of a multinational state. As the above analysis made clear, the benefits of federalism are not only confined to mono-national federations: multi-level governance may lead to political and policy experimenting. Federalism may not only give rise to new parties assuming executive power at the regional level of government, but insofar as the sub-units of a region have autonomous law-making or administrative possibilities, federalism may also lead to policy innovation; for instance in the field of educational policies or in applying the newest government budgeting techniques, etc.

Having said this, the above analysis equally made clear that federalism is not without its faults. Obviously, in a federal state the steering capacity of the central government is weakened. As a result of the density of the intergovernmental framework, responsibilities are more dispersed and therefore it is more difficult to hold accountable all of the public involved in intergovernmental policy-making. Administrative federations, which usually require intense co-operation between the federal and regional levels of government for the formulation and implementation of policies can often result in sub-optimal outcomes, reflecting the 'lowest common denominator'. Furthermore, federal arrangements always in one way or another violate the majority principle. The small regions are likely to be over-represented in federal institutions (for instance having been guaranteed a disproportionally high share of the seats in the second chamber, cabinet or even lower house). Likewise the smallest regions benefit from the formulae required to amend the constitution or by their representation in the intergovernmental mechanisms discussing federal-regional or inter-regional relations. By the same token, if a substantial part of the population strongly identifies with the regions, a violation of the majority principle may be the necessary price to pay in order to bind these units in a larger polity. In any case, federalism requires that both levels are willing to play the game (in Germany this concept is referred to as *Bundestreue* or federal loyalty). Federalism by itself is no panacea for containing extreme forms of regional or local nationalism.

Devolution touches upon many of the issues that were discussed in this paper. First, as in Spain and Belgium, devolution means asymmetric decentralisation. Second, devolution means political experimenting: experimenting with proportional representation and coalition governments. Third, devolution is likely to be a first step in conceding more regional autonomy to the regions: the policy and fiscal autonomy of the regional levels of government remains by comparative standards limited. The crucial factor concerns the dispersal of power within the 'federation-wide' parties (Labour, Conservatives and Liberals) and the popular support for extreme regionalist parties such as the Scottish and Welsh Nationalists. However, devolution is only one of two territorial challenges facing the future of the United Kingdom. It is frequently asserted that the stronger autonomy of the Welsh and Scottish regions could not have been accomplished without their and Britain's full integration into the European Union. Since the enactment of the Treaty of Rome, which aimed for the creation of a common market, the European

Union has developed into a quasi-federal political structure. European primary legislation (Treaties) and secondary legislation (regulations, directives, decisions) are supreme to domestic law and have direct effect within each of the EU Member States. The gradual removal of European trade barriers is as much a challenge as it is a threat to the newly regained autonomy of the Scottish and Welsh regions. A challenge, insofar as the Scottish and Welsh economies can foster intense trade links with other EU Member States or regions and in such a way promote their cultural distinctiveness. A threat insofar as the Scottish and Welsh governments are equally bound by the European Treaties and secondary legislation as is the United Kingdom. This implies that both regions should be given sufficient institutional autonomy to articulate their interests at the European level whenever matters are being discussed that fall within their (domestic) competencies. Since common European decision-making mechanisms do not allow a Member State's vote to be split up along regional lines, intergovernmental mechanisms at the domestic level must ensure that the Welsh and Scottish policy views are adequately expressed at the European level.

## Notes

[1] Pierson, P., 'Fragmented Welfare States: Federal Institutions and the Development of Social Policy', in: *Governance*, vol.8, October 1995, no.4, pp. 449-478.

[2] On the principles of confederation, see Croisat, M., *Le fédéralisme dans les démocraties contemporaines*, pp. 25-31.

[3] The concepts of 'bringing-together' and 'holding-together' constitutions were first used by Juan J. Linz and Alfred Stepan, see their *Problems of Democratic Transition and Consolidation*, Baltimore: John Hopkins University Press, 1996.

[4] Elazar, D., 'Constitution-making, the pre-eminently political act,' in: Banting, K. and R. Simeon (eds.), *The Politics of Constitutional Change in Industrial Nations. Redesigning the State*, Macmillan: London, 1986, pp. 232-247.

[5] This is not to deny that some provisions of the German Constitution are impossible or very difficult to amend. For instance, Article 79 of the German Basic Law states that amendments affecting the division of the federation into *Länder*, the participation on principle of the *Länder* in legislation or the basic principles laid down in Articles 1 (protection of human dignity) and 20 (the recognition of Germany as a *democratic* and *social federal* state) are inadmissible. Furthermore changes to the territorial structure of the federation (creation of

new regions or the merger of existing regions) require the popular consent of the people living in the affected regions.

[6] Watts, R. L., *Comparing Federal Systems in the 1990s*, pp. 118-122 for a comparative overview of the distribution of competencies between federal and regional levels of government.

[7] Braun, D. (ed.), *Public policy and federalism.*

[8] For a more detailed overview, see Swenden, W., *'How (A)Symmetric is Belgian Federalism?'*

[9] The term 'executive federalism' was first used by Donald Smiley, see his *Canada in Question. Federalism in the Eighties.*

[10] The prime aim of German federalism as a means for deconcentrating rather than decentralising political power was aptly discussed by Charlie Jeffery, 'Party Politics and Territorial Representation in the Federal Republic of Germany', in: Brzinski, J.B., Lancaster, T.D. and C. Tuschhof (eds.), *Compounded Representation in Western European Federations*, London: Frank Cass, 1999, pp. 130 – 166.

# Devolution in the United Kingdom
*The EU dimension*

## Alan Butt Philip

Devolution to a new Scottish Parliament and a new Welsh Assembly marked such a major shift in UK politics at the end of the 1990s that it is not surprising that the impact of these constitutional changes upon the European Union and upon Britain's relations with the EU have been largely over-looked. Any attempt to assess these impacts, within less than three years of the coming into being of these new institutions, is necessarily tentative. Nevertheless, there have already been some clear departures from the usual patterns of UK politics in relation to the European Union for such an assessment to be worthwhile. This chapter will consider the issues arising in terms of the political structures and institutions now in place; the impacts on EU policies; the impacts upon individuals involved in politics; and the changed dynamics of relationships between different levels of government in an EU context.

### Political structures and institutions

The creation of a Scottish Parliament and a National Assembly for Wales evidently called forth a re-appraisal of how Scottish and Welsh interests were to be represented in the EU institutions and how far the EU needed to change the quality of its institutional relationships with Scotland and Wales. The issue of Scotland's relations with the EU was discussed in some depth in the 1997 White Paper on devolution to a Scottish Parliament, but this did not become an issue in the public debate before the referendum held the same year. The key issue was how should Scottish interests continue to be represented by the UK Government within the Council of Ministers – as Scotland would still not be represented separately in that body – given that there would now be a separate Scottish 'government' accountable to the Scottish Parliament in addition to Scottish representation in the UK Government and Parliament. Even with weaker devolution to Wales, the same issues of co-ordination of policy and its implementation were to arise there also. Up until 1999 the Scottish, Welsh and Northern Irish Offices of the UK Government had overseen the administration of great swathes of domestic UK policy (such as health, education, agriculture, environment, local government, transport, social security) although the policies devolved were not all the same (e.g. the police function was not devolved to the Welsh Office, but was to Scotland and Northern Ireland). Thus the administrative apparatus was largely in place to oversee policy. What devolution changed was the pattern of accountability and political representation to the Brussels level.

Strictly speaking the UK Government is still the channel through which policy and administrative issues with a European dimension should be represented to the EU institutions, but the UK Government is usually no longer responsible for the policy itself. Hence the formal relationships within the UK governmental structure have had to change, and this has had a knock-on effect upon the relations of Scotland and Wales with the EU. The conventional pattern of ad hoc representation of Scottish and Welsh interests on the UK delegation in Council of Ministers negotiations (especially the Council working groups) has had to be strengthened and systematised. Contacts between the Scottish and Welsh executives and the European Commission have had to be established; in the case of Wales, the presence of Neil Kinnock, a former Welsh MP, as one of the UK-appointed Commissioners has obviously been helpful behind the scenes. Scottish and Welsh representation in Brussels, above and beyond the presence of 9 Scottish and 5 Welsh MEPs, has been strengthened by the separate offices representing a combination of Scottish and Welsh governmental, economic and educational interests – Scotland Europa and Wales European Centre. This trend for representation of separate Scottish and Welsh interests to the European Union has also extended over time from Scottish fishermen and Welsh farmers through to employers, higher education, economic development and local government. The new Scottish executive has in addition organised its own separate representation in Brussels in order more closely to monitor the work of the EU institutions and to network with other regional interests.

A parallel development has begun to be noticed among UK parastatal agencies such as the Environment Agency. Because their lines of communication to central and EU levels of government have been altered by devolution, so these agencies have to break up their structures geographically to reflect newly separated roles. Thus in 2001 the Environment Agency appointed a high ranking official to monitor and represent English environmental interests in Brussels for the first time, Welsh and Scottish agency interests already having been catered for.

Pressure to co-ordinate the messages emanating from Scotland, Wales and Northern Ireland being conveyed to the EU institutions has intensified, so members of the Economic and Social Committee (ECOSOC) and the Committee of the Regions, as well as MEPs, are receiving briefings from their governments in Belfast, Cardiff and Edinburgh and, on many occasions, these representatives are happy to work together across the political divide in order to maximise the weight of their regional case.

The English regions have been the Cinderellas in the field of political and administrative reform since the 1970s. The English regional economic planning boards and councils instituted in February 1965 by the Wilson Government were immediately swept away when Mrs Thatcher and her Conservative government came to power in 1979. The lack of administrative apparatus and resource in the English regions to co-ordinate regional responses to EU initiatives proved an ever-increasing handicap. The reforms of the structural funds in 1984 and 1989 required more and more regional projects eligible for EC funding to be presented under the umbrella of regional development programmes and sub-programmes, which the English regions were singularly ill-equipped to devise. It was left to the Major administration to decide to bite the bullet and reverse the direction of government policy. A new regional government presence in the English regions was organised from 1994 with each of the eight administrative regions hosting a Government

Office for the Region combining senior officials from Whitehall departments including trade and industry, environment and employment among others. The role of GORs is to promote a coherent approach to competitiveness, sustainable economic development and regeneration using public and private resources. This significant reconstruction of regional administration in England thus owed its origins to policy changes in Brussels, agreed by the UK Government up to a decade earlier.

As far as the English regions are concerned, the Blair Government has made it very clear since 1997 that enhanced regional government may be on offer in England, subject to evidence of local demand, but only on the basis of existing administrative regional boundaries. Meanwhile each region was to be endowed with a Regional Development Agency. This in turn has galvanised most English regions to establish 'regional chambers' of local interests (local government, employers, trade unions) as a first step along this road. In the case of the South West of England one of the first decisions taken by the new Regional Chamber was to rally unanimously behind the demand from Cornwall for Objective One status under the new EU structural fund arrangements, subordinating all other regional demands of EU level to this one goal. It did not take this Regional Chamber and the parallel Regional Development Agency very long to work out that they too needed to have separate representation in Brussels, not least to match the efforts of the neighbouring Welsh authorities. A similar knock-on effect of devolution is to be observed in the representation of the interests of the North of England to Brussels. A new structure for London, with an elected mayor and assembly acting in a strategic capacity, has also intensified its relations with the European Union.

Viewed from a Brussels perspective, the emergence of the Scottish Parliament and the Welsh Assembly have also prompted changes at EU level. The representation of the European Commission in Edinburgh and Cardiff long preceded devolution, but it has had to be strengthened. The Scottish, Welsh and Northern Irish press and broadcast media have given proportionately more coverage to EU affairs because they had more direct financial interests at stake than England. Now the new parliaments are scrutinising the EU dimensions of policy and administration much more carefully than the House of Commons was prepared to do with separate European committees, and, accordingly, more political intelligence and information is needed in these capitals for and from the Commission. Brussels lobbyists have also set up links, if not local offices, in Edinburgh and Cardiff to exploit new commercial opportunities and in particular to keep an eye on any legislative developments in Scotland that may feed through, via the well-known ratchet effect, to subsequent EU legislation. This kind of monitoring is also carried out across the German *Länder* and the Belgian regional structures for the same reason. Equally the Commission and the Brussels lobbyists will be watching out for examples of where regional as well as national legislation and administrative practice is not conforming with EU norms. The scope for this is immeasurably greater with the advent of devolution and thus looser co-ordination, with divided responsibilities between national and regional governments, for the implementation of EU legislation across a wide range of fields.

**Policy development and administration**

A core principle that the EU applies to all policy matters that are dealt with away from Brussels by the Member States is that each national government is fully responsible for and accountable to the EU institutions for what is done within its territory. Thus even if the Member State has devolved responsibility for a policy area that has substantial EU origin (e.g. agriculture) to a sub-national tier of government, it is the national government of that Member State that is still responsible for the actions of the sub-national government (or local authority) as far as the EU is concerned. This principle is necessary to ensure clear accountability to the EU for the implementation of EU decisions or legislation and to ensure consistency of policy application across many disparate regions. It thus imposes upon national governments an obligation to monitor and to report to Brussels on what sub-national governments are doing on behalf of the European Union and to ensure that they are not contravening EU law, for example in the area of state aids. The penalties for any such contravention are applied to the national government. This obligation may in turn lead to a certain centralisation of policy development in areas previously subject to local initiative in order to conform to EU requirements

– a trend noted in the field of environmental policy in the UK as long ago as the early 1980s.[1] Some policy areas remain strictly and solely under Westminster control – e.g. foreign relations, defence, immigration and nationality, macro-economic policy and taxation. But most policy areas are now subject to concurrent responsibility between the national and sub-national levels (in Scotland, Wales and Northern Ireland) if not sole responsibility at this 'regional' level. The broad scope of EU policy means that very few domestic policy areas do not have some EU dimension.

The two most significant EU spending areas for the new parliaments are represented by agriculture and the structural funds. High spending by the Union is also accompanied by substantial regulatory and administrative requirements to be followed by national and sub-national governments as well as the recipients of funding. It is clear that Whitehall is still acting as the 'gatekeeper' of policy in regard to the EU in these areas, and has a controlling handle over the slowly strengthening direct regional relations with the European Commission. Yet there are important signals that regional level governments are trying to emerge from the shadow of Whitehall. In the wake of restrictions on meat exports from the UK following on from the BSE crisis and the foot and mouth disease epidemic, Scotland, Wales and Northern Ireland have all sought to de-couple their territories from restrictions imposed on England – Northern Ireland achieving some success with this tactic. With the ending of the special headage payments, licensed under the Common Agricultural Policy since UK accession in 1973, the Welsh agriculture secretary tried hard to introduce an alternative subsidy for the hill farmers of Wales, only to be told that this was illegal under EU law.

The majority of the structural funds have, by convention and of necessity, been spent in the UK outside of England. Devolution to Scotland and Wales has made more transparent the already highly decentralised system for generating programmes eligible for structural fund money and for monitoring and evaluating those programmes. The Welsh Executive has taken this function so seriously that it has set up a separate executive agency, the Welsh European Funding Office, to administer it. The availability of genuinely additional funding from EU sources ought to be made clearer by the new financial arrangements for Wales and Scotland, and there is certainly more parliamentary scrutiny in Cardiff and in Edinburgh concerning the speed, allocation and status (in terms of Brussels-prescribed objectives) of such funding. The take-up of EU funds, which is always dependent upon some matching funds organised locally or regionally, can be expected to improve under the pressure of such scrutiny as heated debates in the Welsh Assembly early in 2001 demonstrated. The new structure of regional development agencies in England, with increasing funding provision from 2001, also promises to make these agencies pay more attention to EU funding opportunities now that they are so much more able to provide the matching funds portion at regional level.

It should not be forgotten that Northern Ireland has been the beneficiary of special EU funding since the early 1980s. One of the first two special integrated operations under the European Regional Development Fund was devoted to Belfast. It succeeded in bringing together a number of local agencies (including, uniquely, the local housing authority) to maximise the synergies of co-ordinated policy for long-term economic development. The European Parliament's much disapproved of initiative in commissioning its own assessment of how the EC might contribute to bring inter-communal peace in Ulster, known as the Haagerup Report of 1982, also paved the way for EU-led cross-border economic initiatives and institution-building which many political actors now acknowledge played a vital part in making the Good Friday Agreement of 1998 possible. Although it is not obvious that any comparable opportunities for EU initiatives exist within the rest of the United Kingdom, the possibility of the EU acting as an honest broker, when national-led governments appear to have run out of options, cannot be ruled out.

The devolved governments have a continuing interest in a whole range of EU policies and legal obligations which may cut across their own territorially specific policies. Transport, environment, labour market, energy, technology, taxation, financial institutions, enterprise and small business policies all fall into such a category. The EU's competition policy, which embraces restrictive practices and mergers inter alia, is of particular salience because of the treaty-based provisions which enable the European Commission to monitor, authorise and, at times, to disallow state aids, which include all national, regional or local government incentives – in case or in kind – to encourage the development of local industry and employment. The slow demise in 2000-1 of Corus, Britain's leading steelmaker, might have been expected to call forth a vigorous financial response from the new Welsh and Scottish administrations in an attempt to rescue a very major regional manufacturer and employer. However, the devolved governments have found themselves very severely constrained by EU rules about the scale and nature of any financial aid offered as well as by the exigencies of the high value of sterling/low value of the Euro which were well beyond their span of control.

One of the most unexpected and perverse interventions into domestic politics by the EU occurred in 1999 in relation to the Scottish Executive's determination, under pressure from its Liberal Democrat junior coalition partner, to abolish tuition fees for Scottish students attending Scottish universities. Tuition fees had been introduced across the whole UK higher education system with great speed in 1998 by the Labour Government in London, and Labour in Scotland seemed prepared to toe the Whitehall line had Scottish coalition politics not determined otherwise. The elimination of tuition fees for Scottish students going to Scottish universities could not be carried out legally under EU law unless the same terms were offered to students from all other EU Member States. This was conceded by the Scottish Executive, leaving English, Welsh and Northern Irish students having to face paying fees, unlike their Scottish, French or German counterparts!

**Individuals as political actors**

The impact of devolution upon individuals active in politics is still emerging and the implications for relations between the regions, the Member States and the EU are as yet unclear. However not only do the devolved governments and parliaments offer alternative career paths of substance to the conventional Westminster-based career, but this change may have knock-on effects at EU level. The emergence of influential politicians with their political base in a UK region is now on the cards, and some leading MPs have already abandoned the House of Commons as a result (e.g. Henry McLeish and Jim Wallace in Scotland, Dafydd Wigley and Rhodri Morgan in Wales). The new elected mayor of London, Ken Livingstone, has used his position to demand the early entry of the UK into the Eurozone in order to safeguard the economic interests of the London region. We can expect more such interventions on the European stage from leading regional politicians as they and their administrations become established. The new regional constituencies for European Parliament elections also point in the same direction. The regions no longer need only to look to London for practical support: Brussels and Strasbourg beckon as well. Career paths to and from these latter destinations are increasingly likely to by-pass London altogether.

Equally the enhanced politicisation of government in Scotland and Wales, following from the election of the Scottish Parliament and Welsh Assembly, can be expected to lead to a greater politicisation of public appointments in those two countries, including appointments to the EU's Economic and Social Committee and the Committee of the Regions, and even in regard to secondments from the civil service to Brussels. The arrival of coalition governments, in Scotland from 1999 and in Wales from 2000, will also encourage Labour and Liberal Democrat coalition partners to tap into parallel political networks in Brussels to seek either political advantage or at the very least to sustain their domestic policy positions.

The political parties have their links to pan-European political federations, or at the very least to political groups in the European Parliament, which provide political resources and networking opportunities for individual politicians. The nationalist parties of Scotland and Wales have rather fewer contacts with other political parties than the Liberals, Socialists and Conservatives, but have worked with a number of smaller political parties in the European Parliament, which in the 1999-2004 Parliament combined to form a group some thirty MEPs strong under the banner of the Greens-European Free Alliance. The present fine political balance of the European Parliament probably offers the best opportunities for Liberal Democrats seeking influence, as their MEPs hold the most obvious and effective swing votes (Hix, 2000). But there is little evidence so far that the Scottish and Welsh Liberal Democrats have attempted to link up with their MEP affiliates to achieve common goals.

**The dynamics of integration and devolution**

Devolution offers the chance of stronger bilateral relations between the EU (specifically the Commission) and the regions with devolved governments. It also offers the possibility of more balanced triangular relationships between the EU, the UK central government and the new devolved governments. So far there is little to suggest that much has changed in this respect. The UK Government still appears to be an effective gatekeeper concerning EU policy and most EU relations, and has applied strong pressure to keep the Scottish and Welsh governments in line when there appeared to be threats to the unity of policy stance emanating from the UK. However, the issue of tuition fees for students in higher education has shown how one devolved government can destabilise the policy position of the UK central government on an issue with EU legal resonance if that devolved government persists with an independent policy. The devolved parliaments have also put in place new scrutiny committees, which should enhance their ability to set a different agenda on EU affairs from Westminster and to win any ensuing arguments.

It is also possible that with the rise of devolution and decentralisation across Western Europe – the UK being last as usual onto the scene – implementation of policy and policy outcomes, at the behest ultimately of the European Union, under conditions of devolved government will give rise increasingly to inconsistencies and a loss of cohesion across the Member States. The licence to vary environmental standards confirmed by the European Court of Justice, following the Single European Act of 1986 is the clearest but by no means the only example. This poses a major strategic dilemma for the authorities in Brussels. Should they insist on more centralised EU monitoring and control over national and sub-national governments in order to insist on policy consistency (as most multinationals in the EU would like)? The alternative is to be more open about tolerating diversity of policy implementation and outcomes, especially after the anticipated Eastern enlargement of the Union, in the expectation that in the long term with rising prosperity the and sharing of best practice across borders policy harmonisation on the ground will occur across all the Member States. The latter approach may offend integrationist purists, the big corporations and the bureaucrats, but may prove politically the wiser course if the EU is to retain legitimacy and consent for the exercise of its authority across a whole continent.

The devolution experience in the UK as elsewhere is a complication for Brussels and introduces more untidiness into policy development and administration as viewed from Brussels. The EU institutions have to learn to live with this fact of political life and to adapt their culture to it rather than to fight the consequences.

*Notes*

[1] Haigh, N., 'Devolved Responsibility and Centralisation: Effects of EEC environmental policy', in: *Public Administration*, vol. 64, 1986, pp. 197-207.

# A Federalised Polity
## *An alternative to Scottish 'independence' in Europe?*

## Alex Wright

'The role of regional democracy and of regional Parliaments and Governments is only wakening up. Our time has finally come. The debate will be about sharing sovereignty at a European level, and about what the use of national sovereignty at the beginning of the century will be about and what the contribution of real, bottom-up democracy will be.' (Hans de Belder, Secretary General of the Assembly of European Regions, at a seminar on Scotland and Europe arranged by the Scottish Parliament, February 2001)

### Legislative devolution and the EU: Maximalists versus minimalists

Even before the Scottish Parliament first re-convened in 1999, there was a measure of concern about how Scotland could enhance its influence in the EU. The 1997 White Paper, which set out the UK Government's proposals for a Scottish Parliament devoted a whole chapter to the subject, and civil servants acknowledged privately that this was a difficult issue. In part that was a result of the SNP's 'Independence in Europe' campaign; the implication being that Scotland's interests in Europe would be served better if Scotland became a Member State in its own right. Furthermore, there was the perception amongst a swathe of Scottish interest groups that Scotland's influence in the EU was far too modest prior to legislative devolution. Consequently the onus lay with the unionist parties in Scotland – especially the Scottish Labour party which was to become the major partner of the governing coalition – to demonstrate that Scotland's interests in the EU could be promoted and defended more vigorously than had been the case hitherto. But as the White

Paper portended, and the Scotland Act (1998) confirmed, responsibility for foreign affairs – including relations with the EU – was to be reserved to the Westminster Parliament.

So there was good reason to suppose that involvement of the Scottish Executive (or 'Government') would be quite *minimal*.

- It would be concerned primarily with overseeing the implementation of EU policies and co-ordinating bids for EU funds.

- As regards the representation of Scottish interests, the Executive would be merely relegated to transmitting the Scottish view on a particular issue of policy upwards to whichever 'lead' department in London was responsible for representing the UK in the Council of Ministers (currently the EU's supreme decision-making body).

- The handling of EU matters would be primarily an administrative affair, which would be left largely in the hands of Scottish civil servants.

- By virtue of its reserved status it would be inappropriate for there to be any substantive ministerial leadership in Scotland - there would be no minister with a 'European' or external affairs portfolio.

Conversely the Executive might opt for a more *maximalist* approach to the EU, the constituent elements of which would be as follows:

- One or more Scottish minister holds an external affairs portfolio

- The Executive formulates a distinctively Scottish agenda which may not necessarily complement the UK's position on the European Union (EU) at a particular moment in time – it might be divergent.

- The Executive develops its own linkages with the EU's institutions and the governments of the Member States.

- The Executive joins pan-European networks designed to enhance sub-state influence in the EU.

- The Executive joins other sub-state governments in demanding that the EU's regions and stateless nations have greater influence over decision making.

Given the legal constraint exercised by its reserved status the maximalist perspective on Scotland's relations with the EU seems unlikely. But that leaves us with a conundrum. It could equally be argued that the minimalist scenario is simply not feasible either. It is unimaginable that the Scottish Executive could somehow avoid becoming intimately involved in European affairs despite its reserved status.

- Scotland's interests in the EU can be quite distinct from those of the rest of the UK – there is no assurance that the UK Government could accommodate them satisfactorily when it formulates its own position vis-à-vis a given EU policy.

- EU policies can impact directly on areas of policy devolved from Westminster to Scotland – Scottish ministers would have little option but to attempt to influence the EU directly from time to time.

- More contentiously perhaps, the EU is beginning to displace the UK as Scotland's primary loci of government. In part this can be attributed to the supranational characteristics of the EU, which ensure that its legislation takes precedence over UK law. In addition there have been occasions when the other Member States adopted a particular policy, which impacted on Scotland directly. Regardless of whether the UK Government agreed to it or not – e.g. the EU ban on the export of beef products during the BSE crisis in the late 1990s – there could be times when the Scottish Executive might have little choice but to forge alliances with the governments of the Member States.

- The EU remains for the time being an evolutionary polity the outcome of which is of considerable importance to Scotland's future wellbeing.

- Scottish ministers cannot afford to ignore it because the consequences could be too great for Scotland. They therefore have little alternative to formulate an EU strategy if they wish to remain in office.

Faced with such conflicting pressures the Executive found itself in an unenviable position during the early years of legislative devolution. Legally it was duty bound not to breach the terms of the Scotland Act. Thus in theory it would not be responsible for foreign affairs. Yet, the EU's impact on Scotland was such that it was difficult to avoid becoming involved not least because there was no clear dividing line as to what constituted domestic and EU matters. That then raised a number of questions. To what extent would the Executive attempt to move towards a maximalist approach? Would it hold back at first for fear of upsetting the UK Government in London and thereby avoid provoking a constitutional crisis during the early years of legislative devolution? If eventually it could no longer hold back, then to what extent would the Government in London *allow* the Executive a measure of leeway?

## The Scottish Executive, the Scotland Office and the EU

Once the Scottish Elections had been held, the former Scottish Office was succeeded by the Scottish Executive and the Scotland Office. The Scottish Executive was responsible for devolved matters; the First Minister stood at the apex of its political leadership and he and his ministers were accountable to the Scottish Parliament. The Scotland Office's functions included responsibility for matters which were reserved to Westminster, it was headed by Scotland's Secretary of State who was a member of the cabinet and who along with his or her ministers was accountable to MPs at Westminster. Given that foreign affairs was a reserved power it could be expected that the Secretary of State would play a leading role regarding Scotland's relations with the EU. Certainly the incumbent was a member of a cabinet committee on the EU but apart from that to all intents and purposes to-date the post-holders have adopted a low profile on European matters.

As mentioned above the Executive's room for manoeuvre was circumscribed by the Scotland Act. But the White Paper did offer some guidance. It affirmed that the Executive and Parliament would have an 'important role' with regard to those 'aspects of European integration which affect devolved areas.'[1] However for the most part it appeared little had changed. Scottish ministers did not have the automatic right to attend the meetings of the Council of Ministers; instead they could only do so with the agreement of their colleague from the lead department in London. Even so, the White Paper affirmed that they could be 'involved' in EU Councils[2] – but this did not seem to amount to a substantive change as ministers from the former Scottish Office had attended meetings in Brussels for years. In the main the tone of the White Paper emphasised the need for the Governments of Scotland and the UK presenting a united front over foreign affairs; the Scots would be part of 'a UK team'. But it did mention that the Scottish

Executive might wish to open its own links with other territories in the EU, implying that Scotland might enjoy some autonomy over foreign affairs.

During the second half of 1999 civil servants formulated draft proposals for a Memorandum of Understanding, Concordats and a Joint Ministerial Committee (JMC). In this instance we are interested primarily in their relevance to Scotland's relations with the EU. The Memorandum of Understanding maintained that in principle the UK and territorial governments should have a constructive and collaborative relationship; in essence, conflict between the two should be avoided. The Concordats, one of which dealt with international relations went some way to formalising intergovernmental relations between the different layers of authority – albeit that they were not legally binding. Subsequently a raft of 'functional' Concordats was agreed between departments in London and the territorial administrations (e.g. on Fisheries). Although the JMC lacked executive authority, where necessary it could act as a forum for resolution of disputes between the territorial and UK Governments. If that failed to settle the matter then it might be brought before the Judicial Committee of the Privy Council. So, there were two sides to these arrangements. On the one hand they appeared to offer Scotland the means to challenge the actions and perhaps even the competence of the UK Government – something which is particularly salient as more and more power is transferred to the EU. On the other they appeared to constrain the autonomy of the Scottish Executive. This was particularly so in relation to the EU – for instance under the fisheries concordat Scottish civil servants were not supposed to receive direct approaches from the European Commission and if they did then they were obliged to inform the then Ministry of Agriculture Fisheries and Food.[3] In effect the Executive should not embark on 'expansionism' – that is to say it should involve itself in areas of policy where it had no right to be, because they are the preserve of Westminster and the departments in London. Arguably much of this related to the civil service, because for the first time it would be answerable to different political leadership and in theory at least it had little desire to be caught up in turf wars between the territorial and UK Governments.

The first twelve months of the Executive's existence were notable for its reluctance to adopt a high profile approach to external relations. There was no single minister responsible for 'Europe'; it was claimed that since the EU covered many areas of policy that were devolved to Scotland it made more sense for each of the 'functional' ministers to have a measure of involvement (finance or rural affairs). Yet it was difficult to avoid the impression that external relations was potentially controversial when legislative devolution was in its infancy and that consequently the Executive had chosen a minimalist approach to this. It should be remembered that this was a moment in time when there was a degree of ambiguity over the existing constitutional settlement. Some (including apparently Donald Dewar, then the First Minister) viewed it as part of a process (or as Dewar put it 'stable but not rigid') but others – including Dr John Reid, then the Secretary of State for Scotland – argued that it was to be 'final'.[4] If the Scottish Executive had embarked on a maximalist strategy towards external affairs when this was reserved to Westminster that might have cultivated the impression that it supported the argument that the existing arrangements were temporary and that it was keen for Scotland to attain more autonomy.

Following Dewar's untimely death in the autumn of 2000, Scotland's external relations strategy changed markedly. Mr McLeish, his successor, assigned the portfolio for the EU and external affairs to Jack McConnell who was also responsible for education and Nicol Stephen was to act as his deputy. Within a short while McConnell was calling publicly for greater powers for territorial governments in the EU, whilst Jim Wallace, the deputy First Minister, argued in a speech in Barcelona, that they had to be more closely engaged in EU affairs. During March 2001 the Executive and the Convention of Scottish Local Authorities presented a joint submission to the EU on governance, part of which stated: 'We think it essential that the EU Governance debate addresses the potential for giving a greater role to Scotland and the other regions with legislative powers.' (See appendix, p. 259) It was later announced that Scotland would have its own civil servants in the UK embassy in Washington. This should not be exaggerated as it related primarily to trade and Scottish officials had long been active in the USA – but symbolically it was significant because of its high profile. Likewise McLeish undertook a number of overseas trips where he met the Pope and, as part of the tartan day celebrations, the American President. Following the UK election in June 2001, Robin Cook was replaced by Jack Straw. News reports indicated that there was some alarm in the Scottish Parliament that Scotland's external affairs policy might be circumscribed by London and officials at the Foreign and Commonwealth Office (FCO) stressed that Scotland's participation in the 2004 Intergovernmental Conference (IGC) would be relegated to dovetailing into a pan-UK position.[5] It would seem that by adopting a maximalist approach the Scottish Executive took a step too far.

Whilst there might be limited room for manoeuvre if the same parties were in office in London and Edinburgh, the situation would be markedly different if they were not (e.g. the Conservatives in London and the SNP in Edinburgh). Despite the existence of the Joint Ministerial Committee, the Concordats and the Memorandum of Understanding – all of which are supposed to underpin intergovernmental relations between Edinburgh and London - Scotland's needs might be too divergent from the rest of the UK as far as the EU is concerned.

All in all, Scotland's relations with the European Union could well be one of the issues (another being devolution finance) that unravels the current constitutional settlement in the UK. If that were to happen then legislative devolution may have been little more than a staging post to a completely new arrangement resulting perhaps in a federal UK, or an 'independent' Scotland in the EU or maybe simply an 'independent Scotland' (i.e. akin to Norway or Switzerland). The potential for change in the UK is mirrored at the European level, where the EU itself appears to be in transition from a confederation to a federation (that is if the pro-integrationists get their way at the next Inter-governmental Conference in 2004). As we shall see below, some argue that it is unlikely that Scotland could become a member of the EU if it ceded from the UK. In turn, another way to resolve the pressures of European integration is that aspirations for greater Scottish autonomy could be 'accommodated' in a federal UK which was itself part of a federalised EU – in effect a 'federalised polity'.

**The next step: a federalised polity?**

There are a number of features of a federal polity which suggest Scotland would enjoy more autonomy compared to legislative devolution.

• A federal system constitutionally 'entrenches' the powers of the various tiers of government, whereas legislative devolution was enacted by the Westminster Parliament. In theory Westminster could rescind the Scotland Act if it so chose or suspend legislative devolution (as has occurred from time to time in the North of Ireland).

• A federal system usually ensures that sovereignty is shared between the different tiers of government, whereas under legislative devolution, the Parliament at Westminster maintains that only it is sovereign.

• A federal system usually has a supreme or constitutional court which can adjudicate in the event of constitutional disputes over competence, whereas under legislative devolution as it stands in the UK this is dealt with by the Judicial Committee of the Privy Council, the legitimacy of which is questionable on the grounds of potential bias and the absence of transparency.

Some suggest that a federal system could transform Scotland's situation (Smith, 1995). Instead of the Concordats and the Joint Ministerial Committee, relations between the Scottish and UK Governments would be conducted on a more formal basis. As mentioned above the Concordats are essentially informal devices and the JMC lacks executive powers. They are little more than a continuum of the pragmatic approach which successive governments in the UK have adopted towards Scottish aspirations for more autonomy. In short, they are inherently flawed.

Despite the existence of a Scottish Parliament the relationship between Scotland and the UK is hierarchical with the result that Scotland remains politically dependent on the UK Government. That may not appear contentious. But it is. Pragmatic arrangements *can be* valuable by virtue of the potential for flexibility. However, the *very* fact that there is a measure of in-built flexibility can also be disadvantageous. It ensures that the party in government at Westminster can be pivotal to Scotland's welfare. In the aftermath of legislative devolution, this relates especially to the allocation of financial resources but it also includes relations with the EU and the rest of the world. Prior to Mrs Thatcher's premiership the relationship between Scotland and the UK was pragmatic and it was based primarily on the willingness of both the UK Government and the administratively devolved

Scottish administration to compromise. Scottish ministers were relegated to bargain hunters within the UK polity and the bulk of their lobbying took place behind closed doors in Whitehall. By their intrusion into Scotland's political arena (e.g. the introduction of the poll tax, the weakening of the powers of local government, the creation of quangos) both she and John Major revealed just how little autonomy Scotland really possessed. Consequently, whilst Scots were more hesitant about constitutional change in 1979 they overwhelmingly supported it in 1997.

Under the existing constitutional arrangements there is too much reliance on a government in London that is both willing and able to respond to Scotland's needs. If another party held office that could change. Yet, even Tony Blair's 'devolutionist' credentials are open to challenge on the grounds that the constitutional reform programme related more to winning the 1997 election than assigning more autonomy to Scotland. Would Scottish aspiration for autonomy be resolved by a federal system? Providing a federal arrangement was based on equity between the levels of government in theory this would prevent a UK government from interfering in Scotland's affairs and it would also ensure that Scotland's (relative) autonomy would be secure.

Federal systems are regarded by some as the most propitious forms of government by virtue of their capacity to accommodate territorial diversity. Burgess commented:

'The genius of federation lies in its infinite capacity to accommodate and reconcile the competing and sometimes conflicting array of diversities having political salience within a state. Toleration, respect, compromise, bargaining and mutual recognition are its watchwords and 'union' combined simultaneously with 'autonomy' is its hallmark.' (Burgess and Gagnon, 1993)

Burgess was not alone in referring to compromise; Smith claimed that the federal idea is,

'Generally conceived as a compromise, conveyed by the image of checks and balances between unity and diversity, autonomy and sovereignty, the national and the regional.' (Smith, 1995)

Yet others observed that effective federal systems do not inherently resolve conflict, but instead manage it successfully.

'The success of federal systems is not to be measured in terms of the elimination of social conflicts but instead in their capacity to regulate and manage such conflicts.' (Burgess and Gagnon, 1993)

Gagnon subsequently qualified this with the rider that the capacity of a federal system to protect minority and territorial interests could rest with the willingness of the various parties to 'strike a deal that has the potential to satisfy communities sharing a common territory for the long haul.'

So far so good, but a federal system has its deficiencies too.

If a federal system is to succeed or for that matter if it is even to come into existence a number of preconditions need to be satisfied. First there needs to be some acquiescence on the part of the actors involved that it is desirable – in the words of Elazar (1987) there has to be a 'federally inclined political culture' – effectively one that is committed to 'power sharing', 'political restraint', and 'some orientation towards the involvement of large numbers of people in the political process'. Second, it is likely to be more successful if there is a reasonable balance between the various component parts. In this context, population, landmass and GDP are all relevant: one territorial unit should not be dominant. Third, it can be vulnerable to external forces – for instance, a third country might view it as a threat. Each of these applies if the UK were to become a federal polity.

At the time of writing there does not appear to be any desire on the part of the UK's citizens for a federal polity. To date in Scotland the constitutional debate has focused on union versus independence. England is overwhelmingly larger than the other territories of the UK. A common argument goes along the lines of the inequity of parity with Scotland or Wales or Northern Ireland when the 'English' comprise roughly 85 per cent of the population of the UK. In the context of devolution in England with the regions as units in a federal UK, it is possible to envisage various 'solutions', possibly involving some form of qualified majority voting.

The third potential deficiency referred to above relates to the EU. It may not be a third country as such but it does have the potential to destabilise a federation at the state (UK) level.

Although much was made of a 'Europe of the regions' during the late 1980s much of this is little more than a myth. What we do have is a Europe *with* Regions. In practice, for the most part European integration has the potential to exacerbate intergovernmental relations between the state (i. e. UK) and territorial level. In Scotland's case it extended the chain of communication between decision-makers and citizens and prior to legislative devolution at least, it reduced the extent to which Scottish institutions and organisation could influence public policies which affected Scotland (i.e. those policies which fell under the EU's competence). The reason for this was relatively straightforward; whereas before the UK joined the EU the Scottish administration dealt directly with those who governed the country in London it now had to use the departments in London as a conduit to influence the Council of Ministers in the EU. The same problem applied to federal systems. For example the German *Länder* recognised that as more and more power was assigned to the EU, this impinged on their autonomy. After the Single European Act new mechanisms were agreed between the *Länder* and the Federal Government to ensure that they had a greater say over how the Federal Government voted in the Council of Ministers.

Some considered Germany's co-operative federalism a possible pacesetter for Scotland. The German constitution was amended in 1992 so that the *Länder* would be more directly involved in the Council of Ministers in those areas of policy that applied to their responsibilities. Jeffery suggested that the 'the system is deemed to work satisfactorily'. Others have reservations. One reason is that when deciding on how the Federal Government should respond to a legislative proposal from the EU, the *Länder* vote by simple majority not by unanimity – there is no right of veto. Benz is even more dismissive:

> 'The analysis [...] can also explain why the endeavour of the German *Länder* governments to promote their interest in European institutions are doomed to fail. Not only does such a strategy ignore the divergent objectives of German *Länder*, but it also underestimates the intricacies of the EU's political system. It is simply not possible to transfer the German practice of joint policy-making between federal and *Länder* governments to a system of multi-level governance as is characteristic for the EU.' (Benz in Le Galès and Lequesne, 1998)

Despite Jeffery's earlier assertion concerning the EU and the *Länder*, this perspective rather tallies with the concluding section of his paper, which he entitled 'from co-operative federalism to competitive federalism?' In sum there may now be rather too much competition between the *Länder* for consensual politics and this could well be exacerbated by the EU. If the UK were a federation and the current German model was adopted then Scotland could be outvoted by England in its entirety on EU matters. Moreover, the German experience outlined by Benz, Loughlin and Jeffery raises the question as to whether the relationship would be one of competition rather than co-operation.

Thus, as far as relations with the EU are concerned it is difficult to see whether a federal UK would enhance Scotland's influence in the EU. Influence has tended to be used in favour of the Member States and business. Although the EU did flirt with regionalism for a while in the end it largely rested with each Member State to determine how its territories were represented in the EU. The net result was that the citizens of the EU's territories perceived that they were inadequately represented by their 'national' governments. That could well explain why some *Länder* are calling for entrenchment of the powers of territorial governments in an EU constitution at the next European IGC in 2004 – the underlying aim being to constrain the EU and by default the Member States from subsuming any more of the *Länder's* power.

As far as the 2004 IGC is concerned there is little sign that territorial empowerment is at the forefront of the Member States' plans. In an address at Humboldt University during May 2000, Joschka Fischer, the German Foreign Minister called for a 'European federation'. He observed:

> 'European integration can only be successfully conceived if it is done on the basis of a division of sovereignty between Europe and the nation state. Precisely this is the idea underlying the concept of 'subsidiarity' a subject that is currently being discussed by everyone and understood by virtually no one.'

The paradox could not be more stark – there is no mention of territorial governments. Subsidiarity in this instance relates to the EU/Member State relationship – not with decision-making being devolved to the most appropriate level. The following month, in a speech at the *Bundestag* Jacques Chirac, the president of France affirmed the continuity of the 'national state',

'Neither you nor we are envisaging the creation of a super European state which would supplant our national states and mark the end of their existence as players in international life. Our nations are the source of our identities and our roots. The diversity of their political, cultural and linguistic traditions is one of our Union's strengths. For the peoples who come after us, the nations will remain the first reference points.'

From a French perspective this is relatively straightforward inasmuch as arguably there is only one French nation (the Bretons might disagree), whereas the UK is a multi-nation state. Although Chirac referred to 'clarifying the division of responsibilities between different levels of the European system', there is no reason to suppose that this refers to territorial empowerment. Such a scenario would be unlikely from a French perspective – at the time of writing France is now more centralised than the UK: when Scotland sought membership of a pan-European inter-parliamentary body, allegedly it was blocked by the French.[6] Tony Blair trod a similar path in his speech in Warsaw the following October. Insofar as nation states remained pre-eminent, he rejected any notion that there should be a constitution. He argued instead that there should be a 'statement of principles' – which would not be too far removed from the UK's unwritten constitution, much of which is based on custom and precedent. He called for a second chamber of the European Parliament comprising 'representatives of national parliaments', the task of which would not be to engross itself in the minutiae of legislative scrutiny but to 'help implement the agreed statement of principles.' Although 'national parliament' could include Scotland, the position of the FCO is not encouraging. Scotland belongs in the UK camp: it is not a player in its own right in the EU.

The dilemma confronting the EU's leaders as they themselves acknowledge is that the EU lacks democratic legitimacy. In contrast with the Member States, the EU has a government (Commission) which does not emerge directly from the Parliament elected by the EU's citizens: hence the German calling for a European federation, and Chirac's reference to a pioneer group of Member States forging ahead in closer integration. They have paid scant attention to the EU's regions and stateless nations, which for the most part have been the victims of European integration. The EU itself is at a momentous point in its evolution – Economic and Monetary Union and the next enlargement will have substantive ramifications not only for the Member States but also for its territories. The European Commission itself warned in its Agenda 2000 paper, that in the aftermath of these events some territories would be affected adversely and that there was a risk of 'economic and political tensions'.

In the absence of any substantive reform of the EU which enables them to participate directly in its decision-making it might make more sense for its regions and stateless nations to secede from their state (i.e. the UK), and become states in their own right with a view to joining the EU. So in some respects this represents a pistol to the EU's head. This is reinforced by the fact that more and more states set to join the EU – some of which are smaller geographically and in terms of population than Scotland for example. But if this became something of a landslide what would happen to the existing Member States? It is partially for this reason that some view a federal polity as resolving the conundrum vis-à-vis territorial empowerment, the sovereignty of the Member States as well as the competence of the UK. But as Anderson surmised, would federalism in the UK be little more than an attempt to 'buy off' Scottish independence (Anderson in Smith, 1995) and if it is, will it succeed? He was far from convinced due to the twin tensions of European integration and territorial diversity. He believed that there would be neither a Europe of the Regions nor a fully-fledged European federation comprising the Member States. A more likely scenario was what he termed 'selective confederation', a concept not dissimilar from the Scottish National Party's (SNP) position on EU. This too is based on the continuity of a confederal EU, whereby the states would retain sovereignty. Although that seems increasingly ephemeral as European integration progresses, we will end with a brief analysis of independence in Europe or perhaps even 'independence' as being Scotland's final constitutional destination.

### A final step: Scottish 'independence' in Europe?

'The SNP stands for Scotland in Europe. The Scottish National Party believes that membership of the European Union will give Scotland real advantages. It will secure for Scotland a voice at the heart of Europe, with full membership of the important decision and policy-making bodies.'

As mentioned at the beginning of this chapter the SNP's 'Independence in Europe' campaign has served its purpose in so far as it ensured that the government of the day, first in London, and now in Edinburgh and London had to demonstrate that it could adequately promote and defend Scotland's interests in the EU. As European integration has gathered pace an open-ended commitment to the EU became less realistic for the party and even in the 1990s it maintained that its approach related to a 'confederal' EU - e.g. the Member States must retain a veto. There are two reasons why this is paramount. First the notion that Scotland would be an 'equal partner' in the EU is integral to its European policy – the implication being that the union with England has been fundamentally unequal. Second, if the EU were to become a federation in the sense that it becomes a state in its own right, then there would presumably be more opposition from within the SNP over jumping from one union to another. If the EU were to progress down that road then the SNP may simply opt for another form of independence more on the lines of Norway or Switzerland. If such a strategy were to emerge it would not be alone as the Scottish Socialist Party has already adopted this line.

During the last twelve months a number of scholars have evaluated the consequences of the SNP's policy. In *Scotland's Place in Europe* (2001), Murkens offers the reader a thoughtful and provocative analysis. It starts with the premise that 'Scotland would have the natural right to be a player in Europe' and it then explores whether this would be feasible under international law. It is at this point that the paper's first deficiency is exposed. The author conceded that Scotland would be something of an anomaly if it were to secede from the UK and apply to join the EU, and concluded that it would not automatically be entitled to join. According to Murkens the 'worst case scenario' would be if Scotland 'found itself outside the EU' but in a subsequent section the author acknowledged that this situation would be 'unrealistic'. This epitomises the tenor of what is a circular and rather inconclusive paper. The second flaw relates to Scotland's influence in the EU in the aftermath of devolution, compared to its position post independence. The author makes a series of assertions which are not sustained by sufficient empirical evidence concerning Scotland's influence before, during and potentially after legislative devolution. Rather it focused on the weighting of votes in the Council of Ministers, or the number of MEPs and European Commissioners – this is far too narrow given the characteristics of policy-making in the EU, much of which is based on trans-national bargaining and coalition building within the Council.

Scheiren (2000) ploughed much the same furrow as Murkens in a paper published in *Scottish Affairs*. Once again the emphasis was on the legal aspects of Scotland's application for EU membership. Once more the author argued that were Scotland to choose this path, then the outcome would be dependent on the consent of 'all contracting parties' (i.e. the Member States of the EU). Much the same arguments were aired about whether the Member States would condone the dissolution of the UK because of the possible ramifications for them. This is not the place to assess the 'ins and outs' of independence in Europe *per se*; the response to Murkens and Scheiren merits a more substantive reply than there is space for here.

Nonetheless, there is one fundamental theme that has been at the heart of this chapter. As we have seen, Scotland is not alone in its concern over the potential loss of influence – as Keating observed: 'European integration has posed a series of political and constitutional challenged to regions.' Scotland's interests in the EU can be quite distinct from the rest of the UK and under the existing constitutional arrangement there is no assurance that this will improve. As we have seen the situation for territorial governments in federal systems offers little encouragement and as far as the EU is concerned the current debate about moving from a confederal to a federal polity ignores for the most part the territorial dimension. If that were to come to fruition and if the EU's territories were to be excluded from participating more directly in EU decision-making at the 2004 IGC, then it would be perfectly rational for some of them to secede from their states and apply to join. Scotland, therefore might be no more than one in a line of territories from within the EU opting for 'independence' in Europe.

From a neo-functionalist perspective European integration is the product of collaboration between trans-national political and economic elites. For the most part the EU's citizens have had a minimal impact on its evolution.

When the Irish recently rejected the terms of the Nice Treaty in a referendum, it was apparently viewed by the EU as a minor irritant rather than a major constitutional crisis. As the EU moves from confederation to federation its future stability may well depend on its democratic legitimacy. This can best be constructed from the bottom-up – with citizens as the bedrock. In this context, territorial governments have the potential to act as the EU's building blocks – something that ministers in the Scottish Executive have already implied. Do the EU's leaders have the vision to recognise this and if so will they be willing to allow their territorial governments to participate in the EU as more equal partners? A federal polity could be the last chance saloon before territorial fragmentation; if it is not realised what will become of the EU, not to mention Scotland and the UK?

## Notes

[1] Scottish Office 1997, Cm 3658, Scotland's Parliament, 5.1.

[2] Scottish Office 1997, Cm 3658, Scotland's Parliament, 5.2.

[3] The Scottish Executive (SE) would not normally expect to receive direct approaches from the Commission relating to new policy initiatives. Should it do so, it will inform MAFF as soon as possible of such approaches and will pass on to MAFF its views in good time for them to be taken into account. Equally, SE will provide information on any direct contacts with other Member States or third countries. (Concordat between the Ministry of Agriculture, Fisheries and Food (MAFF) and the Scottish Executive (SE), 1999)

[4] Kenny Farquharson, in *Sunday Times*, 06 August 2000, p. 2.

[5] 'Although Robin Cook encouraged the Scottish Executive's links with the EU during his tenure as foreign secretary, his successor, Jack Straw, has already raised concerns in the Scottish Parliament over the leeway likely to be given to Scotland to build on its links with other European areas.' A Foreign Office spokesman explained to the Sunday Times: 'The intergovernmental conference [in 2004] is a matter for Member States to deal with as Member States, but Scotland will be involved in participating through helping to formulate the UK position.'

[6] The author was informed of this by one of the individuals involved in Scotland's application for membership/observer status.

# 5

# Conclusion and Beyond

# A Summary

## Stanley Henig

Any short summary of the substantive contents of this book is inhibited by two factors. The first relates to the richness of the material, covering as it does a significant part of the current politics of the United Kingdom and its component parts and placing them also into their historic context. The importance of that history is especially underlined in the chapters on Northern Ireland and Scotland. The notion that our constitution is the product of evolution, and in no sense the result of revolution or revolutions, is deeply ingrained. Whatever the other challenges posed by 'New' Labour, a revolutionary overturn of the constitution is not one of them. As demonstrated by the book's contributors, modernisation is an ongoing and evolutionary process: the *revolutionary* strategy of 'immediate action concentrated on one limited but decisive point' (as described in the Schuman declaration, which is often considered the launch-pad for what is now the European Union) remains alien to the British political process. The second factor militating against any pithy summary, let alone a conclusion, flows naturally from this: there is, as yet, no obvious end to the story. This is the reason why the final words in this book are those of Louise Ellman MP.

Evolutionary processes are not necessarily any easier to control than revolutionary. Louise Ellman's visionary voyage is far from being one to an unknown destination. She offers a clear view of a political structure which might operate in 2015. This view may, at one level, be making a virtue out of necessity; what is critical to it is that 'the 'institutional mess' – Ines Newman's graphic phrase – and the diversity described and analysed by many contributors are transformed into being pillars of a new system of governance. Louise Ellman does not actually use the word 'system', but the notion is surely implicit in the 'settled constitutional outcome' postulated.

Such a quintessential New Labour view faces twin challenges, both of which are present in the book although in different forms. They are most starkly expressed in the chapters on Scotland. Jane Saren uses the words of prominent members of the Scottish Labour Party to highlight conflicting possible destinations. Devolution according to Wendy Alexander can be equated to 'modern governance in the information age' and indeed most of Saren's chapter is devoted to describing what we might term the new political system in Scotland – substantial home rule but still very much a part of the United Kingdom. By way of contrast Saren also quotes Tam Dalyell's scathing description of devolution as a 'motorway with one exit'. As is so often the case with such graphic phrases, they are evocative rather than strictly accurate. Motorway exits are mostly onto other roads and they usually offer a choice of directions: such possibilities are explored in Alex Wright's chapter. Tam Dalyell himself comes from a very different school of thought.

This book is about the process of modernisation. The concentration is on the essence of devolution and its major features. It cannot deal in detail with all the related political battles involved, although – particularly in the case of Northern Ireland – it is certainly impossible to ignore them completely. Amongst a shoal of complexities in the chapter by Elizabeth Meehan we come across the concept of 'pro-' and 'anti-' agreement parties. The latter, largely drawn from the unionist community, share Dalyell's fears. Instinctively they might want to go back – were that only possible – to the Stormont regime prior to its suspension in the 1960s. In the real world this probably puts them into the anti-devolution camp and in this sense they can be considered alongside potential 'allies' in both Scotland and Wales. Barry Jones reminds us of the closeness of the referendum contest in Wales, where there had not previously been a clear historical pattern to 'demands for devolution, still less for independence'. On the other hand if he ends with the assertion that the 'devolution settlement is not yet finalised', he finds little to suggest that it will actually be reversed.

The Conservative Party has become the great champion of a single unified Great Britain and has played a leading role in the anti-devolution camp in Scotland, Wales and the English regions. In the 1997 general election the Conservatives won no seats in either Scotland or Wales (four years later they won just one seat in Scotland) and only a handful in those northernmost regions of England most favourable to some form of devolution. Scotland, Wales and Northern England between them elect around two fifths of members of the House of Commons (274 out of 659). In 1997 just 17 of the 274 were Conservative and in 2001 the number only rose to 18. Back in 1970 when the Conservatives last won a close electoral contest, they captured more than a third of the seats in what might be termed 'the peripheries' (Scotland, Wales and the three northern regions of England). Conservative attitudes to devolution are clearly not the sole reason for this electoral collapse, but they go hand in hand with a popularly perceived failure to identify with those parts of the UK. It is easy enough to point to inherent political instability in new constitutional arrangements which technically can always be withdrawn by Westminster when they are juxtaposed with a situation in which one of the two major parties is opposed to devolution. In terms of real politics this latent instability is more likely to be ended by a change in Conservative policy than by a unilateral Westminster decision to end devolution. Going back in history to the Great Reform Act (if not earlier) that is, of course, precisely the way in which constitutional evolution has always operated in the UK.

Motorway exits remain part of the debate on both Scotland and Northern Ireland. Alex Wright looks at the possible options for Scotland in its future relations with both the rest of the United Kingdom (although he is primarily concerned in this context with England) and with Europe. Federalism and federal thought are major features of his analysis. In Northern Ireland the majority in the nationalist camp has dropped the use of force as a means of unification with the Republic. Insofar as this remains a political goal, its future attainment depends on a combination of democratic choice, the impact of the European Union and, perhaps, demographic change.

The settlement in Northern Ireland is, of course, underpinned in a different way from those in Scotland and Wales. Devolution with its plethora of special constitutional arrangements was a means of resolving sectarian conflict. In effect the settlement is underpinned by international agreement with another sovereign state, reached through the good offices of a third. Institutionalisation of the North-South Ministerial Council and the British-Irish Intergovernmental Conference are permanent reminders that this devolved settlement legitimated a limitation on 'Queen in Parliament'. The variety of new institutions and their complex inter-twining also introduce another feature. It is impossible not to look at them and note the similarities with avowedly federal structures elsewhere: Belgium – another country with sectarian conflict – is the obvious parallel. In introducing his chapter on the 'English question' John Tomaney points to the difficulties inherent in any schematic federal constitution for the United Kingdom. Nonetheless the British-Irish Council is nothing if not an embryonic federal type institution.

If devolution is, at least in practice, irreversible for Northern Ireland, Scotland and Wales, the jury is still 'out' for the English regions. John Tomaney and Ines Newman describe ongoing developments and write in expectation that the northern 'peripheries' will gain the opportunity to elect assemblies and with them some rights of control through accountability. Thus far or any further? For the immediate future Alan Whitehead, a Government Minister in the DLTR, suggests two qualifications to the spread of devolution envisaged by Louise Ellman. The English regions must opt for it in some kind of referendum and they must already have a 'predominantly unitary form of local government'. He offers no definition of 'predominantly'. However, it is hard in practice to envisage exclusion on these grounds of the North West region where unitary local government covers two thirds of the population but only a small proportion of the geographic area. My own chapter on local government points to some ambivalence in attitudes, not incompatible with the statesmanlike introduction by Jeremy Beecham, Chairman of the LGA. Meanwhile there is not the slightest evidence of any governmental desire to re-open the 'can of worms' labelled reform of local government! Partial resolution of the institutional mess may be a legitimate expectation of the White Paper and subsequent legislation, but some muddle may remain. Baron Isherwood's chapter has a relatively narrow focus on the inter-relationship between RDAs and GORs: it suggests that the machinery of government is far from being attuned to the constitutional reality of modernisation. The report by the Performance Innovation Unit (PIU) of the Cabinet Office lends support to this view.

London as ever stands slightly apart from the rest of England. Alex Bax reminds us that its boundaries are hardly compatible with contemporary economic realities. Indeed it is hard to see quite how London fits into the regional map of England. In effect it is a city region with tentacles that go well beyond the defined geographic boundaries. If London is indeed in reality a city region it presumably has to be cut to size for the sake of the rest of England and especially the South East and Home Counties. Even so, London's boundaries still cause all kinds of complications for adjacent regions. Rail travellers on the West Coast main line may have time for reflection on journeys to the capital, but it is doubtful if their thoughts often stray to the logic of regional boundaries. Were they to do so, they might find it odd that when they reach Milton Keynes they are – still fifty miles North West of London - temporarily in the South East region. Milton Keynes is perhaps itself the ultimate frontier town: West Midlands, East Midlands, East of England and South East regions all meet. Thereafter the railway proceeds more or less along a straight line to London – only it passes en route through part of the Eastern region. Immediately after the 1997 election John Prescott - then Secretary of State at the DETR and now as Deputy Prime Minister still retaining overlordship for regional devolution in England - was explicit that the process would not be delayed by any attempts to re-open boundary issues. It follows that all of Cumbria is in the North West, even though the northern parts of the county identify far more strongly with the North East; the South West region stretches from Lands End to the Warwickshire border and its boundary with the South East resembles the proverbial 'line in the sand' whereby colonies were once demarcated. Potential implications for referenda voting have been ignored.

We in Britain like to think of ourselves as different and it is certainly the case that some of our constitutional procedures can only be described as *sui generis* – literally one of a kind of which there is only one. But I am not sure that devolution fits into this categorisation. Wilfried Swenden accepts the basic differences between devolution and federalism, but he also shows how the short British experience to date fits into the European mainstream.

Devolution in Spain and Belgium means 'asymmetric devolution' which may offer rather more to the spin doctors than 'institutional mess'. Swenden is another who visualises devolution as a first step towards conceding more regional autonomy. He also links the process to membership of the European Union. The chapters by Alan Butt Philip and Ines Newman demonstrate the extent to which the dynamics of the Union are a powerful additional force behind the devolution process. John Major's half-way house of Government Offices of the Regions accountable only to central government could not ultimately satisfy the European imperative for regional partners.

One of the objects of this book is to look at the extent to which federal thinking has played, or might in future play, a role in the devolution process. There is no single federal model; rather, federalism is a way of thinking and a mode of organisation. A provisional judgement can be made on the basis – as indicated in the introduction – that federalism is about the dispersal of political power, and particularly the division of constitutional competences between different tiers of government and its entrenchment.

Political power in the United Kingdom has become more dispersed. Irritation on the part of Westminster politicians with political decisions made in Cardiff or Edinburgh offers a kind of reverse proof as do, in a rather different way, the concerns expressed by the authors of the PIU report. At a technical constitutional level the Northern Ireland, Wales and Scotland settlements are reversible by Westminster fiat, but not in the world of real politics. In that sense national devolution is entrenched and its detail can only be altered by mutual agreement. The dispersal of power is reinforced by proportional representation, also used in London. Such voting methods militate against single party control of the executive: to that extent they are part of the programme of power dispersal.

Few constitutional experts would describe our current political state as 'Federal Britain in a Federal Europe'. Despite New Labour's commitments to both strengthened European integration and regional devolution, its architects would probably consider the concept as little more than a flight of fantasy when described in such words. Nonetheless many of the ingredients for a 'Federal Britain in a Federal Europe' are in place, and there is, indeed, as yet no certain end to the story.

# Looking Forward
## *Reuniting politics and economics*

## Louise Ellman MP

Labour has long advocated regional government though its leaders have become adept at avoiding commitment to the implementation of this potentially major constitutional change. Following the setting up of the Scottish Parliament and the Welsh Assembly, not to mention the GLA and Northern Ireland Assembly, it may at last be the turn of the English regions. A White Paper, due early in 2002, could be followed by referenda, where requested by individual regions, with elected assemblies established within the lifetime of this parliament.

The UK's regionalism has both economic and political strands. The dysfunctional nature of the British economy in the 1980s with its overheating in the South East and de-population of the North made the case for regional economic regeneration self-evident. The independent, but party-supported, Millan Commission made a strong case for the Regional Development Agencies as instruments of economic regeneration. Implemented by the Labour Government in 1999, these are already making an impact.

Government appointed RDAs were not matched at the time by structures of political accountability, although the mainly indirectly elected regional assemblies partially fill the vacuum. Neither was the yawning democratic deficit, posed by the increasingly powerful regional quangos, resolved. Political regionalism was moving more slowly than its economic arm.

Prior to the 1997 election, Labour produced a document entitled *A Choice for England* which set out the case for elected regional assemblies but created a formidable hurdle by stipulating that before any progress could be made, England should have a unitary system of local government. To those still smarting from the attention of the Banham Commission, this was a potentially fatal blow to devolution's progress.

However there were a number of changes during Labour's first term of office which have changed the political landscape.

First, the successful negotiation of devolution to Scotland and Wales has created a justifiable feeling that devolution should be an option for the regions of England, with the Northern regions being most vocal in this call. Second, the establishment of the Greater London Authority, while not strictly devolution, has reawakened concerns about London's dominance. Third, the uncompleted reform of the House of Lords has recognised the legitimacy of regional representation with the Government's limited proposals for direct elections focused on regional representatives. Fourth, the concept of a 'Europe of the Regions' has been progressing as Europe introduces notions of subsidiarity. The pattern of democratically accountable regions managing substantial devolved services and strategies is now firmly established among European states. The Committee of the Regions is a serious pole of political influence in the making of regional decisions in Europe. The absence of regions in England that can pull equal weight with their continental counterparts looks increasingly problematic. Finally, the overall theme of much of Labour's agenda of constitutional reform has been about accountability. Devolution in the 1980s and early 90s was strictly administrative: integrated government offices represented government in the regions, not the regions in Whitehall.

Meanwhile the strength of feeling in the English regions about the democratic deficit has grown deeper as the still extensive quango state persists. Labour has been consistent in its devolutionary message: what has changed over recent years is the pressure to act. In Labour's 2001 manifesto, the commitment was repeated:

'[...] In 1997 we said that provision should be made for directly elected regional government to go ahead in regions where people decided in a referendum to support it and where predominantly unitary local government is established. That remains our commitment.'

The changed political landscape between 1997 and 2001 has allowed Labour to bring together once again economic and political regionalism, recognising the overwhelming logic of marrying the two aspects into a stable and workable outcome.

Obstacles to implementation remain. The long-standing debate about whether regions need to be created simultaneously is resolved in the manifesto. Democratic regional government will be introduced over an extended period of time, probably becoming established first in the North of England, where support is strongest, although this is also growing in the South West. The potential difficulty of uneven development is resolved because there is now in place an effective system of Regional Development Agencies, streamlined government offices and some degree of indirect accountability through regional assemblies. It will be possible, therefore, to live with a patchwork of regional powers, for an extended period.

The formula that is likely to be adopted is a period where regions establish a popular will for a transition to democratically accountable institutions through affirmative referenda and then move to establish directly elected assemblies. The decision on whether these will follow a 25 member GLA strategic type model concentrating on economic development, arts, transport, environment, and planning or be closer to the powers of the Welsh Assembly is yet to be resolved.

A key role of regional assemblies will be to guide and plan the work of the development agencies. Indeed, the more advanced the work of the Agencies, the more issues of demonstrative accountability become pre-eminent. One clear example is the question of regional planning. The devolved bodies must, at a minimum, absorb or oversee quangos and take powers from Whitehall. They must work in tandem with strong local government.

The manifesto condition that regional government can occur only where 'predominantly unitary local government is established' could remain a second obstacle. These words represent a departure from the original hard line of the *A Choice for England* document in 1995, but still present a challenge. Four regions already possess 'predominantly unitary' local government, and therefore 'qualify' as they stand: but they might still consider reorganisation following the successful establishment of assemblies. In other parts of the country, establishing at least the architecture for possible reorganisation may well be required for any affirmative referendum. The defining consideration will probably rest on service provision. Shire or District could become the unitary.

So what might we contemplate for the year 2015? Early successful referenda could create the impetus for regional devolution, just as the Scottish Parliament has raised the debate in the North of England. We might, by 2015, see a settled constitutional outcome based on positive consent: across England, democratically accountable regional government enjoying powers that are substantial though not necessarily identical to those in Wales, Scotland or London. This will ensure that many of the regional functions not clearly accountable will become the responsibility of an assembly regularly asked to submit to a renewed mandate and led by regional figures able to act as champions and entrepreneurs for their regions. It also means that national decision-taking would have to take much more explicit account of regional interests. In short we would achieve normalisation of a method of governance which is not centralised at Westminster and Whitehall and which includes strong political players not reliant on London for their clout. This in itself would add weight to the already emerging ability of regions to enhance the running of their economies. It would be indeed the uniting of economic and political regionalism. That would be good for the national economy. Beyond that the emergence of strong and accountable regional bodies would be a boost for national politics. It would place decision-making and transparency at appropriate levels for participation and delivery. A political system that achieves this will only gain in strength.

# Appendices

# Scotland

| | |
|---|---|
| Population | 5.1 million |

## The Scottish Parliament

| | | |
|---|---|---|
| Number of members | 129 | |
| Current composition | 55 Scottish Labour Party | 1 Scottish Green Party |
| | 35 Scottish National Party | 1 Scottish Socialist |
| | 19 Scottish Conservative and Unionist Party | 1 Independent |
| | | 1 Presiding Officer |
| | 16 Scottish Liberal Democrats | |
| Voting System | Additional Member System | |
| | 73 members by First-past-the-post | |
| | 56 members by regional lists | |
| Committees | Audit | Local Government |
| | Education, Culture and Sport | Procedures |
| | Enterprise and Lifelong Learning | Public Petitions |
| | | Rural Development |
| | Equal Opportunities | Social Justice |
| | European | Standards |
| | Finance | Subordinate legislation |
| | Health and Community Care | Transport and the Environment |
| | Justice 1 | |
| | Justice 2 | Private Bills Committee |
| Budget | £16.7 billion | |
| Legislative powers | Primary and secondary legislative powers | |
| Tax-raising powers | Power to vary basic rates of income tax and business rates (by approx. 3 pence per pound) | |
| Devolved policy areas | Agriculture, Forestry and Fishing | Local Government |
| | Economic Development, Planning and Financial Assistance to Industry | Natural and Built Heritage |
| | | Police and Fire Services |
| | | Social Work |
| | Education and Training | Sports and Arts |
| | Environment | Statistics, Public Registers and Records |
| | Health | |
| | Housing | Tourism |
| | Law and Home Affairs (most aspects of criminal and civil law, the prosecution system and the courts) | Transport (Scottish road network, bus policy and ports and harbours) |

## The Scottish Executive

| | |
|---|---|
| Head | First Minister |
| | nominated by the Parliament; apppoints ministers |

| | | |
|---|---|---|
| Ministers and departments | Deputy First Minster and Minister for Justice | Finance and Public Services |
| | Education and Young People | Health and Community Care |
| | Enterprise, Transport and Lifelong Learning | Parliamentary Business |
| | | *Law Officers:* |
| | Environment and Rural Development | Lord Advocate |
| | Tourism, Culture and Sport | Solicitor General for Scotland |
| | Social Justice | |

## History

| | |
|---|---|
| White Paper | *Scotland's Parliament*, July 1997 |
| Referendum | 11 September 1997 |
| | turnout 60.4% |
| | Yes votes for Scottish Parliament 74.3% |
| | Yes votes for tax-raising powers 63.5% |
| Parliamentary Act | Scotland Act, November 1998 |
| First election | 6 May 1999 |
| First sitting | 12 May 1999 |
| Official opening | 1 July 1999 |

## The region in Europe

| | |
|---|---|
| Number of MEPs | 8 |
| Number of CoR members | 4 |
| The Scottish Parliament and Europe | 1 MSP is a CoR member |
| | European committee hears evidence from MEPs |
| Office in Brussels | *Scotland House*, including: |
| | Scotland Europa, the Scottish Executive EU Office, Convention of Scottish Local Authorities (CoSLA), the Highlands and Islands European Partnership and several other offices from both public and private sector |
| | 36 staff, 9 for the Scottish Executive |
| | since 1992; Scottish Executive Office since 1999 |

# Wales

| | |
|---|---|
| Population | 2.9 million |

## The National Assembly for Wales

| | |
|---|---|
| Number of members | 60 |
| Current composition | 28 Labour |
| | 17 Plaid Cymru |
| | 9 Conservatives |
| | 6 Liberal Democrats |
| Voting System | Additional Member System |
| | 40 members by First-past-the-post |
| | 20 members by regional lists |

Committees

*Subject Committees:*
Economic Development
Culture
Education and Lifelong Learning
Agriculture and Rural Development
Health and Social Services
Environment, Planning and Transport
Local Government and Housing

*Regional Committees:*
North Wales
Mid Wales
South Wales
South East Wales

*Standing Committees:*
Audit
Legislation
Equal Opportunities
European Affairs
Standards of Conduct

*Committees which meet in private:*
Business
Planning Decision
House

| | |
|---|---|
| Budget | £8.5 billion |
| Legislative powers | Secondary legislative powers, no primary legislation |
| Tax-raising powers | No |

Devolved policy areas

Agriculture
Ancient Monuments and Historic Buildings
Culture
Economic Development
Education and Training
Environment
Health and Health Services
Highways

Housing
Industry
Local Government
Social Services
Sport and Leisure
Tourism
Town and Country Planning
Transport and Roads
WelshLanguage

## The Executive

| | |
|---|---|
| Head | First Minister |
| Ministers and departments | Culture, Sports and the Welsh Language / Finance, Local Government and Communities<br>Education and Lifelong Learning / Health and Social Services<br>Assembly Business / Rural Affairs<br>Environment |

Ministers and departments:

Culture, Sports and the Welsh Language  
Education and Lifelong Learning  
Assembly Business  
Environment  

Finance, Local Government and Communities  
Health and Social Services  
Rural Affairs

## History

| | |
|---|---|
| White Paper | *A Voice for Wales*, July 1997 |
| Referendum | 18 September 1997<br>turnout 50.3%<br>Yes votes 50.6% |
| Parliamentary Act | Government of Wales Act 1998 |
| First election | 6 May 1999 |
| First meeting | 12 May 1999 |
| Designation | 1 July 1999 |

## The region in Europe

| | |
|---|---|
| Number of MEPs | 5 |
| Number of CoR members | 1 |
| The Welsh Assembly and Europe | 1 Assembly member is CoR member<br>MEPs and CoR members are invited to meetings of European Affairs Committee |
| Office in Brussels | *Brussels Office of the Assembly*<br>since September 2000, 3 staff<br>*Wales European Centre* represents over 70 public bodies, including:<br>the Welsh Assembly, the Welsh Development Agency, the Welsh Local Government Association, local government, further and higher education institutions, social partners, environmental organisations etc.<br>since 1992 |

# Northern Ireland

| | |
|---|---|
| Population | 1.7 million |

## The Northern Ireland Assembly

| | |
|---|---|
| Number of members | 108 |

| | | |
|---|---|---|
| Current composition | 28 Ulster Unionist Party | 3 United Unionist Assembly Party |
| | 24 Social Democratic and Labour Party | 2 Northern Ireland Women's Coalition |
| | 20 Democratic Unionist Party | |
| | 18 Sinn Féin | 2 Progressive Unionist Party |
| | 6 The Alliance Party | 1 UK Unionist Party |
| | 3 Northern Ireland Unionist Party | 1 Independent Unionist |

| | |
|---|---|
| Voting System | Single Transferable Vote |
| Committees | Chairmen and Deputy Chairmen allocated using d'Hondt system |

| *Statutory Committees:* | Health, Social Services and Public Safety |
|---|---|
| Agriculture and Rural Development | Regional Development |
| Culture, Arts and Leisure | Social Development |
| Education | *Standing Committees:* |
| Employment and Learning | Procedures |
| Enterprise, Trade and Investment | Business |
| Environment | Committee of the Centre |
| Finance and Personnel | Public Accounts |
| | Committee on Standards and Privileges |

| | |
|---|---|
| Budget | £5.7 billion |
| Legislative powers | Full legislative and executive powers |
| Tax-raising powers | No |

| Devolved policy areas | Agriculture | Health |
|---|---|---|
| | Culture, Arts and Leisure | Local Administration |
| | Education | Rural, Regional and Social Development |
| | Enterprise, Trade, Investment | |
| | Environment | Social Services |
| | Housing | Training and Employment |

## The Executive

| | |
|---|---|
| Head | First Minister |
| Ministers and departments | Executive Committee selected by Assembly using d'Hondt system |

| | |
|---|---|
| Agriculture and Rural Development | Environment |
| Culture, Arts and Leisure | Finance and Personnel |
| Education | Health, Social Services and Public Safety |
| Employment and Learning | Regional Development |
| Enterprise, Trade and Investment | Social Development |

## History

| | |
|---|---|
| White Paper | *Good Friday Agreement*, 10 April 1998 |
| Referendum | 22 May 1998 turnout 81.1% yes votes 71.1% |
| Parliamentary Act | Northern Ireland Act 1998 |
| First election | 25 June 1998 |
| First meeting | 1 July 1998 |
| Designation | Powers were devolved to the Northern Ireland Assembly on 2 December 1999 |

## The region in Europe

| | |
|---|---|
| Number of MEPs | 3 |
| Number of CoR members | 3 |
| The Northern Ireland Assembly and Europe | 1 Assembly member is CoR member |
| Office in Brussels | *Office of the Northern Ireland Executive in Brussels* since March 2001, 4 staff *Northern Ireland Centre in Europe* Partnership of economic and social interests, including local councils, trade unions, private and voluntary sector organisations |

# London

| | |
|---|---|
| Population | 7.1 million |
| Area covered (boroughs) | Barking & Dagenham, Barnet, Bexley, Brent, Bromley, Camden, Croydon, Ealing, Greenwich, Hackney, Hammersmith & Fulham, Haringey, Harrow, Havering, Hillingdon, Hounslow, Islington, Kensington & Chelsea, Kingston, Lambeth, Lewisham, Merton, Newham, Redbridge, Richmond, Southwark, Sutton, Tower Hamlets, Wandsworth, Westminster, Corporation of London |

## The London Assembly

| | |
|---|---|
| Number of members | 25 |
| Current composition | 9 Labour |
| | 9 Conservatives |
| | 4 Liberal Democrats |
| | 3 Green |
| Voting System | Additional Member System |
| | 14 members by First-past-the-post |
| | 11 members by regional list |

| | | |
|---|---|---|
| Committees | Appointments | Transport Operations Scrutiny |
| | Audit panel | Transport Policy and Spatial |
| | Budget | Development Policy Planning |
| | Economic Development | Short Term Scrutiny |
| | Environment | Investigations |
| | Scrutiny Management | |
| | Standards | |

| | |
|---|---|
| Number of staff | 550 |
| Competences | Veto on budget |
| | Scrutiny of Mayor |
| | Appointment of Chief Executive and other senior staff |
| | Development of proposals |
| | Provide members for functional bodies |

| | | |
|---|---|---|
| Main areas of responsibility | Transport | Planning |
| | Policing | Culture |
| | Fire and Emergency Planning | Environment |
| | Economic Development | Health |

## The Mayor

| | |
|---|---|
| Voting system | Directly elected by Supplementary Vote |
| Cabinet | Advisory cabinet of 21 members (Assembly members and others) |

| | | |
|---|---|---|
| Responsibilities | Propose budget | Develop *Strategies*: |
| | Appoint members to TfL, MPA, LDA, LFEPA* | Air Quality |
| | | Ambient Noise |
| | General power of competence | Culture |
| | | London Development Agency |
| | | Transport |
| | | Spatial Development |
| | | Biodiversity Action Plan |
| | | Waste Management |

## The GLA budget

| | | |
|---|---|---|
| Total | £3.7 million | |
| Breakdown | GLA | £36.2 million |
| | TfL | £781.3 million |
| | LDA | £308.4 million |
| | MPA | £2258.3 million |
| | LFEPA | £351.4 million |
| Funding | Government grant, tax precept on council tax, income from congestion charges (in planning) | |

## History

| | |
|---|---|
| White Paper | *A Mayor and Assembly for London*, March 1998 |
| Referendum | 7 May 1998 |
| | turnout 34.6% |
| | yes votes 72% |
| Parliamentary Act | Greater London Authority Act, November 1999 |
| First election | 4 May 2000 |
| Designation of Assembly and Mayor | 3 July 2000 |

## The region in Europe

| | |
|---|---|
| Number of MEPs | 10 |
| Number of CoR members | 3 |
| The London Assembly and Europe | 1 Assembly members is CoR member |
| Office in Brussels | *London House Brussels* |
| | financed by GLA and partner organisations (TfL, LDA, LFEPA and London Health Authorities) |
| | includes Office of Association of London Government |
| | since November 2001, 5 staff |

| | |
|---|---|
| * TfL | Transport for London |
| MPA | Metropolitan Police Authority |
| LDA | London Development Agency |
| LFEPA | London Fire and Emergency Planning Agency |

# East of England

| | |
|---|---|
| Population | 5.5 million |
| Area covered | Bedfordshire, Cambridgeshire, Essex, Hertfordshire, Norfolk, Suffolk, Luton, Peterborough, Southend-on-Sea, Thurrock |

## Regional Assembly

| | |
|---|---|
| Number of members | 42 |
| Composition (local authorities : other stakeholders) | 28:14 |
| Sub-committees | Regional Planning, Europe, Health and Social Inclusion, Liaison with RDA |
| Number of staff | No own staff, Local Government Conference staff works for Assembly |
| Number of meetings per year | 4 plenary, 4 committees |
| Venue | Assembly meetings rotate Secretariat in Bury St. Edmunds |
| Regional Planning Guidance | No, the Regional Planning Body is the Local Government Conference |
| Budget | No own budget other than the £500k government grant |
| Funding | Partner organisations make sources available; government grant |
| Date of formation | 12 March 1999 |
| Date of designation | 21 July 1999 |

## The region in Europe

| | |
|---|---|
| Number of MEPs | 8 |
| Number of CoR members | 2 |
| The Assembly and Europe | Europe Panel (EERA and EEDA*) |
| | Brussels Office Senior Management Team (EERA, EEDA, TECs & CCTEs, GO-East*) |
| | Quarterly MEP briefings by EEDA |
| Office in Brussels | *East of England European Partnership* (EEDA, EERA, EELGC, TECs & CCTEs) managed by EELGC |
| | *Essex International* |

| | |
|---|---|
| * EEDA | East of England Development Agency |
| EERA | East of England Regional Assembly |
| EELGC | East of England Local Government Conference |
| TECs | Training and Enterprise Councils |
| CCTEs | Chamber of Commerce Training & Enterprise |
| GO-East | Government Office for the East of England |

# East Midlands

| | |
|---|---|
| Population | 4.2 million |
| Area covered | Derbyshire, Nottinghamshire, Lincolnshire, Leicestershire, Rutland, Northamptonshire |

## Regional Assembly

| | |
|---|---|
| Number of members | 105 |
| Composition (local authorities : other stakeholders) | 70:35 |
| Sub-committees | Steering Group, Integrated Regional Strategy Policy Forum, *Task Groups*: Energy, Environment, Housing, Lifelong Learning, Public Health, Social Inclusion, Transport, European Strategy Forum |
| Number of staff | No own staff, secondments from regional LGA and other member organisations |
| Number of meetings per year | 3 plenary |
| Venue | Assembly meetings rotate Secretariat in Melton Mowbray |
| Regional Planning Guidance | No, overall responsibility is with LGA, but regional planning has been the spatial theme of the Assembly's Integrated Regional Strategy since 17 September 1999 |
| Budget | No own budget other than the £500k government grant |
| Funding | Partner organisations make sources available; government grant |
| Date of formation | 17 December 1998 |
| Date of designation | 18 May 1999 |

## The region in Europe

| | |
|---|---|
| Number of MEPs | 6 |
| Number of CoR members | 1 |
| The Assembly and Europe | All 6 MEPs are members of the Assembly 1 future CoR member will be Assembly member |
| Office in Brussels | *East Midlands Regional European Office* since 1992 funded by local authorities and other organisations Secretariat provided by EMLGA* |

*EMLGA    East Midlands Local Government Association

# North East

| | |
|---|---|
| Population | 2.6 million |
| Area covered | Northumberland, Tyne & Wear, Durham, Tees Valley |

## Regional Assembly

| | |
|---|---|
| Number of members | 63 |
| Composition (local authorities : other stakeholders) | 44:19 |
| Sub-committees | Executive Committee, *Fora*: Inclusivity, Promotion of the North East, Regional Development, Social Issues |
| Number of staff | 12 |
| Number of meetings per year | 2 plenary, 4 Executive Committee |
| Venue | Assembly meetings rotate<br>Secretariat and Executive Committee meetings in Newcastle |
| Regional Planning Guidance | Yes, but only local authority members vote |
| Budget | £861k, plus £500k government grant |
| Funding | Subscriptions, mainly from local authorities, some from other partners; government grant |
| Date of formation | 1 April 1999 |
| Date of designation | 22 June 1999 |

## The region in Europe

| | |
|---|---|
| Number of MEPs | 7 |
| Number of CoR members | 1 |
| The Assembly and Europe | 1 MEP and 1 CoR member are Assembly members |
| Office in Brussels | *North of England Office*<br>Core Partners are: Association of North East Councils (regional LGA) and OneNorthEast (RDA for North East)<br>since 1992 |

# North West

| | |
|---|---|
| Population | 6.9 million |
| Area covered | Cumbria, Lancashire, Greater Manchester, Merseyside, Cheshire |

## Regional Assembly

| | |
|---|---|
| Number of members | 80 |
| Composition (local authorities : other stakeholders) | 56:24 |
| Sub-committees | Planning, Environment and Transport, European Affairs, Knowledge Economy, Economy and Society |
| Number of staff | 15 |
| Number of meetings per year | 4 plenary |
| Venue | Assembly meetings rotate Secretariat in Wigan |
| Regional Planning Guidance | Yes, but final decision by local authority members only (=regional LGA) |
| Budget | Approx. £1 million, plus £500k government grant |
| Funding | Local authority subscriptions; government grant |
| Date of formation | 3 July 1998 |
| Date of designation | 19 May 1999 |

## The region in Europe

| | |
|---|---|
| Number of MEPs | 10 |
| Number of CoR members | 2 |
| The Assembly and Europe | MEPs and CoR members report to Assembly |
| Office in Brussels | *North West Regional Assembly/ North West Development Agency Office* <br> Also offices from Cheshire, Lancashire, Greater Manchester and Merseyside councils |

# South East

| | |
|---|---|
| Population | 8 million |
| Area covered | Berkshire, Buckinghamshire, East and West Sussex, Hampshire, Isle of Wight, Kent, Oxfordshire, Surrey |

## Regional Assembly

| | |
|---|---|
| Number of members | 111 |
| Composition (local authorities : other stakeholders) | 74:37 |
| Sub-committees | Regional Planning, Health, Europe, Sustainable Development |
| Number of staff | 12 |
| Number of meetings per year | 3 plenary, 8 executive, 3 Regional Planning |
| Venue | Assembly meetings rotate Secretariat in Guildford |
| Regional Planning Guidance | Yes, since April 2001 |
| Budget | £1.2 million, plus £500k government grant |
| Funding | Local authority subscriptions; government grant |
| Date of formation | 20 January 1999 |
| Date of designation | 21 July 1999 |

## The region in Europe

| | |
|---|---|
| Number of MEPs | 11 |
| Number of CoR members | 3 |
| The Assembly and Europe | Joint Assembly/ SEEDA* Europe Committee (JEC) to which CoR members are invited |
| | Regular meetings between JEC chairs and MEPs |
| Office in Brussels | *South East England House*, including: |
| | Hampshire/ Isle of Wight/ West Sussex Partnership, Kent Partnership, East Sussex/ Surrey/ Brighton&Hove Partnership; joint representative for SEEDA and Assembly; Partnership of Thames Valley local authorities |

*SEEDA          South East England Development Agency

# South West

| | |
|---|---|
| Population | 4.8 million |
| Area covered | Avon, Cornwall, Devon, Dorset, Gloucestershire, Somerset, Wiltshire, Isles of Scilly |

## Regional Assembly

| | |
|---|---|
| Number of members | 117 |
| Composition (local authorities : other stakeholders) | 83:34 |
| Sub-committees | Executive Committee, Planning Policy Advisory Group, Transport, Regional Economic Strategy, Waste, European and International Vision Group |
| Number of staff | 12 |
| Number of meetings per year | 3 plenary, 4 executive |
| Venue | Assembly meetings in Devon County Hall, Exeter Secretariat in Taunton |
| Regional Planning Guidance | Yes, since July 2001, but only local authority members vote |
| Budget | £600k, plus £500k government grant |
| Funding | Local authority subscriptions; government grant |
| Date of formation | 2 July 1998 |
| Date of designation | July 1999 |

## The region in Europe

| | |
|---|---|
| Number of MEPs | 7 |
| Number of CoR members | 2 |
| The Assembly and Europe | MEPs and CoR members report to Assembly in plenary meetings |
| Office in Brussels | *South West UK Brussels Office* funded by local authorities |

# West Midlands

| | |
|---|---|
| Population | 5.3 million |
| Area covered | Birmingham, Black Country, Worcestershire & Herefordshire, Shropshire & Telford, Staffordshire & Stoke, Warwickshire, Coventry & Solihull |

## Regional Assembly

| | |
|---|---|
| Number of members | 100 |
| Composition (local authorities : other stakeholders) | 68:32 |
| Sub-committees | No standing committees, but time-limited task groups; European Policy Forum |
| Number of staff | No own staff, secretariat from WMLGA*, also support from other member organisations |
| Number of meetings per year | 3, plus Annual Conference |
| Venue | Assembly meetings rotate Secretariat in Birmingham |
| Regional Planning Guidance | No, only advice and endorsment to WMLGA |
| Budget | Virtually no budget other than the £500k government grant |
| Funding | Sustained by WMLGA and other member organisations; government grant |
| Date of formation | 28 January 1999 |
| Date of designation | 22 April 1999 |

## The region in Europe

| | |
|---|---|
| Number of MEPs | 8 |
| Number of CoR members | 2 |
| The Assembly and Europe | 1 MEP per political party is co-opted Assembly member; future CoR member will be Assembly member |
| Office in Brussels | *Birmingham & West Midlands Office* funded by Birmingham Council and WMLGA |

*WMLGA    West Midlands Local Government Association

# Yorkshire & Humberside

| | |
|---|---|
| Population | 5.1 million |
| Area covered | North Yorkshire, West Yorkshire, South Yorkshire, Humberside |

## Regional Assembly

| | |
|---|---|
| Number of members | 35 |
| Composition (local authorities : other stakeholders) | 22:13 |
| Sub-committees | Advanced Economy, Robust Infrastructure, Skilled and Flexible Workforce, Sustainability, Quality of Life |
| Number of staff | 18 |
| Number of meetings per year | 4 plenary, 8 committees |
| Venue | Assembly meetings rotate Secretariat in Wakefield |
| Regional Planning Guidance | Yes, since 22 October 2001 |
| Budget | £1 million, plus £500k government grant |
| Funding | Subscriptions from local authorities; government grant |
| Date of formation | 20 July 1998 |
| Date of designation | 27 July 1999 |

## The region in Europe

| | |
|---|---|
| Number of MEPs | 7 |
| Number of CoR members | 1 |
| The Assembly and Europe | MEPs and CoR members report directly to the Assembly |
| Office in Brussels | *European Office* funded by regional LGA, Yorkshire Forward (RDA), TECs, South Yorkshire Passenger Transport Executive, Environment Agency since 1997; 3 staff |

## Joint submission by Scottish Executive and COSLA to the European Commission, March 2001

Under Appendix A the key principles were:

**Principle 1**: Effective European governance should facilitate citizens' participation in and influence over EU policy-making.

**Principle 2**: We need to find ways of better engaging regional and local organisations in the EU decision-making process.

**Principle 3**: It is particularly important to involve regional and local levels of government, because they are democratically elected and implement much EU legislation. We think it is essential that the EU Governance debate addresses the potential for giving a greater role to Scotland and the other regions with legislative powers.

**Principle 4**: Decisions should be taken at the lowest level (i.e. closest to the citizen) consistent with effectiveness (the subsidiarity principle). This becomes all the more important with enlargement.

**Principle 5**: The EU institutions must respect the Member State's role in deciding the internal allocation of competences between it and sub-national authorities.

**Principle 6**: A greater sense of participation can only be achieved if there is wider consultation of all those affected by proposed legislation before final versions are drafted by the Commission. Enlargement will make wide consultation more challenging but even more necessary.

**Principle 7**: Any policies with an impact at the regional or local level (e.g. agriculture, fisheries, environment, education) should be made available on a consultative basis to the relevant authorities at the earliest possible stage (i.e. before adoption by the College of Commissioners).

**Principle 8**: The EU institutions should take better account of the potential financial impact of legislation on the implementing authorities and other concerned parties (whether private or public sector).

**Principle 9**: Those involved in the attainment of targets should be involved in setting them.

**Principle 10**: The Commission and implementing authorities should aim for a consensual approach whereby the Commission assists in achieving the objectives of a policy (e.g. cleaner rivers) rather than simply resorting to infraction proceedings if there appears to be a problem.

**Principle 11**: In the present Union, and especially after enlargement, the Commission needs to find more flexible ways of implementing policy which draw on the resources and expertise present at Member State and sub-Member State level, allowing implementation to take account of local needs on the ground. This should apply to policies such as agriculture, environment and fisheries.

# Bibliography

Atkinson, H. and Wilks-Heeg, S., *Local Government from Thatcher to Blair. The politics of creative autonomy*, Cambridge: Polity, 2000

Bogdanor, V., *Devolution in the United Kingdom*, Oxford: Opus, 1999

Bradbury, I. and J. Mawson, *British Regionalism and Devolution*, London: Jessica Kingsley, 1997

Braun, D. (ed.), *Public policy and federalism*, Aldershot: Ashgate, 2000

Bulpitt, J., *Territory and Power in the United Kingdom*, Manchester: Manchester University Press, 1983

Burgess, M., *Federalism and European Union*, London: Routledge, 1989

Burgess, M. and A.-G. Gagnon (eds.), *Comparative Federalism and Federation*, Hemel Hempstead: Harvester Wheatsheaf, 1993

Butt Philip, A. and O. Gray (eds.), *Directory of Pressure Groups in the European Union*, Harlow: Catermill, 1996

Calder, A., *Revolutionary Empire. The rise of the English-speaking Empires from the Fifteenth century to the 1780s*, revised edition, London: Pimlico, 1998

Chandler, W. M. and M. A. Chandler, 'Federalism and Political Parties', in: *European Journal of Political Economy*, vol.3, Nos. 1-2 (1987), pp. 87-108.

Croisat, M., *Le fédéralisme dans les démocraties contemporaines*, Paris: Montchrestien, 1992

Dungey, J. and I. Newman, *The New Regional Agenda*, London: LGIU, 1999

Dungey, J. and I. Newman, *The Democratic Region*, London: LGIU, 2000

Elazar, D., *Exploring Federalism*, Alabama: University of Alabama Press, 1987

Elazar, D., *A Handbook of Federal, Confederal and Autonomy Arrangements*, 2nd ed., Harlow: Longmann, 1994

Fearon, K., *Women's Work: The Story of the Northern Ireland Women's Coalition*, Belfast: The Blackstaff Press, 1999

FitzGerald, G., *All in a Life: An Autobiography*, Dublin: Gill and Macmillan, 1991

Forsyth, M. (ed.), *Federalism and Nationalism*, Leicester: Leicester University Press, 1989

Galligan, B., *A Federal Republic*, Cambridge: Cambridge University Press, 1995

Garside, P. and M. Hebbert, *British Regionalism 1900-2000*, London: Mansell, 1989

Greenwood, J., *Representing Interests in the European Union*, London: Macmillan, 1997

Harvie, C., *The Rise of Regional Europe*, London: Routledge, 1994

Harvie, C., 'English regionalism: the dog that never barked', in: B. Crick (ed.), *National Identities. The Constitution of the UK*, Oxford: Blackwell, 1991

Hassan, G. and C. Warhurst (eds.), *The New Scottish Politics: The First Year of the Scottish Parliament and Beyond*, London: The Stationery Office, 2000

Hazell, R. (ed.), *The State and the Nations: The First Year of Devolution in the United Kingdom*, Thorverton: Imprint Academic, 2000

Hazell, R. (ed.), *Constitutional Futures. A History of the Next Ten Years*, Oxford: Oxford University Press, 1999

Hebbert, M., *London, more by fortune than by design*, Chichester: J. Wiley, 1998

Hesse, J. J. and V. Wright (eds.), *Federalizing Europe? The costs, benefits and preconditions of federal political systems*, Oxford: Oxford University Press, 1996

Hicks, U. K., *Federalism: Failure and Success*, London: Macmillan, 1978

Hix, S., 'How MEPs Vote', ESRC 'One Europe or Several' Programme, Briefing Note 1/00, University of Sussex, European Institute, 2000

Hobsbawn, E. J., *Nations and Nationalism since 1780: Programme, Myth, Reality*, Cambridge: Cambridge University Press, 1990

Jeffery, C., *Multi-Layer Democracy in Germany: Insights for Scottish Devolution*, London: The Constitution Unit, 1998

Jones, B. and D. Balsom (eds.), *The Road to the National Assembly for Wales*, Cardiff: University of Wales Press, 2000

Keating, M., *The New Regionalism in Western Europe*, Cheltenham: Edward Elgar Publishing, 1998

Kellas, J. G., 'Some Constitutional Aspects of Devolution', in A. Wright (ed.), *Scotland: the Challenge of Devolution*, Aldershot: Ashgate, 2000

Le Galès, P. and C. Lequesne (eds.), *Regions in Europe*, London: Routledge, 1998

Leonardy, U., 'The Institutional Structures of German Federalism', in: C. Jeffery (ed.), *Recasting German Federalism. The Legacies of Unification*, London: Pinter, 1999

Loughlin, J., *Subnational Democracy in the European Union*, Oxford: Oxford University Press, 2001

Mackintosh, J. P., *The Devolution of Power: Local Democracy, Regionalism and Nationalism*, Harmondsworth: Penguin, 1968

Marquand, D. and J. Tomaney, *Democratising England*, Paper for the Regional Policy Forum, available on www.rpf.org.uk, 2000

Marr, A., *The Battle for Scotland*, 2nd ed., Harmondsworth: Penguin, 1995

McLeod, A. J., 'Regional Participation in EU Affairs: Lessons for Scotland from Austria, Germany and Spain', Scotland Europa Paper 15, Brussels, 1999

Mitchell, G., *Making Peace: The Inside Story of the Good Friday Agreement*, London: William Heinemann, 1999

Murkens, J. E., *Scotland's Place in Europe*, London: The Constitution Unit, 2001

Nairn, T., 'The Three Dreams of Scottish Nationalism', in: L. Paterson (ed.), *A Diverse Assembly: The Debate on a Scottish Parliament*, Edinburgh: Edinburgh University Press, 1968

Osmond, J. (ed.), *The National Assembly Agenda*, Cardiff: Institute of Welsh Affairs, 1999

Performance and Innovation Unit/Cabinet Office: *Reaching Out – The Role of Central Government at Regional and Local Level*, London: The Stationary Office, 2000

Rawlings, R., 'The New Model Wales', in: *Journal of Law and Society*, vol. 25, No. 4, Oxford: Blackwell, 1998

Regional Policy Commission (the Millan Report): *Renewing the Regions: Strategies for Regional Economic Development*, Sheffield: Sheffield Hallam University, 1995

Roberts, P., *The New Territorial Governance: Planning, Developing and Managing the UK in an Era of Devolution*, London: Town and Country Planning Association, 2000

Royal Commission on Local Government in England, London: HMSO, 1969

Royal Commission on Local Government in Greater London, 1957-60, Report, Cmd. 1164, London: HMSO, 1960

Royal Commission on the Constitution, London: HMSO, 1973

Salmon, T., 'An Oxymoron: the Scottish Parliament and Foreign Relations?', in: A. Wright (ed.), *Scotland: the Challenge of Devolution*, Aldershot: Ashgate, 2000

Sandford, M., *Next Steps for Regional Chambers*, London: The Constitution Unit, 2001

Sandford, M. and P. McQuail, *Unexplored Territory: Elected Regional Assemblies in England*, London: The Constitution Unit, 2001

Scheiren, S., 'Independence in Europe: Scotland's Choice?', in: *Scottish Affairs*, No. 31, Spring 2000

Schmitter, P. C., *How to Democratize the European Union…and Why Bother?*, Maryland: Rowman and Littlefield Publishers Inc, 2000

Scottish Executive, *Joint Paper on European Governance*, Scottish Executive and COSLA, 2001

Smiley, D. V., *Canada in Question. Federalism in the Eighties*, Toronto: McGraw-Hill Ryerson, 1980

Smith, G. (ed.), *Federalism. The Multiethnic Challenge*, Harlow: Longman, 1995

Swenden, W., 'How (A)Symmetric is Belgian Federalism?' Paper prepared for a Conference on Regionalism in the European Union, EU Centre, Georgia State University, Atlanta, 20 April 2001

*The Marshall Inquiry on Greater London*, Report to the Greater London Council by Sir Frank Marshall MA, LLB. GLC, 1978 (The Marshall Inquiry)

Tomaney, J., 'New Labour and the English Question', in: *The Political Quarterly*, vol. 70, No. 1, 1999, pp. 74-82.

Travers, T. and G. Jones, *The New Government of London*, York: Joseph Rowntree Foundation, 1997

Trench, A. (ed.), *The State of the Nations 2001. The Second Year of Devolution in the United Kingdom*, Thorverton: Imprint Academic, 2001

Urwin, D., 'Territorial Structures and Political Development in the United Kingdom', in: Rokkan, S. and D. Urwin (eds.), *The Politics of Territorial Identity: Studies in European Regionalism*, London: Sage, 1982

Walker, D. B., *The Rebirth of Federalism*, 2nd edition, Chatham N.J.: Chatham House, 1995

Watts, R. L., *Comparing Federal Systems in the 1990s*, Kingston, Ontario: Institute of Intergovernmental Relations, Queen's University, 1996

Weir, S. and D. Beetham, *Political Power and Democratic Control in Britain*, London: Routledge, 1999

Wilford, R. (ed.), *Aspects of the Belfast Agreement*. Oxford: Oxford University Press, 2001

Wilford, R. and R. Wilson (eds.), *Northern Ireland Quarterly Reports (QR)* for the Devolution Monitoring Programme, funded by the Leverhulme Foundation and the Economic and Social Research Council, available on www.democraticdialogue.org, 2000 and ongoing.

Wilford, R. and R. Wilson, *A Democratic Design? The Political Style of the Northern Ireland Assembly*. London: The Constitution Unit, 2001

Wilson, R. (ed.), *A Guide to the Northern Ireland Assembly: Agreeing to Disagree*, Norwich: The Stationery Office, 2001

Wright, A., *Scotland and the EU: a Case of Subsidiarity or Dependency?*, unpublished PhD Thesis, University of Dundee, 1998

Wright, A., 'The Europeanisation of Scotland. A Driver for Autonomy', in: M. Graves and G. Girrard (eds.), *Europe United, the United Kingdom Disunited?*, University of Brest, 2000

# Abbreviations

APNI    Alliance Party for Northern Ireland

BIC     British-Irish Council

BIIC     British-Irish Intergovernmental Conference

CoR     Committee of the Regions

DETR    Department for the Environment, Transport and the Regions (until June 2001)

DfEE    Department for Education and Employment (until June 2001)

DTI     Department of Trade and Industry

DTLR    Department for Transport, Local Government and the Regions (since June 2001)

DUP    Democratic Unionist Party

EU     European Union

FCO    Foreign and Commonwealth Office

GLA    Greater London Authority

GLC    Greater London Council

GOR    Government Office for the Region

IGC     Intergovernmental Conference

IRA     Irish Republican Army

| | |
|---|---|
| JMC | Joint Ministerial Committee |
| LGA | Local Government Association |
| MLA | Member of the Legislative Assembly (Northern Ireland) |
| MEP | Member of the European Parliament |
| MSP | Member of the Scottish Parliament |
| NIWC | Northern Ireland Women's Committee |
| NSMC | North-South Ministerial Committee |
| OFMDFM | Office of the First Minister and Deputy First Minister |
| QR | Quarterly Reports (of ESRC project, see chapter on Northern Ireland) |
| RDA | Regional Development Agency |
| SDLP | Social Democratic and Labour Party |
| SF | Sinn Féin |
| SNP | Scottish National Party |
| UUP | Ulster Unionist Party |